LAW'S ENVIRONMENT

JOHN COPELAND NAGLE

Law's Environment

HOW THE LAW SHAPES THE PLACES WE LIVE

Yale UNIVERSITY PRESS

NEW HAVEN AND LONDON

Published with assistance from the foundation established in memory of James Wesley
Cooper of the Class of 1865, Yale College.

Set in Scala type by Westchester Book Group.

Library of Congress Cataloging-in-Publication Data

Nagle, John Copeland, 1960–
    Law's environment : how the law shapes the places we live / John Copeland Nagle.
        p.   cm.
    Includes bibliographical references and index.
    ISBN 978-0-300-12629-7 (pbk. : alk. paper)
    1. Environmental law.   2. Law—Environmental aspects.   I. Title.
    K3585.N34 2010
    344.04'6—dc22   2009051028

A catalogue record for this book is available from the British Library.

For Laura and Julia

CONTENTS

THE STORIES OF ENVIRONMENTAL LAW have always fascinated me. My first high school research paper reported on the pending Supreme Court case involving the endangered snail darter versus the Tellico Dam. My undergraduate thesis told the story of the Sagebrush Rebellion that pitted the advocates of state or private ownership of western lands against federal land managers and environmentalists. Law school, of course, brought story after story told by judges in court opinions, and my practice as a trial attorney with the Justice Department often involved uncovering the stories of how old industrial facilities became hazardous waste cleanup sites.

Most legal scholarship will not be mistaken for literature. Bill McKibben has observed that writing has been crucial to the environmental movement and specifically to the development of environmental law, but he adds that lawyers are "not a species known for eloquent prose" (*American Earth: Environmental Writing Since Thoreau* [New York: Penguin Putnam, 2008], 348). That is not to say that writing about environmental law has been unhelpful. There is great value in academic writing that identifies the appropriate principles that should guide the law and that analyzes the operation of a particular law. I have done some of that writing myself, and I am indebted to those whose scholarly writing facilitates our understanding of the law.

Yet my early fondness for stories of environmental law never quite disappeared. It was rekindled by the untimely death of my mother in 2001, which prompted me to write an essay about how her life and death shaped my view of the natural world around me. Soon thereafter, I served for five months as a Fulbright scholar with the privilege of teaching and lecturing in China. My travels in China demonstrated the contrast between what environmental law says and the actual conditions of local environments. China's environmental laws are surprisingly detailed and powerful, but the country's environment remains polluted. Why doesn't the law make more of a difference? Returning from China, and struggling to craft an examination question, I seized upon the plight of the Aleutian shield fern, reputed to be the rarest plant in North America. My interest in the fern survived the immediate context of the exam and blossomed into a fascination with the plant's home of Adak Island, far out in the Aleutians yet buffeted by the changing commands of environmental law. Soon I began to envision this project, which explores the actual effect that environmental law has on the natural environment in five places scattered throughout the United States.

The resulting book benefits immeasurably from the time and insights shared by the many people who talked to me in each place. For Adak Island, I am grateful to Mike Boylan, Peter Dunlevy, Steve Ebbert, Steve Hines, Chuck Lyon, Jenna Mueller, Jennifer Roberts, and Lisa Scharf. In Colton, California, thanks to Greg Ballmer, Gail Egenis, Robert Gonzales, Mark Nuaimi, Daryl Parrish, Larry Sheffield, and Dan Silver. I learned about North Dakota's badlands from Gary Foli, Bruce Key, Cindy Klein, Ron Ness, Dale Patten, Dave Pieper, Deborah Reichman, Wayne Schafer, John Schulz, Mark Trechock, and Gene Veeder. Along the Susquehanna River, I talked with Tom Beauduy, Woody Cole, Mitch Cron, James Curatalo, Sara Dueling, Janet Gleisner, Larry Johnson, Chip McElwee, Brian Mangan, and Bob Wasilewski. My first and last trips were to Alamogordo, New Mexico, where I interviewed Ray Backstrom, Jackie Diehl, Bruce Gillespie, David Gottula, Frank Martinez, and Lynn Rice.

My research continued as I conducted my interviews. The staff members at the Anchorage Museum of History and Art, Alamogordo Public Library, Colton Public Library, and Osterhout Free Library in Wilkes-Barre, Pennsylvania, helped me to locate documents and photographs that greatly aided my understanding of each community. Back home at Notre Dame, research librarians Dwight King, Chris O'Byrne, Patti Ogden, and Warren Rees located documents that were invaluable to my project and that I never could have found on my own. My student research assistants— Elizabeth Adams, Jenn Curfman, Geoff Gisler, Annalee Jenke, Jared Jodrey, Stephen Leys, and Carlos Rodes—taught me about New Mexico's nocturnal animals, riparian rights along the Susquehanna River, the unique legal status of North Dakota's grasslands, and many more items than I cannot recall now. I am even indebted to two students whom I have never met—Alicia Casner and Melissa Quintana— whose paper studying brownfields in Colton was featured on the geography department's website at the University of California, San Bernardino, and who generously discussed the results of their research with me.

Numerous colleagues read drafts of chapters and discussed my experiences with me. I am especially grateful to Amy Barrett, Jamison Colburn, Nicole Garnett, Rick Garnett, Alex Klass, J. B. Ruhl, Jim Salzman, Julian Velasco, and Sandi Zellman for their thoughtful comments on earlier drafts. I also had the privilege of presenting chapters of the book to my colleagues and students at the Notre Dame Law School, the Rocky Mountain Mineral Law Foundation's Natural Resource Law Professors biannual conference, the conference "Environmental Stewardship: An Exploratory Program for Religious Leaders" sponsored by the Foundation for Research on Economics and the Environment (FREE), and the University of Colorado Natural Resource Law Center's Twenty-fifth Anniversary Summer Conference. And when I received another Fulbright to return to China in 2008, I presented chapters from the book at Shantou University in Guandong Province and at the Southwest University School of Law in Chongqing.

As with all of my work, I have benefited greatly from the communities in which I have worked. These include the University of Hong Kong Faculty of Law, which generously hosted me for five months in 2008, and a remote cabin in Jackson Hole, Wyoming, where I nonetheless cultivated relationships that I look forward to developing in the coming years. My friends at Notre Dame are a constant source of inspiration and encouragement. Notre Dame supported my work with generous financial assistance; thanks especially to Dean Patricia O'Hara (who approved numerous stipends and travel requests) and to the Matthews family (who endowed my professorship). The final community that I thank resides in my home, where my wife, Lisa, facilitated the travel that was necessary for me to undertake this project and cheered me on in my writing. My daughters, Laura and Julia, were not able to join me on any of my research trips, but they were able to accompany me to Antarctica and Borneo, respectively. They already manifest a love and concern for the kinds of places that I describe in this book, which I dedicate to them.

ABBREVIATIONS

AMNWR	Alaska Maritime National Wildlife Refuge
CERCLA	Comprehensive Environmental Response, Compensation, and Liability Act
EPA	Environmental Protection Agency
ESA	Endangered Species Act
FERC	Federal Energy Regulatory Commission
FWS	Fish and Wildlife Service
NPS	National Park Service
ORV	off-road vehicle
PADEP	Pennsylvania Department of Environmental Protection
PCBS	polychlorinated biphenyls
SRBC	Susquehanna River Basin Commission
TRNP	Theodore Roosevelt National Park

Introduction

THIS IS A BOOK about how the law affects the natural environment in which we live. Environmental law tells us how much pollution we must tolerate. It forbids additional pollution in seemingly clear places while declining to remove worse pollution from others. Environmental law also chooses which areas are worth preserving. The law insists on the preservation of some areas, through such designations as national parks and wildlife refuges, while ignoring pleas to preserve other landscapes. These choices about the law go far in determining the state of the natural environment in each place.

Often, these choices are made in response to stories of pollution and preservation that capture the public's consciousness. Environmental law thrives on stories. Writers such as John Muir, Rachel Carson, Roderick Nash, and Wendell Berry have reached popular audiences with their accounts of remarkable places and the need to preserve them. Bill McKibben credits environmental writers with inspiring environmental laws in his anthology *American Earth: Environmental Writing since Thoreau,* which contains nearly one thousand pages of excerpted work by a diverse collection of more than one hundred authors. Environmental law results from such stories. One of the themes that runs through the scholarship about environmental law is the crucial role of anecdotes in prompting Congress to enact significant environmental legislation. The burning of the Cuyahoga River in Ohio resulted in the Clean Water Act of 1972; the oozing contamination at Love Canal in New York helped yield the Superfund law in 1980. Once the statutes are in place, judicial opinions tell stories of disputes that result in litigation between contested claims to the use of forests, lakes, grasslands, and wetlands large and small, near and far. And the laws are sometimes stories themselves. Again, consider *American Earth,* which includes the text of the Wilderness Act of 1964, a dissenting opinion written by Justice William O. Douglas, Theodore Roosevelt's remarks upon designating the Grand Canyon as a national monument, and Lyndon Johnson's statement upon signing the Highway Beautification Act of 1965.[1]

Legal scholars and others who are interested in environmental law have long depended on such stories for multiple purposes. We use casebooks that are filled with judicial opinions that tell stories about cases that illustrate and *teach* the operation of the law. We tell stories in order to *remind* us of environmental law struggles in the past, as Oliver Houck did in his article about five cases that "came early in the history of environmental law and" whose "impacts were huge." We use stories to *illustrate* theoretical arguments in legal scholarship, such as the discussion of the regulation of the California Bay Delta that is contained in an article about modular environmental law written by Jody Freeman and Daniel Farber. We rely on stories to *persuade* courts to reach a certain decision or to *encourage* Congress to enact a new law. We tell stories to *exhort* individuals to action, a tradition that extends at least from John Muir to Al Gore. We also use stories to *study,* to examine a legal issue without a preconception about what one will learn.[2]

Somehow, this ubiquitous use of stories in environmental law has gone unnoticed by the scholars who have studied the role of stories in legal scholarship. For example, the book *Law's Stories: Narrative and Rhetoric in the Law* contains twenty-one essays examining how stories influence the creation of specific laws and how they are employed in specific judicial cases. None of those essays discusses the role of narrative in natural resources law or environmental law; they focus instead on issues of constitutional law, civil rights, and criminal law. Even so, the insights of those essays and of related legal scholarship can help those who are interested in environmental law to better understand the use of stories. Stories elicit a different kind of response than other kinds of writing. Stories "can produce an experience, an insight, and one or more emotional responses," wrote Martha Minow. Stories are also especially suited for challenging the status quo. Richard Delgado reported that "stories, parables, chronicles, and narratives are powerful means for destroying a mindset—the bundle of presuppositions, received wisdoms, and shared understandings against a background of which legal and political discourse takes place." More modestly, Minow added that stories are welcome "'as a healthy disruption and challenge' to legal doctrine and theories." But there is also a cautionary note. Dan Farber and Suzanna Sherry warned that "even if a story is true, it may be atypical of real world experiences." They emphasized that "the point of all scholarship—including the nontraditional forms—is to increase the reader's understanding (here, of law)."[3]

Historians are often the best storytellers, and writing about environmental history has flourished during the past few decades. Some of that writing focuses on particular places, including recent studies of Seattle, the Fox River in Wisconsin, and William Cronon's famous examination of the environmental history of New England. Other writings engage the entire sweep of American environmental history. And many of these authors highlight the role of the law in shaping the American environment. Consider Ted Steinberg's *Down to Earth: Nature's Role in Environmental History,* which credits legal changes for two of the three major "turning points" in American environmental history. One turning point resulted from the Land Ordinance of 1785, which "allowed the land to be bundled up and sold in one of the most sweeping attempts on record to put nature up for sale, the legacy of which is still visible today." The "rise of consumerism" is another of Steinberg's turning points, and he attributes that development to "changes in the law [that] made the corporation legally bound to pursue what was in the best interests of its shareholders, regardless of the impact on the natural world or the public welfare," thereby "profoundly affecting not just the American landscape but the entire planet." Most environmental historians study the full range of scientific, cultural, economic, and other factors that join with the law in affecting the natural environment. That project, although immensely valuable, is distinct from my attention to the role of the law and what an examination of specific places tells us about the law, those places, and the ongoing relationship between them.[4]

The stories that I tell in this book are designed to help us learn more about environmental law. More specifically, they are intended to supplement the existing literature that often overlooks stories of how environmental law affects the natural environment. My focus is the reverse of the typical accounts of how particular incidents prompted the enactment of a new law, instead considering how existing laws affect the natural environment in certain places. One would expect that a legal regime premised upon the importance of preserving or recovering certain conditions within the natural environment would pay more attention to what those conditions actually are. Similarly, a body of law designed to incorporate holistic ecological principles should recognize the importance of a holistic examination of all of the laws that affect the natural environment, but too often that has not been the case. There are stories about why laws are enacted, and stories about how one specific law is applied in numerous different places, but there are not as many stories about the role of the law in shaping the environmental conditions in specific places. Stories that focus on one environmental statute or regulation overlook the ways in which many environmental laws combine to influence the natural environment in a single place. To cite just one example: many excellent books and journal articles examine the management of national wildlife refuges, the cleanup of hazardous wastes, and the management of fisheries, but very little writing seeks to explore how the laws governing those three issues relate to one another in a place such as Adak Island, the subject of my first chapter. Nor has the work of environmental ethicists on place-based theories of why we value the environment prompted similar research into the role of specific places in environmental law. Likewise, there are many excellent scholarly and popular accounts of the environmental history of particular places, but most of these writings do not emphasize the ways in which environmental law determines the natural environment in those places.

This omission led Aaron Sachs to assert in *The Humboldt Current: Nineteenth-Century Exploration and the Roots of American Environmentalism* that recent environmental setbacks have occurred because "environmental thought has been disconnected from" travel narratives and other stories about the natural environment that the law seeks to govern. The same concern is echoed in recent writing about environmental law. For example, in his book *The Making of Environmental Law*, Richard Lazarus argues that "environmental law must necessarily be responsive to the types of problems that it seeks to address." Similarly, Eric Freyfogle, in *Why Conservation Is Failing and How It Can Regain Ground*, contends that environmentalism "is stymied . . . because it lacks good overall direction." And in *Saving Our Environment from Washington*, David Schoenbrod argues that "the 'law' in environmental law was critical to the field's climb to respectability, but environmental law today is not the rule of law." The common theme of these books and of many other authors is that environmental law has lost its sense of direction because it too often neglects the places that it is intended to govern.[5]

My thesis is that existing studies of environmental law overlook how multiple laws operate to affect the natural environment of specific places. This way of approaching the relationship between the law and the environment has numerous advantages. It connects how we think about environmental law to what we actually observe about the environment. It recognizes that many laws combine to influence a given environment, and those laws produce different results in different places. It encourages further study of how environmental law is actually applied, and how other laws produce significant effects upon the environment as well.

I tell the stories of five places. Chapter 1 considers Adak Island, whose remote location in the middle of the Aleutian Islands would seem to insulate it from the effects of human manipulation of the environment. Instead, shifting human uses of the island have transformed it. The introduction of foxes, caribou, and rats during the past several centuries has literally altered the appearance of the island's landscape; as the new mammals preyed upon native seabirds, the vegetation changed because the nutrients provided by the seabirds disappeared. Now the law is trying to return the landscape to its prior condition. But Adak is still cleaning up the contamination from a military base that operated there from World War II until it was closed in the 1990s. The federal Superfund law decides what that cleanup will look like. And the future of the tiny human community remaining on the island may depend on the decisions embedded in federal fishery management laws.

Chapter 2 describes the unsuccessful efforts of Colton, California, to accommodate both the endangered Delhi Sands flower-loving fly and pressure for expanding human development. Colton hosts a rapidly growing and relatively impoverished human population, and the city's economic needs have produced a sharp conflict between the desires of the local zoning officials and the habitat preservation demands of the federal Endangered Species Act. Colton is also an old industrial city that is struggling with a century of contamination and the current challenge of the extreme air pollution produced by the millions of vehicles that travel along Interstate 10 as it bisects the city.

Chapter 3 explores Theodore Roosevelt National Park, located in the desolate badlands of western North Dakota that once were home to Teddy Roosevelt. North Dakota's badlands experienced a long struggle for designation of the area as a national park that succeeded only after President Harry S. Truman vetoed an earlier park proposal because the area lacked the requisite scenic qualifications. The park never became the national tourist attraction that its boosters expected, and now it is immersed in an administrative and legislative battle to decide what to do with its exploding elk population. Outside the national park, much of the land is part of the Little Missouri National Grassland, which is under the jurisdiction of the Forest Service but which was long effectively governed by county grazing associations. The advent of ecological interest in the grasslands has produced a management conflict as the Forest Service seeks to abide by its governing statutes while acknowledging the area's historical realities. The badlands also face the irony of providing national park status to an area whose economic development is now constrained by more stringent air pollution regulations imposed by the National Park Service Organic Act and the Clean Air Act.

Chapter 4 examines the Susquehanna River, which flows from upstate New York through Pennsylvania and into the Chesapeake Bay. The river has long been used for multiple purposes such as fishing, transportation, and waste disposal. In 2005, American Rivers, a leading environmental organization, named the Susquehanna as the most endangered river in the United States because of the water pollution legacy of decades of coal mining and the failures of the outdated sewage facilities operating in the old cities located along its banks. Congress thought that it solved the river's management problems when it created the Susquehanna River Basin Commission in 1970, but the ineffectiveness of that body has left a legal gap that is being filled by innumerable laws, such as the federal Clean Water Act, Pennsylvania's Clean Streams Law, local zoning decisions, and regional efforts to restore the Chesapeake Bay.

Chapter 5 discusses the efforts of Alamogordo, New Mexico, to preserve the area's dark skies for professional and amateur astronomers. I first learned about Alamogordo when I read that it has the most stringent light pollution ordinance in the country. That ordinance has been used to protect the dark skies through civic pressure and the development of social norms instead of through the legal enforcement actions that are associated with most pollution control efforts. To Alamogordo's northeast, the Lincoln National Forest struggles to implement the shifting national regulations and norms concerning wildfires. To the city's southwest, the White Sands National Monument narrowly missed becoming a national park during the 1920s, but the current proposal to name it a World Heritage Site has generated opposition from those who fear that the United Nations would then employ international law to rule the region.

I selected these places with a number of criteria in mind. I sought places that illustrate different kinds of environmental problems, such as air pollution, wildlife preservation, and the removal of hazardous wastes. I sought places that illustrate a broad range of federal, state, and local laws affecting the natural environment. I sought geographic diversity within the United States and a diversity of environmental conditions within those places. I also sought to examine places that have not gained the significant popular attention already experienced by places such as the Everglades, the Love Canal hazardous waste site near Niagara Falls, and the Gulf Coast after Hurricane Katrina. Perhaps the most difficult challenge was limiting myself to five stories. I wish I could tell many more stories, such as Taiyuan, the Chinese city reputed to have the worst air pollution in the world; the Grand Kankakee Marsh in Indiana, a vast swamp whose size was second only to the Everglades until federal and state laws caused it to be drained; Brunswick, Georgia, which has been described as the most polluted zip code in the United States; or a place that illustrates the relationship between Native Americans and their environment amidst the development pressures of the twenty-first century. I hope to examine some of those places in the future, and I also hope that other scholars will conduct their own investigations into cases that are of special interest to them.

I did not approach these five places with any preconceptions about the utility of environmental law. Instead, I hoped to answer many questions. What difference does the law really make? What do we want a place to look like? Who should make that decision? What happens when we change our minds? I studied Adak Island, Colton, North Dakota's badlands, the Susquehanna River, and Alamogordo with such questions in mind. My hope was that through rich anecdotal experiences we may come to learn the questions that we should be asking—questions that we are capable of formulating only through observed experience. I examined the documents that comprise the traditional sources of environmental law, and I researched the local history of each place. I also visited each place, usually more than once, so that I could interview those individuals who are involved in or affected by the law's impact on the local environment. It was tremendously helpful simply to see the places that I was writing about.

The resulting stories seek to illustrate the process by which we use the law and other devices to manage the natural environment. Although no set of case studies can yield definitive proof about the operation of the law, the five stories that I tell suggest three overriding themes. First, the elusive nature of environmental values is seen in the conflicts about how the law should affect the environment, the often rocky transitions from one value to another, the efforts to inculcate new values, and the importance of who gets to decide which values to incorporate in the law. Second, the changing nature of the law means that sometimes the law responds to new environmental values while other times it affirmatively shapes those values. Environmental law often produces unexpected results, while laws that are not ordinarily regarded as environmental laws often play a key role in shaping the environment. Third, the law operates much differently from what is suggested by the stories told in the judicial decisions that are our most familiar accounts of the operation of the law. Few courts have been asked to resolve legal disputes in the five places that I describe. Yet there is a common understanding that the law governs nearly all human activities that affect the environment, for good or ill.

The stories in this book are designed to encourage additional research that will begin to develop a better understanding of the results of our frequent reliance upon environmental law to produce our desired natural environments. My hope is that a better understanding of how environmental law actually affects certain places will aid us in crafting and implementing that law. As Robert Weisberg observed, perhaps legal storytellers "may become what Shelley called poets: the 'unacknowledged legislators' of a nation."[6]

CHAPTER ONE

The End of the Earth

ADAK ISLAND, ALASKA

"ADAK! That place is the end of the earth," exclaimed my colleague, a native of Anchorage. A 1943 documentary produced and directed by John Huston and his father Walter Huston suggests that Adak is even more distant than that. "Remote as the moon and hardly more fertile," the narrator intones, "Adak is next to worthless in terms of human existence." Eliot Asinof, who later wrote *Eight Men Out,* shared that assessment in a *Saturday Evening Post* article recalling his time on Adak during World War II; he described the island as "something worse than hell—barren, bleak, relentlessly ugly." In the middle of the Aleutian Islands about twelve hundred miles southwest of Anchorage, Adak (pronounced *A-dak,* with a long *a* as in *day*) Island is truly isolated. The community there is the westernmost city in the United States and the southernmost city in Alaska. It is nearly as close to Beijing as it is to New York City. I had planned to visit Adak in October, but a U.S. Fish and Wildlife Service (FWS) official there gently suggested that the island's ubiquitous wind and fog and the airport's questionable electrical system made the fall a less than ideal time to visit. My legal research had uncovered a 1981 case arising under the Death on the High Seas Act in which the widow of an experienced pilot who never arrived as scheduled on Adak complained that the federal government's twelve-day search-and-rescue operation had been inadequate. Pilots flying there a few decades ago could not help but notice the wrecked planes that littered the runway. "It was like flying into an old black and white Godzilla movie," one former resident recalled. That is where my Alaska Airlines flight was taking me in the summer of 2005.[1]

I was going to Adak Island to see how environmental law has shaped and continues to shape a tiny spot of land far from most human civilization. Despite the island's remoteness, the shifting human presence there has profoundly affected its natural environment. The arrival of the first Europeans 265 years ago began a chain of events that are still unfolding on the island today. During the past century, the human story of Adak has encompassed three seemingly contradictory phases: an isolated wildlife refuge only occasionally visited by any people, a large military base used to defend the United States during World War II and the Cold War until the base's closure left a legacy of contamination, and most recently the resettlement of Adak by Alaskan natives hopeful of transforming the island into a sustainable fishing community. Those events have been guided by a series of laws governing the wildlife and plants of Adak and its surrounding waters. The alphabet soup of federal laws that have influenced Adak's environment includes ANCSA, ANILCA, BCRA, CERCLA, CERFA, CWA, ESA, FIFRA, NEPA, and SARA, as well as the occasional environmental statute that has not generated its own acronym, such as the Wilderness Act and the Reindeer Act of 1937. Add to this list several federal laws that do not ordinarily affect the natural environment, an international treaty, some Alaska state regulations, a local ordinance, and traditional common law property rules, and the environmental history—and future—of Adak Island would be much different without the intervention of the law.

The story of Adak Island implicates many of the questions that environmental law is designed to address. The first part of the story considers the wildlife management issues that are colored by the designation of the wildlife refuge and the history of the island's uses. The second part of the story examines how the military changed the island's landscape, and how the departure of the military prompted a cleanup dictated by the federal Comprehensive Environmental Response, Compensation, and Liability Act (CERCLA, also known as the Superfund law). The rest of the island's story considers how the law awarded the abandoned property to native Alaskans and how the law is struggling to help Adak develop a sustainable fishery. The interweaving narratives show that Adak Island is a remarkable example of the process by which we use the law to manage the natural environment, for few would imagine that the natural environment of a single, tiny, remote island could be so profoundly influenced by the choices that we make in enacting and applying so many different environmental laws.

THE ISLAND

Adak Island is surrounded by the Bering Sea to the north and the Pacific Ocean to the south. It sits near the bottom of the curve in the Aleutian Islands at the same latitude as Canada's Vancouver Island and is part of the Andreanof Islands, the third of four groups of islands that stretch westward from the Alaska Peninsula to form the Aleutians. Adak is 28 miles long and contains almost 280 square miles of land, making it the second largest island in the Aleutians. The Aleutians, including Adak, are on the northern end of the famed "ring of fire" that circumvents the Pacific Ocean, and volcanoes bookend Adak to the east and to the west. The volcanic Great Sitkin Island jutted out of the Bering Sea on the crystal clear day that I visited Adak's northern coast. Adak's own creation was violent, resulting from the collision of tectonic plates and accompanying volcanic eruptions. The northern part of Adak features the remnants of three volcanoes, the highest of which reaches nearly four thousand feet above sea level. Glaciers, rain, and wind have further molded the island; numerous rocky fjords define the coastline. Adak also experienced significant earthquakes in 1957, 1964, and 1977, and it felt the tremors of nearby earthquakes in October 2005, December 2007, and March 2008.

Adak's weather is legendary. The island has a polar maritime climate, which means that it is overcast, rainy, windy, and often assaulted by violent storms. About sixty inches of rain falls each year at sea level, and winter brings an average of one hundred inches of snow—with more of both at higher elevations. Frequent violent storms buffet the island, making travel there rather exciting. The wind is especially memorable. "It rips roofs off of houses and buildings," one former resident remembered, adding that he had "seen the wind send steel garbage dumpsters tumbling down the road" and push his car "out of the parking lot, across the street, and into a ditch." Adak experiences periodic williwaws, a weather phenomenon defined as "a violent gust of cold

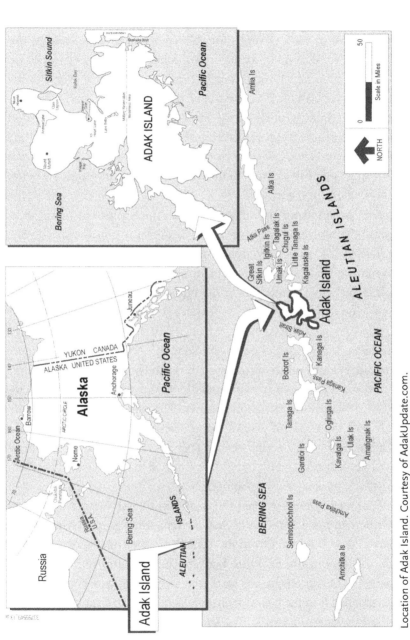

Location of Adak Island. Courtesy of AdakUpdate.com.

wind blowing seaward from a mountainous coast." The writer Gore Vidal, who spent time on Adak during the 1940s and titled his first novel *Williwaw,* described a williwaw as a "big northern storm. Kind of hurricane with lots of snow. Just plain undiluted hell. They come and go real quick, but they do a lot of damage." The skies are persistently overcast, though the sun broke through several times while I visited. The weather changes rapidly, and different parts of the island can experience quite different kinds of weather at the same time. During my three short summer days there, I experienced light rain, steady wind, dense fog, and occasional blue skies. Only the temperature is remarkably stable, usually hovering around fifty degrees in the summer, and rarely dropping below twenty degrees in the winter.[2]

The human history of Adak began with the Aleuts—or Unangas, as they call themselves—who visited the island nearly nine thousand years ago. The Aleuts traveled throughout the Aleutians in pursuit of the abundant marine life in Aleutian waters, hunting otters, sea lions, seals, and whales. They also hunted the many birds that flocked throughout the islands, and they fished both in freshwater streams and in the ocean. The native people gave the island its name: *Adak* is derived from the Aleut word *adaq,* meaning "father." Eventually, the Aleuts established more permanent communities throughout the islands, including Adak, where they lived underground in communal buildings of grass and earth covered by driftwood or whalebone frames. The famed naturalist William Healy Dall, namesake of the Dall's porpoises that are found from Alaska to California, noted "several small village-sites on shell-heaps" when he visited Adak during the 1870s, and he reported that "this island is said at one time to have been very populous."[3]

Adak's fate changed when the Russian explorer Alexei Chirikov arrived there in his ship the *Saint Paul* on September 9, 1741. A storm had separated the *Saint Paul* from the *Saint Peter,* the ship captained by the leader of the expedition, Vitus Bering. The arrival of the Russians at Adak got off to an auspicious start when seven Aleuts who were living there paddled into the bay in their kayaks to greet the *Saint Paul* and to trade fresh water for knives. The Russians claimed sovereignty over all of Alaska, and they traded with the Aleuts throughout the second half of the eighteenth century and the beginning of the nineteenth century. By 1830, the Russians occupied Adak and relocated the native Aleut population hundreds of miles north to other Russian settlements in Alaska. Adak changed hands again in 1867 when Secretary of State William Seward negotiated the sale of all of Russia's Alaskan territory to the United States for $7.2 million. Meanwhile, the Aleuts continued to use Adak for seasonal and subsistence use, but the sea otter and fur seal populations had plummeted by the beginning of the twentieth century because of overharvesting by American, British, Canadian, and Russian businesses.

A REFUGE FOR WILDLIFE

Modern environmental law first touched Adak in 1913. Concerned about the rapidly declining populations of marine animals in the region, President William Taft designated Adak Island as part of a new Aleutian Islands Reservation that encompassed all of the islands. Taft proclaimed that the islands were to be "reserved and set apart as a preserve and breeding ground for native birds, for the propagation of reindeer and fur bearing animals, and for the encouragement and development of the fisheries." The island was redesignated as part of the Aleutian Islands National Wildlife Refuge in 1940, and the name changed again with the congressional enactment of the Alaska National Interest Lands Conservation Act in December 1980, which yielded the Alaska Maritime National Wildlife Refuge (AMNWR). The act also designated the islands, including Adak, as a wilderness area pursuant to the federal Wilderness Act of 1964. The AMNWR now contains twenty-five hundred islands, islets, spires, headlands, and reefs spread over about 4.9 million acres.[4]

"Swirling clouds of seabirds, rare Asiatic migrant birds, beaches of bellowing sea lions and fur seals, and salmon streams in abundance are a few of the wildlife highlights on the Alaska Maritime Refuge." Thus proclaims the refuge's website. Indeed, the AMNWR is "a wildlife paradise." So what wildlife takes refuge on Adak? None, complained Eliot Asinof, who described Adak as "a naked blob, without any of nature's blessings." Other observers encounter multiple types of habitats—including freshwater streams, wetlands, and deep-loam terrestrial and marine habitats—each with its own collection of species. Begin with the birds. In their documentary *Report from the Aleutians*, the Hustons inexplicably claimed that ravens were "the only bird life on the island." But most other observers have a much different experience, especially those birdwatchers who travel thousands of miles and pay thousands of dollars to see the birds of Adak. Adak hosts numerous shorebirds, such as puffins, gulls, cormorants, murres, and auklets. Ptarmigans fly out of the tundra as one approaches. But most of Adak's birds are migratory. All sorts of ducks visit the island. The Aleutian goose, once almost extinct and now touted as demonstrating the success of the federal Endangered Species Act (ESA), sometimes stops there during spring and fall migrations. Nearly three dozen birds that are native to Asia have also been sighted on Adak, which explains its popularity with birdwatching groups. Altogether, 155 species of birds have been seen on the island. I saw several bald eagles during my visit, as well as a rosy finch, one of the most common birds throughout the Aleutians. But I didn't see nearly as many birds as I would have expected on a reputed birdwatching paradise, and the island was surprisingly quiet. The reason why leads us back to the first purposeful efforts to re-create Adak nearly three hundred years ago.[5]

Adak, like many other remote islands, does not have any native terrestrial mammals. It does, however, host numerous marine mammals during their sojourns throughout the north Pacific and the Bering Sea. I watched several sea otters frolic in Clam Lagoon, just where the refuge's colorful interpretive placards said I could find them. Harbor seals are abundant along the island's coasts, and there is a Steller sea lion rookery on the especially inaccessible southwestern coast. Many kinds of whales frequent the seas around Adak. The original Aleut people had engaged in subsistence activities relying on all of these marine mammals, and then the animals attracted the attention of the Russian explorers. The Russians moved quickly to harvest the fur of those animals, and the efforts of the fur traders soon wiped out the resource upon which the Aleuts depended. Steller's sea cow, a species of manatee, became extinct within decades after the Russians arrived. The populations of sea otters and fur seals dropped precipitously over the next century as well, so much so that the Russians had introduced rudimentary conservation measures by the time they sold Alaska to the United States in 1867. The U.S. Navy fought a losing battle with fugitive seal hunters in the Aleutians, giving rise to a legend of a pirate ship that left millions of dollars in gold coins on Adak in 1892. The slaughter of seals continued as an international court rejected a plea to stop it in 1893, over the dissent of U.S. Supreme Court Justice John Marshall Harlan, who wrote his famous dissent in the *Plessy v. Ferguson* separate-but-equal segregation case just three years later. Then, in 1911, the United States joined England, Canada, Japan, and Russia in agreeing to the Treaty for the Preservation and Protection of Fur Seals—the first international wildlife treaty of any type—which banned pelagic sealing and regulated the harvest of seals on land. In 1913, President Taft included Adak Island within the Aleutian Islands Reservation, just ten years after Theodore Roosevelt had created the first national wildlife refuge in Florida.

The Russian fur traders had not been content to watch their business disappear as marine mammal populations plummeted, so they introduced foxes to provide another source of fur rather than seek to create a sustainable population of seals and otters. In 1750—just nine years after Bering's voyage reached Adak—Andreian Tolstykh took a breeding pair of arctic foxes from Russia's Commander Islands and released them on Attu Island at the western edge of the Aleutians. The introduction of just one mating pair of foxes could soon yield a sizeable population on an island—and it did. The foxes feasted on abundant, unwitting, and virtually defenseless colonies of seabirds. The process repeated itself on at least 190 other Aleutian islands as the Russian fur traders, and later the U.S. government, used foxes as a source of income and necessities. In 1882, Secretary of the Treasury (and former New York Court of Appeals judge) Charles J. Folger began to lease Alaskan islands for fox farms, and President Taft added his endorsement to that plan when he listed the propagation of fur-bearing animals as one of the purposes of the Aleutian Islands Reservation. The 1911 treaty protecting fur seals and sea otters made foxes an even more desirable commodity throughout the islands. Henry Swanson, a legendary Aleutian character who told his life's story to local high school students during the late 1970s, recalled that he had stocked Adak with arctic foxes in 1921, though he also related a native story that the Russians had introduced silver foxes to the island long before that. The Seattle-based Adak Ranching Company leased the island for fifty dollars annually during the early 1930s, selling as much as $18,000 in fur during a good year. Altogether, about twenty-seven thousand fox pelts were taken and sold for a price as high as fifty dollars each during the twenty-three years after the establishment of the refuge in 1913.[6]

The decline in fur prices during the Great Depression and the hazardous nature of living in the Aleutians during World War II ended the fox pelt trade. Switching course, the FWS began to eliminate the foxes from the same islands where the federal government had introduced them just a few decades before. Bob "Sea Otter" Jones became manager of the refuge in 1948, and he removed the foxes from Anchitka Island to see whether that would facilitate the recovery of the Aleutian goose, which foxes had decimated throughout the Aleutians by preying upon the birds' nests on the ground. The plan worked. The removal effort reached Adak in 2002, when FWS biologists spread more than one thousand traps on the coastal areas favored by the foxes and up in the island's mountains where foxes had been known to have dens. The trappers killed 276 foxes in 2002 and another 12 in 2003. Studies during the summer of 2005 failed to identify any foxes or signs of foxes on Adak or on several nearby islands, except for some moldy scat that was probably more than a year old. The only fox that I saw during my visit was stuffed and inside a glass case taken from an exhibit at the old FWS visitor's center. "Maybe we got lucky and got them all," said Steve Ebbert, the FWS biologist who led the effort on Adak.

The fox eradication program might have succeeded just in time. Animal rights organizations had voiced concern about the trapping of foxes, and some local residents enjoyed the sight of the animals. Then, in 2005, a fox trap caught the dog of the city mayor's wife, which soon resulted in the city council enacting an emergency ordinance prohibiting the use of the steel-jawed leg-hold traps favored by the FWS. The ordinance's findings state that such traps "present a risk of injury or death to domestic pets and persons, especially small children." The FWS questions the efficacy of the alternative means of removing foxes, but it has complied with the city's ordinance. The ordinance applies only on the relatively small portion of the island that the city owns, and thus it is not in force on the federal refuge. Nor does the ordinance apply to the lands owned by the Aleut Corporation, the native Alaskan organization that manages much of Adak Island today. Perhaps recognizing the claims of other Alaska natives who rely on subsistence hunting, the Aleut Corporation declined to adopt a similar ban on trapping foxes on its Adak lands. But foxes could spread throughout Adak again if a pair escaped the traps, or if the local residents decide that they want to hunt or otherwise enjoy the animals.[7]

Foxes were not the only mammals that people brought to Adak. Caribou were introduced in the late 1950s by the joint effort of the U.S. Navy, the FWS, and the territorial government. A display that was originally located in the FWS visitor's center on Adak indicates that the caribou were intended "to improve [Adak's] wildlife environment." Another reason for bringing the animals there was to provide "an emergency food supply in the event Adak were ever cut off from the nearest supply point, Kodiak, 915 miles away." A third, perhaps more telling, reason was to "provide recreational hunting for military personnel, dependents, and other civilians on the lonely island," who "yearned for something else to do in their spare time," as the FWS explained in a 1959 press release. The original idea was to transport reindeer, not caribou, but an obscure federal statute—the Reindeer Act of 1937—prohibited anyone except native Alaskans from harvesting reindeer. The plan thus shifted to caribou, and Operation Caribou began in 1958. Air force helicopters helped to capture thirty-one calves, each less than one week old, that were taken from a large caribou herd located near Elmendorf Air Force Base just north of Anchorage. Only ten animals survived, and they were flown to Adak by a navy airplane. Once there, several Marines were deployed to bottle feed them. The FWS explained that "much of the labor was volunteer off-hours activity for the Marines; but four country-bred young men who had probably joined the Corps to get away from the farm were assigned to the job." The caribou prospered, and around three thousand of the animals live on Adak Island today. By contrast, a herd of reindeer that was established on the Bering Sea island of Saint Matthew around the same time literally ate itself to death once the rapidly growing number of animals feasted on all of the island's slow-growing lichens.[8]

Rats are another visitor to Adak, albeit an unwelcome one. A Japanese shipwreck first brought Norway rats to what is now known as Rat Island in the eastern Aleutians in 1780. The rats flourished, often at the expense of the native birds. The AMNWR first recognized that rats were an issue around 1995. The FWS contends that "rats are out of place in the Aleutian and Pribilof Islands," even though they have lived on some Aleutian islands for more than two centuries. It is not clear what damage rats have caused on Adak, nor do we know much about their numbers or distribution. Peter Dunlevy, the FWS biologist who studies the island's rats, estimates that Adak's rat population is in the tens of thousands, and that population could continue to grow now that there are no longer any foxes to prey upon them. Dunlevy is engaged in a two-pronged effort concerning the rats. First, he is trying to conduct a census of the number of rats by setting out traps and then estimating the island's population depending on his catch rate. Second, he is identifying the methods that might be used to eliminate them from the island, or at least to reduce their numbers. Rats are targeted by rodenticides, which is just a gentle way of saying that they are poisoned. As such, the Federal Insecticide, Fungicide, and Rodenticide Act (FIFRA) governs. FIFRA provides several categories for the registration of rodenticides. A Section 3 registration allows the rodenticide to be used throughout the United States for a particular purpose. FWS officials have pursued a Section 3 registration for conservation purposes, but Dunlevy says that "it's kind of a touchy subject due to animal rights" concerns. Alternately, a rodenticide can be registered under Section 24(c) of FIFRA, which is essentially a state registration for the limited purpose of special local needs. The refuge has received a Section 24(c) registration that allows the use of certain rodenticides for conservation purposes, but only to bait the rats for trapping as a monitoring and study tool within the refuge. The development of a protocol for poisoning rats on the refuge also triggers the informational duties of the National Environmental Policy Act, as well as the strictures of the Wilderness Act. The FWS began to eradicate the rats on the satellite islands near Adak in 2003, and it is poised to eliminate the rats from the eponymously named Rat Island two hundred miles west of Adak. So far, though, the agency is not actually trying to take rats off of Adak. The work there has been to devise methods for removing rats from remote islands generally, and Adak has been the site of that work because the island's airport makes it accessible. The availability of future funding to remove rats from Adak is doubtful, especially after *Time* magazine identified the $150,000 congressional earmark for the Rat Island project as one of the most outrageous earmarks of 2008.[9]

The human manipulation of Adak's fauna has also affected the island's flora. During my visit, the land was covered by maritime tundra, which can be extremely fragile. "They say that you can walk across [the tundra] and your footprints will still be there thirty years later," recounted one Adak resident. The most common plants on the island include grasses, forbs, shrubs, ferns, mosses, and lichens. Wild snapdragons, crowberry, bog orchid, sedge, alpine azalea, buttercup, wild celery, rush, horsetail, and grass are among the plants that are native to the island. Purple lupine flowered throughout the areas along Kuluk Bay when I visited during the summer. There are also a handful of invasive plants on Adak. The most obvious were a clump of evergreens, now gone, that navy personnel planted near Kuluk Bay and dubbed Adak National Forest in honor of the only trees on the entire island. During World War II, a naval officer arranged for a planeload of fertilizer to be shipped to Adak because his "flower garden had refused to bloom." But there are few such gardens on Adak today, and although no one has actually studied the issue, it does not appear that invasive plants present a problem. Both the climate and the modest number of visitors minimize the likelihood that an exotic plant species will arrive on Adak and displace the native tundra vegetation.[10]

Adak is also home to one of the rarest plants in North America, the Aleutian shield fern. The fern was first discovered on the island in 1932, and then it was not seen again until D. K. Smith found it growing on Adak's Mount Reed in 1975. It has never been sighted anywhere else. Accordingly, in 1988 the Aleutian shield fern was listed as endangered pursuant to the ESA. The FWS declined to designate any critical habitat for the fern, though, reasoning that such a designation was not prudent because it could trigger unauthorized collecting or vandalism and because everyone on Adak was already aware of the plant. The primary threats to the fern are trampling by hikers and grazing by caribou, but its home on the steep slopes of Mount Reed protects it from all but the most intrepid hikers or caribou. Thus far, scientists have been unsuccessful in their efforts to cultivate the fern so that it can be reintroduced into its native habitat in other places.

I did not see the fern during my visit because I was unable to trek across a mile of tundra and up the side of Mount Reed. The plants that I did see, however, may bear little resemblance to those that grew on Adak a few hundred years ago—and that could be growing there again soon. Foxes are the culprits for the disappearance of Adak's native vegetation. The island's original vegetation depended on the rich nutrients contained in the droppings of the native seabirds, which essentially moved nutrients from the sea to the land by eating fish and then leaving their droppings on the land. According to a study coauthored by one of the refuge's biologists and published in *Science* magazine, "the introduction of foxes to the Aleutian archipelago transformed the islands from grasslands to maritime tundra. . . . The more nutrient-impoverished ecosystem that resulted favored less productive forbs and shrubs over more productive grasses and sedges." The removal of the foxes has already helped seabirds return to their original homes on Adak and throughout the Aleutians, and perhaps the landscape will soon begin to show similar changes.[11]

Which brings us back to the marine mammals whose preservation prompted the establishment of what is now the AMNWR in the first place. Populations of the fur seals, sea otters, and other marine mammals recovered nicely throughout much of the twentieth century once the law stepped in on their behalf. A rare white killer whale was even spotted on the north side of Adak in 2000. Recently, however, the numbers of sea otters and sea lions throughout the Aleutians have again plummeted, for reasons that perplex scientists. The possible causes include overfishing, global warming, pollution, the disappearance of kelp, increased predation by killer whales, or some combination of these factors. The sea otters that I watched play in the lagoons of Adak were designated as a threatened species under the ESA just a few weeks after I returned from my visit there. In listing the otters, the FWS admitted that "the cause of the decline is not known with certainty," but it concluded that "the weight of evidence of available information suggests that predation by killer whales (*Orcinus orca*) may be the most likely cause of the sea otter decline in the Aleutian Islands." The explanation remains elusive, but there seems little doubt that parts of the Aleutian ecosystem are in the midst of a striking collapse.[12]

Perhaps no marine species has been affected as much as the Steller sea lion. The species received its name from the German naturalist Georg Wilhelm Steller, who accompanied Vitus Bering on the Russian explorations of Alaska during the early eighteenth century. Steller managed to affix his name to numerous Alaskan species, including a duck, a blue jay, and the now-extinct sea cow. Steller sea lions once filled the Aleutians, and as recently as the 1940s Eliot Asinof reported that the military personnel stationed on Adak Island delighted in the sight of the sea lions sunning themselves on the rocks. By the 1980s, the sea lions suffered a dramatic drop in population, though no one could explain why. Whatever the cause, the FWS listed the sea lions as threatened under the ESA in 1990, and then the FWS listed the lions in the waters of western Alaska as endangered in 1997. As a result, no boats are allowed within three miles of the sea lion rookery on the southwest corner of Adak, and no fishing trawlers are allowed within ten miles. More generally, the regulations flowing from the sea lions' ESA status have generated significant controversy and litigation involving the waters throughout southern Alaska. In July 2000, a federal district court held that fishing in the Aleutian Islands was jeopardizing Steller sea lions, so the court ordered the National Marine Fisheries Service to ban such fishing within the sea lion's critical habitat. That decision, explained a later article in *National Geographic*, "made it hard to be an environmentalist in western Alaska." It "hit the industry hard" because "boats had to go farther out to get the pollock, reducing the freshness of their catch. 'Instead of getting fish less than 40 hours old, you get fish 60 to 80 hours old,'" explained the manager of one of the fish processing plants. "'You can't do much with that. You can't make filets. Roe quality is diminished.'" And "the ban infuriated fishermen and Alaska Senator Ted Stevens, who claimed that it had little scientific basis. Stevens inserted language into an appropriations bill that granted a year to come up with a more palatable plan—today a hodgepodge of protected zones ranging from 10 to 20 miles—and he earmarked more than 40 million dollars for new research to find the cause of the sea lions' decline."[13]

Nearly one hundred years have now passed since environmental law sought to shape Adak's optimal flora and fauna. The creation of the refuge probably saved some marine mammals from extinction, though the same species face different kinds of threats today. The ESA has made the Aleutian shield fern the most favored plant on the island. Meanwhile, the law has targeted other wildlife for elimination. The law has helped to eradicate foxes, it is beginning to grapple with the rat population, and it may be aimed at removing the caribou that have become accustomed to Adak. In each instance, the values incorporated in the law have determined which types of animals and plants are desirable and which are not, and the island's environment has changed as a result. But the biggest changes are attributable to the people who moved to Adak for an entirely different purpose.

WAR AND COLD WAR

Notwithstanding its refuge status, the intentional and accidental manipulation of Adak's animal and plant life belies any image of the island as a pristine outpost far removed from human influence. Still, on a continuum from pristine to polluted, most Aleutian islands fall on the more pristine side of the scale. But Adak has suffered from serious pollution. Large parts of the island are on the National Priorities List—the sites identified by the Environmental Protection Agency (EPA) as the most contaminated places in the country. That pollution was the inexorable result of the events of December 7, 1941. Seven months after Pearl Harbor, in an attempt to divert the U.S. Navy from an imminent attack on Midway Island, the Japanese attacked the Aleutians. They bombed Dutch Harbor at the eastern end of the chain of islands, sent a few troops to visit Adak, and invaded Attu and Kiska islands at the westernmost edge of the Aleutians. The Japanese intended to occupy Adak with a force of twelve hundred men, but the weather required the cancellation of those plans. In August 1942, General George Marshall directed the establishment of a military base in the Aleutians. The military considered several islands as the possible site for the base, and a retired fur trapper was their best source of information about Adak. The air force regarded Adak's terrain as "a nightmare" for a prospective airstrip, consisting of "almost 300 square miles of mountains and tundra, populated mainly by bald eagles and grotesque scavenger ravens." Nonetheless, on August 28, 1942, two submarines delivered thirty-seven commandos to Kuluk Bay on the northeast coast of Adak, and upon finding the island free of Japanese soldiers, eight days later an entire regiment landed amidst a williwaw that "piled barges on the beach, smashed lighters in the water, and spilled tons of cargo to the bottom." Three days after that, the Army Corps of Engineers drained a swampy lagoon and bulldozed an airstrip in the sand on the northeastern part of the island. (Of course, there was no Clean Water Act regulating the drainage of wetlands then.) By the middle of September, a squadron of B-17s, P-38s, and other planes were operating out of the new base. But one lieutenant wrote that "the constant fog and rain make life wet and miserable." Five straight

One of the World War II Quonset huts remaining on Adak Island.

days of Japanese bombings in October 1942 hardly helped matters. Conditions improved somewhat when the navy built an entire city on the island in the space of four months, replacing tents with corrugated metal Quonset huts, and they got even better when each of the military branches established headquarters there.[14]

The base proved invaluable to the U.S. war effort, providing a forward position from which to drive the Japanese out of Attu and Kiska in the summer of 1943. Plane crashes were an unwelcome occurrence for the duration of the war, but the chief enemy of most of Adak's soldiers once the danger of Japanese attack subsided was "pathological boredom." Adak eventually hosted nearly one hundred thousand U.S. military personnel, including Gore Vidal, who wrote his novel *Williwaw* about his experiences there; Dashiell Hammett, author of *The Maltese Falcon*, who recounted that "here in the Aleutians the soldier's needs are many and the country can supply him with literally nothing"; and Eliot Asinof, whose *Saturday Evening Post* article told stories of unimaginable boredom, feigned mental illnesses, and the stark absence of any women among eighty thousand men. USO shows featuring such movie stars as Olivia de Havilland and Errol Flynn visited Adak to entertain the troops. Walter and John Huston lived on the island during the filming of their War Department documentary *Report from the Aleutians,* which contains rare footage of life there during the war. President Franklin D. Roosevelt was another visitor in the last trip that he took to a military field base before he died, and his one day observing life there convinced him to order the troops out as soon as replacements became available.[15]

After World War II, Adak was one of two military bases in the Aleutians to remain open. The U.S. Air Force controlled the military installations there until they were transferred to the navy in 1949. With the development of the Cold War during the 1950s, Adak became part of a vast network of radar and listening posts and hosted a submarine surveillance center. Sometimes, Soviet planes flew so low that they were visible from the island. The navy used Adak for antisubmarine missions, air and sea patrols, reconnaissance flights, search-and-rescue activities, and cold weather training. In 1959, the northern part of the island was formally withdrawn from the wildlife refuge for use by the navy. The small population left after the war grew such that by the early 1990s, nearly six thousand people lived on the island, making it the sixth largest city in the state of Alaska and complicating the state's electoral apportionment. The Naval Air Facility occupied what became known as the "downtown" area along Kuluk Bay on the northeast side of the island, while the Naval Security Group was five miles north along Clam Lagoon. Thanks to the navy, Adak contained airfields, extensive ports, firing ranges, ammunition and ordnance storage and disposal sites, fuel supply tanks, port facilities, and warehouses. But a community other than a strictly military one also developed. Residential housing, a hospital and dental clinic, two chapels, a theater, and other hallmarks of "ordinary" life appeared on the island. Schoolchildren attended the Ann C. Stevens Elementary School, named after Senator Ted Stevens's first wife who had died in a plane crash, while the older students attended the Bob Reeve High School, honoring the pilot who flew supplies to Adak during World War II and who later ran a local airline servicing the island. McDonald's even built a restaurant there in 1984.

Then the law intervened. The seeds of the end of Adak's glory days were sown in 1988 and 1990, when Congress enacted and then amended the Base Closure and Realignment Act to create a "fair process that [would] result in the timely closure and realignment of military installations inside the United States." The act authorized the secretary of defense to create an independent, bipartisan Defense Base Realignment and Closure Commission (BRAC), whose recommended list of which military bases to close could be accepted or rejected by Congress only in its entirety. Adak dodged the first three rounds of base closures, but in 1995 the Department of Defense recommended that the Adak base be closed. It explained that the navy no longer needed its facilities to conduct antisubmarine warfare surveillance and that closing the base could save $354.8 million over twenty years. The department added that no local jobs would be lost and the community would not be adversely affected because there was no community besides the naval base. It even asserted that closing the Adak base "will have a positive effect on the environment" by reducing air pollution in the area. BRAC accepted the military's recommendation, noting that "there were no formal expressions of concern from the local community." Only the Coast Guard lamented the loss of Adak as a support base for law enforcement, search-and-rescue, and navigational assistance operations. Congress accepted BRAC's recommendations, so Adak joined twenty-seven other major facilities that were slated for closure. All of Adak's military facilities closed in 1997, and most people left the island. At the same time, the environmental legacy of forty years of military operations began to be addressed.[16]

THE CLEANUP

Congress enacted CERCLA in December 1980 as a response to the national outcry over episodes like the toxic soup discovered at Love Canal in Niagara Falls, New York, during the 1970s. In the 1930s and 1940s, a chemical manufacturer based in Buffalo, New York, had dumped its wastes in a nearby canal built by and named after William Love in the late nineteenth century. When the company ceased its operations after World War II, it filled in the canal and deeded it to the local school district for free—and for a promise that the school district assumed any liabilities associated with the land. A residential subdivision soon developed on the site, but by the late 1970s the families living there became concerned about the colored liquids oozing into their basements. This story and others like it prompted numerous congressional proposals for federal legislation. The resulting law was intended to require the cleanup of hazardous waste sites first and then to resolve the questions of who should be liable for the costs of that cleanup. Generally, the EPA orders any immediate actions that are necessary to prevent an imminent public health or ecological problem, and then it decides the appropriate final remedy. Most of the continuing debate about CERCLA has involved the liability scheme, which transcends the common law and imposes liability upon a stated group of parties who have been involved with a site, including the current landowner (whether or not that landowner had anything to do with the contamination); parties who had owned the land when hazardous wastes were disposed; and anyone who transported or arranged to transport hazardous waste to the site. There are sometimes thousands of such responsible parties in a CERCLA case.[17]

On Adak, however, there was only one responsible party: all of the contamination there occurred during the navy's forty years of control over the island. The cleanup was thus governed by the additional laws that Congress enacted to address contaminated military facilities. The Superfund Amendments and Reauthorization Act of 1986 (SARA) expanded Section 120 of CERCLA, which governs the liability of federal facilities for hazardous waste cleanups. SARA also established the Defense Environment Restoration Program, the mechanism by which the military identifies, remedies, and funds environmental cleanups at its facilities. Later, in 1992, Congress enacted the Community Environmental Response Facilitation Act, which amended CERCLA Section 120 to require any necessary cleanup actions as part of the closure of any military base.[18]

The investigation of the environmental pollution on Adak began in 1986 and revealed actual or suspected contamination in landfills and other disposal sites, tank farms, pipelines, buildings that housed military operations, the dry cleaning facility, and even the Boy Scout and Girl Scout camps, the old chapel, and the underground storage tanks at the McDonald's. The navy, EPA, and Alaska Department of Environmental Conservation entered into a federal facilities agreement concerning the cleanup in 1993. One year later, the EPA listed Adak on CERCLA's National Priorities List. The first cleanup work occurred pursuant to a 1994 EPA decision documenting the need to engage in interim remedial actions at two inactive landfills that could imminently and substantially endanger the public health, welfare, or environment. Palisades Landfill was located on six acres of land just a few miles north of downtown Adak, and it received all of the island's wastes from the time of the military's arrival in the 1940s until around 1970. The landfill contained lead and mercury batteries, construction waste, solvents, sanitary trash, paint waste, petroleum products, scrap vehicles, and probably countless other unknown substances. Inexplicably, the landfill had been built along Palisades Creek, which flowed into Kuluk Bay, so immediate action was necessary to prevent further erosion of the site and transfer of the buried toxic substances into the bay. The second landfill, known as Metals Landfill, occupied twelve acres just southeast of downtown Adak between Monument Hill and Kuluk Bay. The extant historical records documented such toxic substances as five thousand gallons of polychlorinated biphenyls (PCBs), twenty-five hundred lead batteries, and five hundred pounds of pesticides that had been disposed there, with the caveat that the estimates were "highly uncertain." Metal scrap and debris constituted most of the waste, and part of the landfill contained dewatered sludge. Both landfills were covered, planted with vegetation, and scheduled for ongoing monitoring. Additionally, ninety-six cubic yards of soil contaminated with PCBs were removed and shipped off of the island. CERCLA prefers that hazardous wastes be treated rather than simply buried or moved someplace else, but the EPA determined that "the size of the sites, volumes of wastes and debris, and remote location preclude a practicable remedy that includes excavation and effective

The site of the Palisades Landfill, a few miles north of downtown Adak.

treatment." Palisades Creek was to have been rerouted around the Palisades Landfill pursuant to EPA's 1995 decision, but that action was abandoned at the behest of the FWS in order to preserve the creek's riparian habitat.[19]

One of the most common contaminants found on Adak, petroleum, fell outside the scope of CERCLA. Congress specifically excluded petroleum from the statute both because oil spills were already regulated by the Oil Pollution Act and because the ubiquity of petroleum spills would vastly expand the law's coverage. So in lieu of federal regulation, state law governs the cleanup of petroleum spills on land. The 2000 Record of Decision issued by the EPA identified 128 sites on Adak that were contaminated by petroleum, but the cleanup of these sites has proceeded pursuant to a State-Adak Environmental Restoration Agreement that the navy negotiated with the state of Alaska. The navy and the state integrated the petroleum cleanup into the broader CERCLA process. Some of the sites were addressed by "monitored natural attenuation," which is to say that natural degradation and dispersion caused the contaminant concentrations to drop below the governing standards.

Environmental law did not have much experience with the most unusual contaminants on Adak. Ordnance and explosives (OE) and unexploded ordnance (UXO) were scattered around the island, especially but not limited to areas of past military operations. More than seventy-five thousand such items were recovered between the time of the military's arrival in 1942 and the closure of the base in 1997. Many of those items were simply small arms ammunition, but there were also mines, torpedoes, bombs, grenades, mortars, anti-aircraft munitions, and other weaponry. One resident recalled that "there were over five thousand people out here at one time—women and children—climbing all over everything out here. No one was ever hurt by UXO." Nonetheless, and not surprisingly, the existence of unknown and potentially dangerous ordnance littering the island was of particular concern to many of the residents. Some of the fears attained the status of urban legend, including the persistent belief that mustard gas had been secretly buried at some unspecified place on the island.

Unexploded ordnance was unlikely to have been a concern of Congress when it enacted CERCLA, but nonetheless, the EPA, the navy, and the state decided to employ CERCLA to address Adak's UXO. As one participant put it: "they rewrote the laws for Adak. They came up with their own laws." In 1998, the navy established a separate CERCLA unit for all of the UXO problems, and it began an exhaustive survey of military archives and a careful investigation of the land to identify any latent ordnance. Ordnance was found at nearly two hundred sites comprising twenty thousand acres of land, or 26 percent of the land that the military had used. The search was more limited in parts of the island that were more distant from the military's activities and less likely to cause a problem because they were "inaccessible to reasonably motivated hikers." In 2001, the EPA decided to remove UXO from three sites. Two dozen sites required further excavation to determine whether a threat existed, but the EPA concluded that "due to limitations in current technology and site-specific conditions on Adak, it is not possible to entirely eliminate the potential for encountering OE/UXO."[20]

Instead, all of the sites were subject to "institutional controls," a term that refers to a variety of actions that are designed to prevent exposure to contamination or to prevent additional contamination from being released in the future. The controls feature an educational program that is intended to familiarize Adak residents and visitors with the history of UXO on the island, the characteristics of UXO, and the procedures to follow in the event that UXO is discovered. I did not receive a formal briefing when I arrived at the island, but I did collect several brochures and posters advising me of the dangers of UXO. Actually, I did not need much warning, for the very thought of stumbling onto a live shell while I was hiking through the tundra or along the beach was a powerful deterrent to venturing too far from well-worn paths. Another set of institutional controls includes warning signs and educational materials that advise residents and visitors not to eat too many fish caught in Sweeper Cove or Kuluk Bay, the two bodies of water immediately adjacent to the naval air base in which elevated levels of some toxins had been found in certain species of fish. More restrictive controls were employed in a minefield near Andrew Lake, where the navy has retained control of the affected land for the foreseeable future and has fenced out any trespassers because "no clearance technology can assume 100 percent removal of ordnance materials." Another set of institutional controls sought to ensure that certain areas would never be used for residential purposes and where more stringent standards for the acceptable level of hazardous substances would apply. But reliance on institutional controls is not a panacea. The FWS told the EPA, for example, that the absence of a governmental entity on Adak Island to enforce such controls and the inability of affected wildlife to read warning signs counseled against the use of such measures in lieu of the actual treatment or removal of contaminated sites. "There is much debate and controversy over the effectiveness of institutional controls," according to a study performed by the federal Agency for Toxic Substances and Disease Registry, but the agency concluded that "the Navy has done a remarkable job removing or reducing the numerous hazards on the former military reservation at Adak Island. With the institutional controls in place, people can now safely inhabit and work on the island."[21]

The cleanup of each facility governed by CERCLA has to comply with the statute's national contingency plan (NCP). According to the NCP, nine criteria must be considered when the appropriate cleanup at each site is being decided. Two "threshold criteria" must be satisfied: overall protection of human health and the environment, and compliance with "applicable or relevant appropriate requirements," or ARARs.

CERCLA does not contain any specific standards for acceptable amounts of individual contaminants. Instead, it relies on ARARs that incorporate the provisions of other environmental statutes and regulations. The relevant standards for Adak were contained in dozens of statutes and regulations, including the several parts of the federal Clean Water Act, the Clean Air Act, the Resource Conservation and Recovery Act, the Fish and Wildlife Coordination Act, a presidential executive order for the preservation of wetlands, and the Alaska state water quality standards, clean air regulations, and oil and hazardous substances pollution control regulations. The next five criteria of the NCP are to be balanced against each other. They include the long-term effectiveness and permanence of the remedy; the reduction of toxicity, mobility, and volume of hazardous wastes through treatment; the remedy's short-term effectiveness; the ease of implementation of the remedy; and its cost of implementation. Finally, state and community acceptance of the remedy are considered as two "modifying criteria" under the NCP. The role of these criteria varied at different sites on Adak. The heavy precipitation that Adak experiences influences the long-term effectiveness of any cleanup remedy because of the effect that such water has on the ease with which contaminants can migrate. The cost of differing remedies influenced the decision to rely on fishing warnings at Sweeper Cove and Kuluk Bay, for the EPA concluded that "containment or dredging would cost approximately 20 times more than institutional controls" and that the existing contamination did not threaten human or ecological health once such controls were in place.[22]

The public was involved throughout the cleanup process. A Restoration Advisory Board was formed in 1996 and has met monthly since then with representatives of numerous organizations and several dozen interested private individuals. A series of open houses and public meetings were held on Adak and in Anchorage to report on the progress of the cleanup and to solicit public input. Interested members of the public can be easily informed about the status of the cleanup simply by visiting the website www.adakupdate.com. Thus informed, numerous individuals and organizations offered their thoughts about the cleanup. My general impression, formed by talking with people on the island and reading through the comments submitted for the formal administrative record, is that people are generally satisfied with and keenly appreciate the more than $200 million that the navy has spent to study, contain, and remove all sorts of contamination. Yet there is some concern about the long-term effectiveness of the cleanup, especially when one realizes that warning signs can disappear, buried chemicals can seep away, and forgotten ordnance may suddenly be found. Several residents have complained about all of the decaying buildings and equipment that the navy left behind on the island, but the EPA has responded that CERCLA does not address such aesthetic concerns. The individuals who have commented on the cleanup decisions also stress the importance of the navy's commitment to providing ongoing education to island residents and visitors about the lingering effects of the contamination and cleanup.

Ten years and millions of dollars have removed much of the environmental contamination from Adak Island. Some areas remain off limits to people, and other places are marked with warning signs. The remaining issues concern the sites where the most munitions were fired. The navy would prefer to do a surface cleanup and then be done with the island. The state is willing to allow this, but only as an interim action pending the development of more cost-effective methods of removing UXO from the ground perhaps decades into the future. The FWS has an especially limited budget that makes it unwilling to assume any further costs of managing property that has yet to be approved for unrestricted uses. The cost of the cleanup also invites comparisons to the many other contaminated sites throughout the rest of the United States that await cleanup funding, and those involved with Adak fear that other sites that are closer to areas with larger populations will take priority.

THE RETURN OF THE NATIVES

The extent of a cleanup depends in part on the expected future use of the land because CERCLA considers such uses when designing the appropriate cleanup. Land for industrial activities can tolerate higher levels of remaining contamination, whereas land that will host residential homes must be cleaned up more aggressively. On Adak Island, the future use of the land was a contested question because the cleanup occurred as the naval base was closing. The navy did not want to retain responsibility for the island, but the buildings and other improvements that it had constructed there were valued at an estimated $1.5 billion. "There's so much infrastructure out there, it's unbelievable," recalled one veteran of Adak's cleanup. For example, I stayed in a comfortable two-bedroom duplex, complete with a living room, kitchen, dining room, laundry room, and two bathrooms. It also had cable TV and a telephone. It was located in the Sandy Cove neighborhood, a subdivision that contains 167 identical units, save for the differently colored roofs, and an additional 334 single-family homes. The naval base had also featured a large new high school complete with an Olympic-sized swimming pool, the McDonald's restaurant, an electric power plant, a hospital, port facilities, and an airport capable of handling large jets.

Even so, simply abandoning the island to the wildlife that had always lived there—along with the wildlife introduced during human occupation—was certainly an option. Ordinarily, the preexisting community takes over the property once a military base closes, but there had not been any such community when the commandos arrived on Adak in 1942. Moreover, Alaska's state Land Reuse Authority determined in 1997 that the establishment of a civilian community on Adak was not economically viable. It is just one of hundreds of islands within the AMNWR, most of which do not have a human population. Admittedly, none of these islands ever possessed the infrastructure that the navy had established on Adak, but that infrastructure could be viewed as a curse as well as a blessing. One disgruntled individual complained to Alaska's senators Ted Stevens and Frank Murkowski that Adak "is one gigantic liability; a hole in the ocean in which to throw money." The FWS had no interest in the developed parts of Adak. "It's contaminated, it's got houses," observed an FWS employee, so that part of the island was unhelpful to the mission of the refuge. The FWS probably would have bulldozed all of the buildings and other structures if the entire island had been given back to the agency. The closure of the military facilities could have meant that the permanent human presence on the island would simply end.[23]

But Adak was not abandoned. The next relevant law in its history is the Alaska Native Claims Settlement Act (ANCSA), the statute that Congress passed in 1971 to deal with the native land claims that had been unresolved when Alaska became a state twelve years before. ANCSA settled the native claims to land throughout the state by providing forty million acres and nearly $1 billion to twelve new regional corporations established for native Alaskans. The Aleut Corporation is one of those corporations, established by Congress with a mandate "to create a healthy corporation, generate revenues with substantial profits, provide significant dividends and benefits to shareholders, and create meaningful linkage to the Aleut 'Unangan' people." The corporation received $19.5 million pursuant to ANCSA, along with the surface rights to more than 1.5 million acres of land on the Alaska Peninsula and the Aleutian, Shumagin, and Pribilof Islands. The corporation is now owned by more than thirty-six hundred shareholders, and the largest bulk of its revenue is generated by operation and maintenance contracts with the federal government. The corporation's businesses also include natural resource development, rental properties, and fuel sales in Alaska, as well as a few investments elsewhere in the United States. Altogether, the Aleut Corporation earned a net income of almost $3.6 million in 2008, a 69 percent increase over the year before.[24]

The navy's exit from Adak Island attracted the attention of the Aleut Corporation, which expressed an interest in developing a community there. ANCSA entitles each Alaskan native corporation to select certain lands in the state to which they then receive title, and the Aleut Corporation selected the northern half of Adak. In 2002, Congress approved an exchange by which the FWS and the Aleut Corporation swapped equally sized parcels of 47,150 acres of land, so the Aleut Corporation now owns most of the northern half of the island while the southern half remains part of the AMNWR. About thirty Aleut families moved to the island from elsewhere in Alaska after the naval base closed. The school reopened, as did several other facilities. The island's residents voted sixty-one to six in April 2001 to incorporate Adak as a city for the purposes of Alaskan law.[25]

Now about 120 people live in facilities that accommodated 6,000 people fewer than twenty years ago. My time on Adak was surreal because the infrastructure is more or less intact, but few of the buildings are used or occupied. The grass looks like it hasn't been cut since the navy left, and many of the buildings have broken windows or other evidence of decay. The old McDonald's restaurant is empty, the hospital is closed, and the relatively new church atop a hill is unused. The large elementary and middle schools are also closed, and even though the high school building is open, it is not a high school anymore. Instead, it houses a combination restaurant and store; the city offices, which are surrounded by rows of student lockers; an enormous gym; classrooms for the remaining eighteen students; and a medical clinic, post office, and video rental counter. The community center building is now home to the Adak General Store. It was a very odd experience living in this large, virtually abandoned town.

The Aleut Corporation and the residents of Adak are keenly aware of the need to attract additional people to the island before the infrastructure decays. They are concentrating their efforts on economic development to make Adak a viable community. Toward that end, in 2005 the corporation established the subsidiary corporations of Adak Petroleum, Aleut Fisheries, Adak Marine Services, Adak Commercial Properties, Adak Residential Properties, Frosty Fuels, and Adak Building Inventory. The corporation recently reported that it "is looking at ways of utilizing its fuel tank capacity of 550,000 barrels (or 21 million gallons) of fuel at Adak." It also noted that "substantial improvements are being made to the properties in Adak, and we should see the benefits of those improvements in the long-term." Fishing is perhaps the key part of Adak's future. A subsidiary of the Aleut Corporation and another private entity operate a seafood processing and cold storage plant for cod, crab, halibut, and other bottom fish. The goal is to have more of the fishing work done on the island, including such "value-added" tasks as preparing filets and steaks. Besides fishing, the state economic development agency's website proclaims that Adak's "unique geographic location makes Adak a supply and support center for commercial, nonprofit and government organizations developing opportunities throughout the North Pacific and the Bering Sea." The island's port services foreign fishing fleets in need of refueling or crew transfers, as well as occasional visits by the M/V *Tiglax*, the FWS research vessel that operates throughout the AMNWR. Nearly fifty fishing boats hope to use a new small boat harbor that is being built to accommodate smaller vessels that are unable to operate close to shore. Additionally, in 2003 the Department of Defense selected Adak to serve as the primary support base for the Sea-Based X-Band radar, part of the missile defense program that was being developed by the Bush administration. The radar was expected to arrive in Adak during 2009, but in February 2009 a former Defense Department official told a congressional committee that the failure to station it there yet rendered its suitability "to be operated and maintained in that

environment unknown." At least housing is affordable on Adak: du-
plexes are on sale for $12,500, while $20,000 will buy the most expensive fourplex on the island.[26]

Adak could even become a tourist destination. As one former resident explained, there are plenty of people, "surprisingly enough," who
were stationed at Adak and want to go back to see it today. Tourism in
Adak could succeed "if people played their cards right, and they started
marketing ecotours, and reunion groups, and vet groups." The wildlife
that prompted the establishment of the AMNWR may also help support
the island's economy. An advertisement for one recent birdwatching trip
extolled Adak as "a spectacular birding destination that has only recently
become accessible to the birding public." Such trips promise outstanding birding opportunities and comfortable accommodations (thanks to
the navy's officer housing), but the price is steep: $4,600 for eight days,
not including the cost of traveling to Anchorage. A couple of dozen bird-
ers have visited the island during each of the past five years, and many
people on the island are talking about starting a charter business, but it
takes a lot of money for a boat and insurance. The reward, however, could
be great for Adak's economy. As one island resident explained: "The
hunter is always a very parsimonious guy. He ain't gonna spend money
on nothing. The birder has a $10,000 spotting scope, they're wearing all
of that Patagonia, they're throwing money at boat people to take them
places. They're rich people that have time to go to *Adak* to look at a bird!"
Ironically, most of the birdwatching sites are located on the land owned
by the Aleut Corporation on the northern part of the island, not on the
AMNWR lands to the south. Besides the birds, other marine mammals
in the adjacent waters, such as whales and endangered Steller sea lions,
could lure ecotourists to Adak, though they have not done so yet. Caribou could attract hunters. Two national hunting magazines described
Adak as having the biggest caribou in the world. The AMNWR reports
that both the size of the caribou herd and the size of the individual animals are growing because there is "plenty of food and little to bother
them." Furthermore, it encourages hunting as a means of protecting native plants and ecosystems; there are no legal limits on the number of
caribou that one can take there.

Adak's appeal to all sorts of travelers is limited by the inexplica-
ble failure of any leading travel guides to mention the island. Even the

guidebook publisher Lonely Planet, which is justly famous for promoting travel to all sorts of obscure locations around the world, neglects Adak in its guide to Alaska. A travel consultant based in Anchorage "loved visiting Adak," but he appears to be the only writer praising the virtues of the island as a travel destination. Equally important, the cost of flights to Adak—round trip from Anchorage is more than $1,200—deters many travelers. Perhaps the most promising sources of visitors are Alaska Airlines employees, who can travel for free, and those people who can use Alaska Airlines frequent flyer miles to travel to the island because it is such an exotic place to visit. One former island resident told me that a trip to Adak was the "best use of miles in the world." And the number of visitors to Adak would surely increase if there were ever a repeat of the fare war that occurred when two carriers served the island while the navy was there, pushing flights to Anchorage to as little as $175.[27]

Many other activities could take place on Adak. One of the studies conducted during the CERCLA cleanup identified a wide range of possible future uses, including housing offices for federal agencies with an interest in the region; supporting oceanographic research; and providing communications facilities, an environmental incinerator or remediation programs, a rocket launch facility, fuel distribution, marine transportation and shipping, and coal or zinc storage. The novel *Prisoners of the Williwaw* by Ed Griffin imagines the island serving as a remote prison camp. One correspondent suggested that the AIG executives who received generous retention bonuses after their insurance company received a government bailout should "be given government transportation to Adak Island, where they will live in tents for the rest of their lives." None of these ideas has yet materialized, and it is doubtful whether they ever will.[28]

THE CONTINUING EFFECTS OF ENVIRONMENTAL
LAW ON ADAK ISLAND

Environmental law has much to say about what will happen on Adak next. Three aspects of the natural environment there are especially important for the island's future: (1) the contamination of the northern part of the island leaves a legacy of continuing environmental regulation, (2) the protected refuge and wilderness status of the southern half of the island restrict what can be done there, and (3) the regulation of the fisheries in the waters surrounding the island will help decide the economic viability of Adak's favored approach to economic development.

CERCLA is the key environmental law with respect to the north side, where the navy conducted most of its operations and which is now owned by the Aleut Corporation. Here, the existence of CERCLA meant that the navy had a legal obligation to clean up the site. That statutory mandate should not be underestimated. Thanks to the retroactivity of CERCLA, the military has engaged in the much more difficult task of removing contamination from many of its former properties that closed long before the law was enacted. At Adak, the navy was able to close its bases and engage in the cleanup simultaneously. And Adak would be a much different—and much less hospitable—place today if the navy had not spent the money that it did to remove the chemicals and ordnance from the site of its former operations.

Yet CERCLA only goes so far. The CERCLA cleanup determined how much contamination would be tolerated. For example, the EPA considered requiring the navy to remove *all* UXO from the site, but it declined to do so because of the cost and impossibility of the task. Nor did the navy purify all of the waters adjacent to its old facilities, relying instead on the advisories to limit the amount of fish taken from areas where the contamination could be a problem. Additionally, many island residents object to the sight of all of the junk that the navy left behind, but the EPA has correctly explained that CERCLA does not consider aesthetic harms. A lot of people complain about "going down to the beach and smelling fuel leaking out of the rocks" and seeing "barrels of mysterious things lying around everywhere." All told, CERCLA ensured that Adak would not suffer from levels of chemical contamination and ordnance that would threaten human or ecological health, but it did not require the navy to remove all traces of its four-decade presence on the island. The navy did, however, remove 43,878 Rommel stakes—pointed metal posts designed to pierce the combat boots of invading Japanese troops—even though these defensive weapons were beyond the scope of the hazardous wastes regulated by CERCLA.

The prospective effect of CERCLA is seen in the equitable servitudes and private land use restrictions that constrain what can be done on the island in those areas affected by past contamination. Before the navy conveyed the land to the Aleut Corporation, the EPA had to certify that the cleanup complied with CERCLA's specific provisions governing the suitability of transferring the land to another party. At a number of sites, the EPA decided that the best remedy was to prevent certain future uses of the land. Several areas, for example, may not be used for residential purposes. The legal mechanism for accomplishing this result once the navy surrendered title to the property appears in the equitable servitudes that become part of the title to the property itself. An *equitable servitude* is a binding restriction upon the use of the land that is imposed for the benefit of a neighbor or some other party and that runs with the title to the land itself. Property thus burdened is subject to the restriction no matter who owns it in the future, and the navy will always retain standing to enforce the restriction.

Adak's wildlife receives extra protection within the AMNWR on the southern part of the island. There, the key statutes are the national wildlife refuge statute and the Wilderness Act. The federal statutes governing national wildlife refuges in Alaska identify five purposes to be pursued in the management of such land: (1) to conserve fish and wildlife habitats in their natural diversity, (2) to fulfill international treaty obligations, (3) to provide continued subsistence uses by native Alaskan peoples, (4) to ensure water quality and necessary water quantity within the refuge, and (5) to facilitate scientific research on marine resources. Certain development activities are not allowed in the refuge, though unlike other refuges, there are no trees to cut and no known mineral resources to exploit. Also, federal regulations specifically direct that the area must remain open to some hunting and sport fishing, which means that caribou hunting is permissible on Adak refuge lands.[29]

The refuge is also a wilderness area and thus governed by the more stringent provisions of the Wilderness Act. The most notable restriction imposed by the Wilderness Act is that motorized vehicles are not allowed in a wilderness area, with rare exceptions. This is not an issue in one sense, for the closest road stops a mile's hike short of the wilderness area. But off-road vehicles (ORVs) have become increasingly popular on Adak in the past few years, including some of the vehicles that the navy had used to search for UXO. The FWS had about a half dozen employees on the island while the navy base was operating, but most of those officials left with the navy, and neither the remaining permanent employee nor the occasional seasonal FWS researcher is equipped to enforce the refuge's boundaries from invading ORVs. Helicopters are another type of motorized vehicle that could become a problem within the refuge. Some of the caribou hunting outfitters have explored the possibility of using helicopters to drop off hunters on more remote parts of the island within the wilderness area, but again, the Wilderness Act would prohibit that.[30]

Several laws complicate the effort to remove certain invasive species from the island. The Wilderness Act is frustratingly ambiguous concerning the baseline conditions that the law is designed to preserve. At what point, in other words, does a species qualify as part of the original landscape that the Wilderness Act is designed to protect? Rats, for example, have lived in the Aleutians for more than two centuries; foxes were on Adak nearly that long. Assuming that the Wilderness Act permits the removal of unwanted species, the means of doing so is governed by FIFRA, which mandates an exhaustive registration procedure before poisons are allowed to be intentionally introduced into the environment. And even that may not be enough. The relationship between FIFRA and the ESA has become a contested issue in the Pacific Northwest with respect to the effects of pesticide runoff into streams inhabited by endangered salmon. A federal court of appeals held that compliance with FIFRA is not sufficient in that instance and that the EPA must engage in the consultation with the FWS that is required before any federal agency can do anything that jeopardizes a protected species. The parallel issue for Adak concerns sea otters, which were listed as threatened species under the ESA in 2005 and which could be adversely affected if they are exposed to the rodenticides that are used to kill rats. The biggest legal challenge to the removal of Adak's invasive species is the fact that only half of the island is protected as a national wildlife refuge. The City of Adak and the state of Alaska have jurisdiction over most of the northern part of the island, and if the city and the state either fail to combat a particular invasive species or affirmatively desire its presence, such as caribou and foxes, then whatever the FWS does on its part of the island will always be at the mercy of the animals that move throughout the island innocent of any knowledge of the boundaries imposed by law.[31]

THE FISHERY OF THE FUTURE

One more collection of federal environmental statutes may play a central role in determining the fate of Adak's human community. In 1976, Congress enacted the Magnuson-Stevens Fishery Conservation and Management Act, named after longtime Washington senator Warren Magnuson and Alaska's own senator Ted Stevens. Congress has since amended the statutory regime established by the Magnuson-Stevens Act, first by enacting the Sustainable Fisheries Act in 1996 to address concerns about overfishing, and then by addressing the specific issues of Alaskan fisheries in the American Fisheries Act (AFA) in 1998. Together, these laws have been implemented to reduce foreign dominance of fishing operations, protect the ecological health of the fishery, and aid the small, Alaskan communities that depend on commercial fishing, including Adak.[32]

Traditionally, all fishing in the oceans outside of three miles of a nation's coast was largely unregulated. That approach became untenable by the 1970s as more and more vessels sought to catch a declining number of fish. But it was not the health of the marine ecosystem as such that prompted Congress to act. As one report describes it, "Congress was most concerned first and foremost with the perception that foreign fishing fleets were catching too many fish off American shores." The Magnuson-Stevens Act thus asserted exclusive U.S. jurisdiction over a two-hundred-mile area along the nation's coasts. Still, that did not solve the problem of foreign vessels dominating the fisheries in the Bering Sea and the Aleutian Islands. Therefore, the AFA imposed a series of regulations that were designed to achieve 75 percent U.S. ownership of the vessels and processing facilities operating in the region.[33]

Congress has been concerned about overfishing by Americans as well as foreigners. Generally, the Magnuson-Stevens Act seeks to ensure that marine fishery resources are not overharvested by establishing eight Regional Fishery Councils with authority to regulate fishing within specific areas off the coast of the United States. Each council is composed of twenty-one members representing the federal government, neighboring states, local Indian tribes, fishing interests, and other affected parties. The councils decide how many fish can be caught and who can catch them. A council does this by developing fishery management plans for the areas under its jurisdiction. The National Marine Fisheries Service within the Department of Commerce must determine that each plan satisfies ten national standards prescribed by the statute, including the prevention of overfishing, the achievement of the optimal yield from each fishery, and consideration of the importance of fishery resources for fishing communities. The statute further provides that "if it becomes necessary to allocate or assign fishing privileges among various United States fishermen, such allocation shall be (A) fair and equitable to all such fishermen; (B) reasonably calculated to promote conservation; and (C) carried out in such a manner that no particular individual, corporation, or other entity acquires an excessive share of such privileges."[34]

The North Pacific Fishery Management Council (NPFMC) governs fishing within the Aleutians, the Bering Sea, and the Gulf of Alaska. The council is recognized as the best of the regional councils at managing and conserving the fisheries under its jurisdiction. It issued the fishery management plan for the groundfish fisheries of the Bering Sea and Aleutian Islands Management Area in 1982, and it has amended it more than seventy times since then. The current plan establishes a total allowable catch of two million tons of fish. There are about three hundred species of fish in the Bering Sea, most of which are found at or near the bottom of the sea. One species has commanded the attention of the commercial fishing operations: pollack. Consumer demand for Alaskan pollack has grown rapidly in recent years to supply breaded fish products in the United States and surimi—Japanese for "minced fish"—throughout the world. Pollack account for nearly 70 percent of the two million tons of fish caught in the Bering Sea and Aleutian Islands waters each year. The fish can be found throughout the region in concentrations that depend on the area, the depth of the water, and the season. Pollack are easiest to catch between February and April when the larger fish gather to spawn, though that is also the season when the weather is worst.[35]

Many of the legal disputes arising under the Magnuson-Stevens Act involve efforts by regional councils to restrict the catch of fish whose populations are declining. The pollack in the western Bering Sea and Aleutian Islands, however, do not suffer from that problem. For many years the pollack in the region were ignored by commercial fishing operations, many of which were based in Seattle and could catch all of the pollack that they wanted closer to home in the eastern Bering Sea. The pollack catch in the Aleutian Islands grew from ten thousand tons before 1980 to ninety-eight thousand tons in 1991, and by the mid-1990s, most of the fish were caught in the waters just north of Adak and nearby islands. There are fewer pollack along the Aleutians than there are elsewhere in the north Pacific, so for four years beginning in 1999, the NPFMC recommended against fishing for pollack in the Aleutians because of the modest size of the fishery stock, because the fish were so abundant elsewhere, and because pollack are among the favored prey of the endangered Steller sea lions in the region.

The restrictions on foreign vessels heightened the competition among U.S. commercial fishing operations. Part of the problem was that too many vessels were chasing too few fish; so the AFA pursued decapitalization by buying out certain vessels and restricting future entrants into the fishery, and the law pursued rationalization by encouraging fishing cooperatives and otherwise eliminating the race to catch fish. Furthermore, the NPFMC acted to facilitate economic development in impoverished western Alaskan communities that lacked the capital to establish a commercial fishing fleet. Pursuant to its Western Alaska Community Development Quota (CDQ) program, the council allocates a portion of the permissible fishery catch to six approved groups that represent the Pribilof Islands, the Yukon Delta, and other affected communities. For example, those groups are now entitled to 10 percent of the fishery's pollack allocation. The program has been credited with generating eighteen hundred jobs annually and a total of $650 million in revenues during its thirteen years of assisting many remote fishing communities.

Adak, however, did not benefit from this program because the island had never hosted its own fishing operations. That problem disappeared when Congress intervened to aid Adak's access to the fisheries in the waters surrounding the island. In 2004, Congress added a rider to an appropriations bill that amended the Magnuson-Stevens Act to require the approval and implementation of the fisheries management plan that the NPFMC had adopted. The rider provided that "the non-CDQ directed pollock fishery in the Aleutian Islands is fully allocated to the Aleut Corporation for the purpose of economic development in Adak, Alaska." The provision was inserted at the insistence of Senator Stevens, who told his Senate colleagues that "establishing a small boat fleet will be critical for the economic diversification of Adak and the revenues generated from the use of the Aleutian Islands pollock allocation will allow for greater investment opportunities for this community." More generally, as one environmental assessment described it, "the 'economic development' purpose of the Aleut Corporation is very broad and could encompass any activity funded or undertaken by the Aleut Corporation in or for Adak." The corporation could require that its pollack allocation be focused on those vessels or fishing crews that are based in Adak, but the statutory language does not require that. Another statutory rider gave Adak 2.7 million pounds of the total allowable catch in the western portion of the Aleutian Islands golden king crab fishery that opened in August 2005, the first fishery established under the NPFMC's new crab rationalization program that establishes quotas of permissible catches for vessels and processors involved in the crab fishery.[36]

Acting on that statutory mandate, the National Marine Fisheries Service allocated the nearby pollack fishery and 10 percent of the total allowable annual catch of western Aleutian Island golden king crab to representatives of the Adak community. The establishment of special treatment for Adak provoked objections that the rules would not promote the fisheries preservation for which the Magnuson-Stevens Act was designed and that economic development on Adak was unnecessary, counterproductive (because it could turn Adak into an urban area), and misguided (because it should not be achieved by overfishing in any event). The National Marine Fisheries Service responded that it was powerless to change the statutory mandate, and in any event, no overfishing had or was likely to occur. The FWS added, with notable understatement, that "the nature of the economic development will be decided by the Aleut Corporation and is unlikely to resemble large urban areas in the United States, considering the Aleut culture and the remote location of Adak." Perhaps so, but neither did anyone expect that Alaska would host thirty-two canneries that shipped nearly $3 million worth of salmon two decades after Secretary of State William Seward's purchase of the empty, remote territory.[37]

The allocation of the pollack and crab fisheries to Adak is expressly subject to the continuing dictates of the ESA and other environmental laws. Adjustments to the permissible amount of pollack fishing would trigger the consultation requirement of the ESA because of the possible effects on endangered Steller sea lions. The sea lions eat a lot of pollack, and the existence of ample fish near sea lion rookeries and haulouts is important. Increased fishing could also result in the accidental catching of chinook salmon, which would require the redirection of vessels to fish in areas outside the preferred habitat of the salmon. Moreover, increased visits by ships to Adak also create the potential for more rats, though that is of greater concern for islands that, unlike Adak, have been free of rats to date.

The fishery employs about twenty-five people on Adak throughout most of the year, with a peak of nearly one hundred employees during the busy months between January and March. There are five local fishing vessels, of which two are owned by Adak Fisheries. But the fishing operation has faced significant difficulties. So far, the Aleut Corporation has failed to harvest the pollack allocation that Congress has awarded to it. Adak fishing boats caught only 195 of their 1,200 metric ton allocation during the first year of the program. Part of the problem is the difficulty of having to catch pollack more than twenty miles from shore, as required by the measures protecting Steller sea lions. The city of Adak has already received nearly $90,000 to mitigate the economic effect of the protection of the sea lions. Fishing farther from land is dangerous given the extreme weather in the Aleutians, especially for the smaller vessels that could be based in Adak. The Aleut Corporation has since requested permission to fish in state waters closer to shore, but those waters are within the sea lion's designated critical habitat.

Adak's fledging fishery also depends on the actions of the NPFMC. The crab rationalization program adopted in 2005, which relies on market-based strategies for regulating access to the crab, resulted in the amount of brown king crab processed on Adak dropping from two million pounds annually to only eighty-eight thousand pounds in 2007. As an alternative, Adak Fisheries petitioned the NPFMC for the right to process pollack caught in the Bering Sea, but Dutch Harbor objected that the proposal would limit the pollack that are available to that city under the law's quota. Adak is also objecting to a large fishing corporation based in Seattle that is "draining Adak for cod," according to Adak's mayor, by using a ship to process cod caught near Adak rather than having those fish processed on Adak itself. The administrative decisions of the NPFMC will say much about the future of the fishery operations on Adak.[38]

Those operations have experienced numerous obstacles. Seven people died in October 2008 when their fishing boat capsized while returning to Dutch Harbor with a load of cod that they had caught near

Adak. Pollack appear to be migrating north toward Russian waters, perhaps because of climate change. The corporate arrangements between the Aleut Corporation, the two Norwegian individuals who started the plant, and other corporate partners resulted in the National Oceanic and Atmospheric Administration imposing a $3.44 million fine in 2004 for violating the AFA's crab-processing cap. The corporate arrangements broke down altogether in the summer of 2005 when the ownership of the facilities was litigated in Alaskan state court. Then, in September 2005, the *Anchorage Daily News* published an exposé accusing state senator Ben Stevens of holding a secret option to buy into the Adak fishery operations while his father, U.S. senator Ted Stevens, pushed for the congressional legislation that gave Adak its special rights under the Magnuson-Stevens Act. Ben Stevens had worked as a lobbyist and board member for different entities seeking the pollack allocation for Adak, and he also held an option to buy 25 percent of Adak's fishing company that he did not disclose when the decisions about Adak's pollack allocation were being made in Alaska and in Congress. The federal probe of Ted Stevens investigated possible corruption related to Adak's fisheries, too, but Adak did not play a role in his October 2008 conviction (later overturned for what the trial judge denounced as "outrageous" prosecutorial misconduct) or his November 2008 reelection defeat.[39]

Whatever the cause, the fall of Senator Stevens could result in the demise of the human community on Adak. The island's future depends heavily on federal subsidies. In January 2008, Senator Stevens supported the funding provided by the proposed Indian Health Care Improvement Act by observing that "a pregnant woman living in Adak" who is about to deliver her baby must take a five-hour flight to Anchorage "on a plane that is available only two or three days a week." The Essential Air Service program operated by the U.S. Department of Transportation (DOT) may have the biggest say in Adak's future, even though it is unrelated to environmental law. It is difficult to imagine the community surviving without regularly scheduled flights. Thus, when Reeve Aleutian Airways stopped flying to Adak in December 2000, DOT responded by subsidizing another air carrier to serve the island. "Clearly," DOT admitted, "no community currently relying on subsidized air service is as isolated and dependent on air service as Adak." Moreover, as DOT added, "the very long distance of 1,200 miles to Anchorage, coupled with the very severe and unpredictable weather, almost dictates the use of large aircraft." So I flew to Adak in a Boeing 737, a larger plane than I am able to fly out of my home airport in South Bend, Indiana, thanks to the $1.6 million that DOT pays Alaska Airlines annually to fly to the island. But even with the DOT subsidy, my flight cost more than $1,000. Adak is hardly the only beneficiary of such largesse; thirty-nine other communities in Alaska depend on federally subsidized air service, and, of course, federal spending on highways, Amtrak, and airport improvements go far toward determining the future of communities throughout the country. But DOT warned in 2003 that it would revisit the subsidy "if traffic does not respond or the level of subsidy support needed does not decline." The nine people on my flights into and out of Adak could have fit into three of the twenty-five rows on the Boeing 737, which could concern DOT.

Nor can the people living on Adak Island survive without energy. Gasoline prices there reached $8.65 per gallon in May 2008 (as opposed to only about $4.50 in Anchorage and $3.72 nationally). More ominously, the city owed the Aleut Corporation more than $500,000 for diesel fuel as of September 2008, so it encouraged local residents to leave the island because it could provide electricity only a few hours per day with its limited fuel supplies needed to run the city's power plant. Several bloggers complained that Governor Sarah Palin was too busy campaigning for vice president to attend to Adak's needs. The city's predicament was caused by the failure of Adak Fisheries to pay the hundreds of thousands of dollars that it owed the city, which in turn was caused by "quotas on king crab and an influx of floating fish processors" that had sapped the economic viability of the fishery. In other words, the law—to wit, the Magnuson-Stevens Act as applied by the NPFMC—could produce a cascading effect in which the island's power plant closes, the water pumps are shut down, and the lagoon swamps the facilities that the navy left downtown. The city avoided that fate when its council approved a new agreement to purchase more fuel on credit from the Aleut Corporation, but the city manager and two other officials resigned because they objected to a provision in the agreement that prohibited city officials from publicly criticizing the corporation. If the tenuous agreement fails, then Adak Island could begin to return to the state of nature that the navy commandos found when they landed on the island in August 1942.[40]

CHAPTER TWO

The Mayor's Oversized Flyswatter

COLTON, CALIFORNIA

ONE DAY IN 2002, the mayor of Colton, California, appeared at a press conference wielding a giant flyswatter. Deirdre Bennett did not usually carry such a prop when she spoke, but on that day Mayor Bennett said that her city was being held hostage to a fly—a three-inch, brownish, pollinating Delhi Sands flower-loving fly that the federal government had listed as endangered pursuant to the ESA in 1993. Mayor Bennett's stunt did not work—she failed to persuade Congress to remove the fly from the ESA's protected list—and both the City of Colton and the fly's supporters continue to struggle with each other and the law that brought them together.[1]

This is a story of environmental law not working. The city's economic development has been stymied, the fly and the unique dune ecosystem of which it is a part are disappearing, and everyone blames everyone else. But that is not the only story that Colton has to tell. Founded in the nineteenth century, Colton prospered during the first half of the twentieth century, but since then it has struggled with a legacy of environmental contamination, poverty, and corruption. The western part of San Bernardino County where Colton is located also experiences some of the worst air pollution in the nation. To tell Colton's story, I begin with the city's history, then turn to the pollution problems that it confronts today, and finally recount the saga of the fly and how its federally mandated preservation continues to affect Colton.

COLTON, THE HUB CITY

Colton is a city of fifty thousand people located seventy-five miles straight east of Los Angeles along Interstate 10. The Santa Ana River flows through the southern end of the city as it travels from the mountains of the San Bernardino National Forest en route to the Pacific Ocean at Newport Beach. Colton is bordered by the cities of San Bernardino on the north and east, Rialto to the west, and Loma Linda, Grand Terrace, and unincorporated Riverside County to the south. It is located in the southwestern corner of San Bernardino County and is thus part of the Inland Empire, the name often given to San Bernardino and Riverside counties. The area was long inhabited by many different Native American peoples, including Serrano and Gabrielino villages along the Santa Ana River. Spanish explorers passed through during the 1770s while in search of a route from Mexico to Monterrey. Then, the area came under the control of Catholic missions until 1834, when the Mexican government desecularized the missions and distributed their vast landholdings to various political favorites. During the 1840s, immigrants from New Mexico founded Agua Mansa, which became the first nonmission Catholic parish in Southern California in what is now the southwestern part of Colton. The first American and English settlers arrived when Mormons established San Bernardino in 1851, one year after California became a state. The area was part of San Diego County at statehood; one year later it moved to Los Angeles County, and in 1853 it moved again to the new San Bernardino County.

Colton was settled in 1874 when the Southern Pacific Railroad built a depot there. The town was named after David Colton, one of the railroad's vice presidents who lived in a mansion on Nob Hill in San Francisco. Colton never visited his namesake city before he died at the age of forty-seven. The city was formally incorporated in 1887 upon the favorable vote of 68 percent of the city's 176 residents. Colton is located only a few miles north of Riverside County, which like San Bernardino County stretches east to the Nevada border. Colton's proximity to Riverside County prevented it from becoming the county seat in San Bernardino, thanks to a state law prohibiting any county seat from being located within five miles of another county. The city of San Bernardino received the county seat honor instead, just as that city obtained a Santa Fe rail depot in the 1880s by offering a better land deal than Colton. Colton kept growing, though, expanding from its initial one square mile to about eighteen square miles thanks to the annexation of adjacent areas that were previously unincorporated in San Bernardino County. Now the city even has an annexation page on its city website. Colton has competed with its neighbors for the same unincorporated territory, once winning a lawsuit accusing Rialto of failing to follow the mandated state annexation procedures. Colton also had to rebuff the efforts of its rival city San Bernardino to annex Colton itself in 1930. Usually, though, Colton has been the aggressor in annexation fights. Sometimes, it is too aggressive: in 2006 Mayor Kelly Chastain apologized to the residents of one area that was targeted for annexation, admitting that the city failed to keep them adequately informed of its intentions.[2]

The railroad has always played a central role in the life of Colton. The California Southern Railroad (a predecessor of the Santa Fe) joined the Southern Pacific in Colton in 1883. The San Pedro, Los Angeles, and Salt Lake Railroad reached Colton in 1905 and by the 1920s was operating as part of the Union Pacific network. Thus, Colton earned the moniker "the Hub City," as it was the only place where the two transcontinental railroads met. The railroads soon generated legal disputes. The Southern Pacific—whose interests were defended by Colton's first sheriff, Virgil Earp—tried to block the route of the California Southern Railroad in 1883 until the governor sent a posse to enforce a court order permitting the new railroad. A land dispute involving the lands that the federal government gave to the Southern Pacific reached the U.S. Supreme Court in 1892, with the Court holding that the contested lands were exempted from the 1871 statute that awarded land to the Southern Pacific. During a 1948 campaign stop, President Truman recalled the turmoil of those early days when he observed that Colton had once "had a fight between the special interests and the people, and they organized a freight train of their own and ran mule teams in competition with the railroad until the freight trains came down to a workable rate." The railroads also attracted workers from Mexico, who soon established a thriving community on the south side of Colton near where the Agua Mansa settlers had lived.[3]

The settlers began planting citrus orchards in 1874 despite concerns that the land was inadequate for farming. But once irrigated water was delivered from the nearby Santa Ana River, the citrus thrived in the warm climate, and much of the land was cultivated for oranges, grapes, peaches, and other fruits by the late 1800s. Industry also reached Colton early in its history. In 1861, the Colton Lime and Marble Company began mining Slover Mountain, named after an early settler who died from a grizzly bear attack there in 1854. The marble was gone by 1887, but there was still a lot of limestone left. The California Portland Cement Company took over and expanded the mining operations beginning in 1891, soon overseeing one of the first cement plants in the United States. Cement from Colton has helped to build the Hoover Dam, the Los Angeles City Hall, Dodger Stadium, and countless other projects as the plant continues to operate into the twenty-first century. But the mine and the fruit orchards did not always exist harmoniously. In 1911, the California Supreme Court ruled in favor of the fruit tree growers in their nuisance lawsuit against the mine. It was, the court noted, "the first case in America, so far as this court knew, in which the operation of a cement plant had been enjoined because of the dust produced in the processes of manufacture." The court recognized that the mining company employed the "best, most modern methods in its processes of manufacture, but that nevertheless there is an unavoidable escape into the air of certain dust and smoke." Yet the company's pleas of financial distress failed to persuade the court. "To permit the cement company to continue its operations even to the extent of destroying the property of the two plaintiffs and requiring payment of the full value thereof would be, in effect, allowing the seizure of private property for a use other than a public one—something unheard of and totally unauthorized in the law." Instead of closing, the cement plant bought the affected 125 acres of land within three-fourths of a mile of the plant for $92,450 (plus paying $24,381 in damages).[4]

Dairies, residential homes, and commercial developments were the next to appear on the scene. The citrus orchards began to be replaced by residential housing by the 1930s. The city enjoyed "a strong community identity," local historian Larry Sheffield told me. "Colton started out as a

The Colton cement plant operating in the early twentieth century.

pretty integrated little community, hometown USA kind of place, where people were born and grew up and went to school and worked and got married and raised their family." Colton High School still holds classes in the building that opened in 1923. (No one seems to care about the irony, given the city's controversies over a fly, that the school's nickname—the Yellow Jackets—celebrates an insect.) But the city's cohesion disintegrated as the citrus industry disappeared, then I-10 literally cut the city in half in the 1950s, and the redevelopment efforts of the 1960s caused the city's sense of identity to break down. "Not too many people really seem to identify very strongly with Colton," Sheffield says. "It's just a place for municipal services. They work and play someplace else." Many Colton residents work in Orange County and Los Angeles, spending countless hours each day commuting on the interstate.

Today, downtown Colton has a modest collection of stores and offices, most of which look like they were built during the 1960s or 1970s, and sometimes earlier. The most impressive building is the old Carnegie Library, built in 1907, which now houses the Colton Museum that Sheffield helps to run. The library abandoned the building in 1982 in favor of a bland—and no larger—building a few blocks away. The revitalization of Colton's downtown is often described as one of the city's most pressing needs. The area south of I-10 features the cement plant, the railroad tracks, and numerous industrial facilities. South Colton is also home to "one of the very few barrios in California that offers the opportunity for preserving and maintaining the integrity of a community that clearly reflects the entire scope of Chicano history," according to one study. The southeastern corner of Colton contains numerous recreational vehicle dealerships and a WalMart, Starbuck's, and other franchises that have become ubiquitous in Southern California and elsewhere.[5]

Most of the residents of Colton are poor and people of color. Sixty percent of the city's residents are of Hispanic origin, and another 18 percent are African American, Asian, or Native American. The city's median family income is about $35,000, and 20 percent of the residents live in poverty, making Colton one of the poorest cities in California. Colton's economic fate has long been tied to the rest of the Inland Empire. The closure of nearby Norton Air Force Base during the first round of base closures in 1992, and the attendant loss of defense jobs in San Bernardino County, caused the region to suffer a significant economic recession during the 1990s. The economic plight of the area was illustrated by the creation of the Agua Mansa Enterprise Zone, which was established in 1986 by San Bernardino and Riverside counties and the cities of Colton, Rialto, and Riverside in an effort to lure economic development to a ten-thousand-acre site that included the southern part of Colton. The state law authorizing enterprise zones provides tax breaks, subsidies, and other financial incentives to businesses that are willing to locate in areas experiencing economic distress. A 2006 study found that areas designated as enterprise zones "showed measurable decreases in poverty rates, unemployment rates, and vacancy rates, as well as measurable increases in household income and median rents." The Agua Mansa zone, however, suffered from worsening poverty, unemployment, and income and lower rents compared to other areas of the state between 1990 and 2000. For better or worse, the Agua Mansa zone expired in 2006, and a new San Bernardino Valley Enterprise Zone includes part of Colton.[6]

The regional economy boomed even as the enterprise zone failed. The population of Colton jumped 20 percent between 1990 and 2000, and it grew another 8 percent to just over 51,000 people by 2006. The entire western San Bernardino and western Riverside County region is expected to see even more explosive growth in the future. San Bernardino County alone may host 2.25 million people by 2012, a 62 percent increase over the county's 2000 population. Housing prices shot up as people migrated from Los Angeles and Orange counties in search of homes that they could afford. The *Los Angeles Times* acknowledged in 2006 that although the Inland Empire was "often seen as a manufacturing and transportation hub, with less-expensive homes for those willing to commute to Los Angeles and Orange counties," it is now "featuring the type of upscale houses, stores and entertainment long found in Los Angeles and other coastal enclaves." Evidence of the growth is easy to see as one drives west along I-10, with big-box stores, shopping malls, and billboards advertising expensive new housing developments. Beginning at the western end of San Bernardino County, one encounters the expansive and modern Ontario International Airport, where I flew to visit Colton; the sleek commercial developments of Rancho Cucamonga, especially the stunning new Victoria Gardens Mall, which contains the usual array of high-end chain stores and a cultural center featuring a playhouse and a public library; and the Southridge Development south of I-10 in Fontana, just east of Colton, with new homes moving up into the foothills of the Jurupa Mountains. National Public Radio reported in 2004 that the Inland Empire had also experienced "a surge in Latino home buyers." But alas, the fall has been nearly as rapid as the rise. By May 2008, the San Bernardino–Riverside area ranked number one nationally for the biggest drop in home prices and number two in the number of foreclosure filings. As an article in *Forbes* magazine explained, prices had doubled between 2003 and 2006, "but median incomes didn't rise much quicker than historical norms, leaving a huge disconnect between what people could afford and what housing cost." The problem is somewhat less acute in Colton because it has so many older homes and lacks the new developments that have been plagued by foreclosures, but the economic downturn has still affected the city.[7]

Colton has confronted these ups and downs with a dysfunctional and corrupt local government. Perhaps that is the curse of David Colton himself, who as a county sheriff billed the California legislature nearly $2,000 for a trip to Illinois that was ostensibly to capture a fugitive but that really enabled him to propose to his future wife. Karl Gaytan, the city's mayor from 1997 to 2000, was convicted of accepting bribes for his votes on land use decisions. In upholding an order demanding that he pay restitution to the city, the federal appeals court explained that "the City of Colton lost the honest service of a public servant whose vote was purchased by developers seeking approvals for their projects which, when authorized, entitled them to tax rebates, loans, and loan guarantees. The citizens of Colton may have lost much more, for Gaytan's vice 'endangers the very fabric of a democratic society.'" Gaytan had replaced a mayor who was removed from office by a recall election, and then Deirdre Bennett replaced Gaytan. She wielded her flyswatter until she lost her 2006 reelection bid by nine votes out of thousands cast to Kelly Chastain, her former close friend and longtime city council member. Chastain confronted a June 2008 recall vote at the behest of city residents who were upset with her governing, too, but she survived with 62 percent of the vote. Meanwhile, the city council continues to confront its own ethical scandals. Several council members have been prosecuted for illicit activities during the past twenty years, and in February 2008 the council hired a psychologist to serve as a crisis consultant who could help the members learn to work with each other. Not to be outdone, the executive director of the Colton Chamber of Commerce has been accused of embezzlement.[8]

SOUTHERN CALIFORNIA'S RUST BELT

The railroads, cement plant, and related businesses have long given Colton the reputation as an old industrial city. Like similar industrial cities in the Rust Belt of the Northeast and the Midwest, the environmental legacy of Colton's industrial past has become apparent much more recently. The city has many brownfields that it is trying to clean and rehabilitate. *Brownfields* are urban properties that remain idle because they suffer from environmental contamination caused by past owners, and new developers are reluctant to obtain the land because they could be held liable under CERCLA for the cost of cleaning it up. The EPA has identified nearly two dozen brownfield sites in Colton, including a landfill, former chemical plants, and railroad facilities. The EPA awarded the city $200,000 in 1998 as part of a Brownfields Assessment Demonstration Pilot, recognizing that "little redevelopment . . . has taken place due to the fear of liability associated with environmental contamination." That grant was used to evaluate the contamination and redevelopment potential of numerous sites throughout the city.

Despite those efforts, little actual brownfield redevelopment has occurred in Colton so far.[9]

The state has addressed Colton's hazardous waste sites, too. The operation of the Colton Manufactured Gas Plant during the first decade of the twentieth century resulted in the disposal of lampblack containing polycyclic aromatic hydrocarbons, which the state's Department of Toxic Substances Control (DTSC) began to address in 1991. By 2005, about two thousand tons of contaminated soil had been removed from the property, and a covenant was imposed upon future uses of certain "inaccessible areas" of the site. Then, in 2006, the DTSC began investigating possible contamination at a site that was first used for the manufacture of railroad boxcars in 1899 and later became Colton Iron and Metal, a scrap metal business. Most of the samples tested below the permissible risk levels of contaminants, but the DTSC and the property owner are working on a Corrective Action Consent Agreement for the removal of lead and PCBs found at the site.[10]

Colton also suffers from the environmental consequences of activities outside its borders. The city's website boasts that "an abundant local water supply is one of Colton's greatest assets." At the same time, however, the city has been litigating to remove perchlorate from that water supply. Perchlorate is used in the manufacture of rocket fuel, munitions, fireworks, and other explosive devices. Exposure to perchlorate may interfere with thyroid functions, though epidemiologists are still working to identify the tolerable dose. The chemical is now found in 5 percent of California's sixty-four hundred public water supplies, including the Rialto-Colton groundwater basin, and Colton has had to close or treat twenty of its wells. The apparent sources of the perchlorate include a variety of defense contractors and fireworks companies that operated just north of Colton in Rialto from World War II through the 1980s as well as a county landfill that accepted hazardous wastes from those facilities. In 2003, the EPA ordered B. F. Goodrich (which had operated a rocket motor factory), Black and Decker (whose subsidiary ran a flare and munitions plant), and several other companies to conduct tests to see whether they were the sources of the contamination. The City of Colton sued those companies and the county to recover its more than $600,000 in cleanup costs under CERCLA, but the federal district court dismissed the case because the city failed to follow the cleanup procedures prescribed by CERCLA's National Contingency Plan. One problem, said the court, was that Colton prohibited the use of water containing any amount of perchlorate even though the state health department had advised that the water was potable. More generally, Colton ignored the contingency plan's provisions requiring public participation and cooperation with state officials. Colton had more success when it joined its neighboring city of Rialto in suing San Bernardino County for the county's alleged role in the contamination. Colton settled that lawsuit in March 2008 for $1 million and the right to two hundred acre-feet of water from the county's treatment facility. Additional funding for the cleanup has come from multimillion-dollar earmarks contained in the federal Department of Defense appropriations bills. Numerous environmental organizations assert that "full cleanup of contamination is an environmental justice priority."[11]

The Federal-Aid Highway Act of 1944 was the law that most affected the city's environment before the sudden emergence of the ESA in Colton's history. Passed by a lame-duck Congress as the Battle of the Bulge raged in Europe, this highway law represented a tentative move toward the interstate highway system that President Dwight D. Eisenhower championed during the 1950s. The law authorized the expenditure of $1.5 billion over three years for the construction of highways throughout the United States, and it required states to pay for half of the costs of any roads that were built. Both of those stipulations were modest in comparison to the Federal-Aid Highway Act of 1956, which authorized $25 billion in spending, created the Federal Highway Trust Fund, approved a formula that required states to pay 10 percent of expenses, and is usually credited with creating the interstate highway system. It was the 1944 highway law, though, that established "a National System of Interstate Highways not exceeding forty thousand miles in total extent so located as to connect by routes, as direct as practicable, the principal metropolitan areas, cities, and industrial centers, to serve the national defense, and to connect all suitable border points with routes of continental importance" in Canada and Mexico. The law called for "joint action of the State highway departments of each state and the adjoining States" to select the routes for the new roads. The federal Public Roads

Administration approved the first routes in August 1947, including 240 miles of I-10 that were to stretch from Los Angeles to the Arizona state line.[12]

The route bisected Colton. What had been J Street in the city's commercial center became I-10 instead. Beginning in 1949, the J. C. Penney store, two other department stores, a hotel, and other businesses composing one-third of the downtown commercial district were demolished to make way for the interstate. Once it was completed, most of the traffic passed over downtown on the elevated highway rather than through it. "Longtime Colton residents still lament the loss of downtown, which many of them attribute to the coming of the freeway," reports Larry Sheffield. Today, downtown Colton is in need of revitalization, as the modest amount of commercial growth has occurred in the far southeastern corner of the city. The interstate also separated the Mexican community from the rest of Colton's residents. Even then, the remaining section of downtown continued to be fairly viable until about 1966, when the City Redevelopment Agency deemed most of the buildings downtown to be safety hazards and had them demolished.[13]

As I-10 took away Colton's downtown, it also brought air pollution. San Bernardino and Riverside counties now suffer from some of the worst air pollution in the nation thanks to the mountains that bracket the region and the persistence of temperature inversions that prevent polluted air from rising. The air pollution in Colton was even worse until the Kaiser steel plant in neighboring Fontana closed in 1983. Even so, the area is still ranked number one in the country for particulate and ozone pollution. Much of that pollution comes from the trucks that travel along I-10 and the trains that travel through Colton, carrying goods shipped from Asia to the Los Angeles and Long Beach ports to places throughout the country. Forty-five percent of the containerized cargo that is shipped to the United States arrives at those ports. Additional pollution comes from the increased number of cars resulting from the growth in the surrounding cities that the interstate triggered. Some pollution comes from Los Angeles and Orange County when the prevailing winds blow the fumes east until they are trapped in the mountains ringing the Inland Empire.

Joe Corless, an award-winning pediatrician at Colton's new Arrowhead Regional Medical Center (about which more soon), has estimated that asthma care costs $38 million in the Inland Empire. Corless was testifying at a field hearing of the Senate Environment and Public Works Committee that Senator Barbara Boxer convened in San Bernardino in October 2007. Another witness objected to the continued siting of polluting facilities in the Inland Empire: "Just as federal intervention was necessary to correct the violations of civil rights occurring in the 1960s, intervention is warranted to correct the immoral land use decisions being made in Southern California. . . . Let's be very clear—the continued practice of placing these polluting facilities in low-income communities of color is institutional racism in its most obvious form." The legislation that Senator Boxer proposed at the hearing did not address such land use decisions but instead would "require oceangoing vessels visiting U.S. ports to use cleaner fuel and cleaner engines."[14]

Absent such legislation, Colton must depend on the existing provisions of the federal Clean Air Act, which Congress enacted in 1970 in response to increased public concern about air polluted by such sources as factories, power plants, and vehicle emissions. The heart of the law directs the EPA to establish national ambient air quality standards (NAAQS) that identify the healthy level (plus a margin of safety) for six "criteria pollutants": carbon monoxide, lead, nitrogen dioxide, ozone, particulates, and sulfur dioxide. Each state must then prepare a State Implementation Plan that ensures that the amount of each criteria pollutant in each part of the state is below the NAAQS. The Clean Air Act contains additional provisions for the regulation of air pollution from vehicles, electric power plants that cause acid rain, and especially hazardous pollutants. Congress has always recognized that California confronts unique air pollution challenges, so the act empowers the state to take actions that are not authorized anywhere else.[15]

California has long struggled to reduce its air pollution and to satisfy the demands of the Clean Air Act. Despite these efforts, the south coastal area that includes Colton has not been able to attain the NAAQS for ozone or particulates. Continued failure could result in the harshest sanction imposed by the act: withdrawal of future federal highway funds. The most recent effort to address the problem appears in a report prepared by the California Air Resources Board in September 2007 recommending the replacement of old diesel trucks, the reduction of emissions from commuter trains, and the seeking of federal funding to mitigate locomotive emissions. The board recommended that the state ask the

EPA to take two actions pursuant to the Clean Air Act. First, the board wanted the EPA to reclassify the Southern California area as in extreme nonattainment for the 8-hour ozone standard (0.08 parts per million averaged over eight hours), which would extend the deadline for meeting that standard from 2020 to 2023, in order to achieve the necessary 76 percent reduction in nitrogen oxide emissions. The board also sought a five-year extension of the PM2.5 standard (the standard addressing fine particles in the air) from 2010 to 2015.

The Clean Air Act and state law both provide legal tools for evaluating polluting activities within Colton. For example, the cement plant has faced scrutiny because of the toxic dust that could spread from clinker piles of raw cement, but in May 2008 the South Coast Air Quality Management District advised that the Colton plant was addressing that problem relatively well. "The cancer risk is going to be much less than living next to a freeway or a train yard," reported a district spokesperson in words that probably offered little comfort to many Colton residents. The construction of new facilities is of even greater concern for air pollution regulation. In 2001, the EPA issued an administrative order on consent—essentially, an agency order resulting from a settlement agreement—to approve an emergency application to build two forty-megawatt power plants in south Colton consistent with the new source review provisions of the Clean Air Act. Another proposed facility—the Agua Mansa Commerce Center—has provided the first opportunity for Colton's contributions to climate change to be considered. The proposed industrial business park would be located just north of the Santa Ana River with eleven buildings totaling more than 1.3 million square feet. The February 2007 draft environmental impact report for the project discusses its relation to climate change, presumably in order to satisfy California attorney general (and former governor) Jerry Brown's novel approach to improving air quality in the Inland Empire. Brown sued San Bernardino County for failing to consider the effect of additional development on air quality, especially greenhouse gas emissions, when the county updated its land use plan in 2007. The parties settled the lawsuit, with the county agreeing to amend its plan to address "those greenhouse gas emissions reasonably attributable to the County's discretionary land use decisions and the County's internal government operations." Not wanting to make the same mistake, the draft report for the proposed commerce center devotes five pages to discussing the possible effects of the center on climate change. The report concludes "that the project would contribute less than 0.000001 percent (one millionth of 1%) of the greenhouse gas burden for the planet." The report further implies that the project may even reduce climate change because it will more efficiently distribute the goods arriving in Southern California's ports. But the owners of a Colton cement factory have warned that the $200 million it could cost to comply with AB 32—California's ambitious climate change law—could force them to close.[16]

Colton's predicament was aptly summarized in an EPA report which observed that "the city has experienced economic decline in the commercial, industrial, and residential sectors of the community. . . . Colton is vulnerable to further decline as development projects seek out preferred greenfield sites." The city was thus eager to encourage the development of the relatively few remaining open parcels of land within its borders. As it has suffered both from its own industrial past and from the environmental consequences of its neighbors' development, Colton wanted to share in the benefits of the economic growth that the Inland Empire experienced beginning in the 1990s. It was poised to do so when it planned to open the $470 million, 373-bed, earthquake-proof Arrowhead Regional Medical Center in September 1993. And then. . . .[17]

ENTER THE ENDANGERED SPECIES ACT

Congress enacted the ESA in 1973 during the heyday of federal environmental legislation. The proponents of the law evoked images of bald eagles, grizzly bears, alligators, and other national symbols that were on the brink of disappearing from this land. Almost immediately, though, the act was deployed to protect much less popular creatures. The listing of the snail darter, a small fish, as endangered just months after the ESA became law resulted in the Supreme Court's 1978 decision in *Tennessee Valley Authority v. Hill*, confirming that the multimillion-dollar Tellico Dam project could not be completed because of the threat that it posed to the snail darter's survival. More recently, the law's application has become a focal point for broader debates about logging and river management in the Pacific Northwest; competition over water between urban, agricultural, and wildlife needs in the Southeast; and suburban development in Southern California, Arizona, Florida, and Texas.[18]

Probably, none of the members of Congress who voted nearly unanimously to enact a more stringent ESA could have imagined that the law might address vanishing insects. Nonetheless, the act directs the FWS to list any species, including insects, if they are either endangered or threatened with extinction. The only exception is for insects that the secretary of the interior deems to be "pests," a provision that has yet to be invoked in the thirty-six-year history of the law. Fifty-seven insects are listed under the ESA—fewer than the number of mammals or birds, even though there are far more insect species than any others. Insect champions complain about the failure to use the ESA more zealously to protect endangered insects. One law review commentator concluded that "a lack of qualified entomologists to file listing petitions may be the cause of 'bias' against insects in listing decisions rather than any ESA provisions or FWS regulations." Another explanation is that the FWS gives listing priority to species that are the only ones in their genus, and scientists tend to classify multiple species in the same genus.[19]

California is second only to Hawai'i in the number of species listed under the ESA. Several of those species—including the coastal California gnatcatcher, the Quino checkerspot butterfly, and the San Bernardino kangaroo rat—have provoked significant struggles over the application of the ESA's regulatory requirements. Colton, however, did not have much experience with the act. Perhaps that should not be surprising, for the area had been so thoroughly developed for so long that little natural habitat remained. A glance at the city's few remaining open spaces today shows dry, sandy land littered with trash and surrounded by railroads, I-10, and various active and inactive industrial facilities. It is not the kind of place where one would expect to find rare wildlife.

Desert ecosystems can be deceiving, though. Long ago, the Santa Ana winds picked up sand from Delhi (pronounced *DEL-high*) in central California's Merced County and deposited it over about thirty-five thousand acres of land located about sixty miles east of the Pacific Ocean in Southern California. Thus were born the Delhi sand dunes (also known as the Colton Dunes), the only inland sand dune system in the Los Angeles basin. The Delhi sands that comprise those dunes cover several patches stretching about forty miles between Ontario and Colton. The Delhi sands are a good example of what one finds in a coastal sage scrub ecosystem. Birds such as western meadowlarks and burrowing owls frequent the area. The San Diego horned lizard and the legless lizard live in the dunes, as do insects such as the Delhi sands metalmark butterfly and the Delhi sands Jerusalem cricket. The onset of night entices the Los Angeles pocket mouse, the San Bernardino kangaroo rat, and other small mammals to survey the land. Primrose, goldfields, and other wildflowers flourish after the winter rains, replaced later in the year by wild buckwheat and the colorful butterflies that the plant attracts. The yellow flowers of telegraph weeds appear in the summer.

The growth in the human population produced a corresponding shrinkage of the original Delhi sands. Most of the dunes were destroyed by the cultivation of citrus groves at the end of the nineteenth century, and over the next one hundred years, commercial, industrial, and residential development eliminated much of the remaining dunes. A shopping center replaced seventy acres of dunes in the early 1990s, and a county park split another segment of dunes in 1998. Only about forty square miles of dunes—or about 2 percent of the original sands—exist in several patches stretching between the cities of Colton and Mira Loma. As the Delhi sands have disappeared, so has the native wildlife. Pringle's monardella, a wildflower that once grew only in the Delhi sands, has already become extinct. The number of meadowlarks and burrowing owls has diminished as their habitats have been converted into human uses, though both birds have displayed a surprising resilience in the presence of bulldozers, landfills, and the like. A 1909 ornithology article marveled at how white-throated swifts had thrived in a narrow gulch created when the cement plant blasted away part of Slover Mountain. But a 1986 environmental study preceding the creation of the Agua Mansa Enterprise Zone assured that no rare or endangered species were living on the affected land.[20]

The dunes are also the only place on earth where the Delhi Sands flower-loving fly clings to life. The fly—known to entomologists as *Rhaphiomidas terminatus abdominalis*—is colored orangish and brown, with dark brown oval spots on its abdomen and emerald green eyes. It is one inch long, much larger than a common housefly. Much about the fly remains a mystery to entomologists. It appears that it undergoes a metamorphosis from egg to larva to pupa to adult over a three-year period underground. Once it emerges from the sand at the end of the three years, a fly lives for perhaps a couple of weeks between July and September.

The Delhi Sands flower-loving fly.

The flies are most active during the heat of the day, preferring temperatures over 100 degrees (which are in ample supply during the summer).
Males buzz around defending their territories in the morning and search-
ing for females in the afternoon; females remain perched on plants for
most of the day. As its name suggests, the fly is a pollinator that loves
flowers. It hovers like a hummingbird as it removes nectar from the native buckwheat flowers with its long tubular proboscis.

The fly is one of nearly eighty-five thousand species of flies that scientists have identified around the world so far. It is one of thirty species
that comprise the *Rhaphiomidas* genus, all of which live in arid and
semiarid parts of California, Arizona, New Mexico, and northern Mexico. The fly is distinguished from the other species within the genus by
its bicolored abdomen and its widely separated eyes. It is actually a subspecies of the *Rhaphiomidas terminatus* species; its companion subspecies and closest relative—the El Segundo flower-loving fly—lived in the
sand dunes north of downtown Los Angeles until it was thought to have
been rendered extinct by the expansion of the Los Angeles airport during the 1960s. But the El Segundo fly was rediscovered in 2006 (in a
still undisclosed location).[21]

The first Delhi Sands flower-loving fly was collected in 1888. Arizona State entomologist Mont A. Cazier described it as a separate species in 1941, and then in the twilight of his career in 1985, he examined new collections and concluded that the Delhi Sands flower-loving fly was actually a subspecies. An amateur fly enthusiast named Joe Wilcox collected many of the area's flies, and after he retired he often asked his friend Greg Ballmer whether he had collected "that big fly over near Mira Loma," as Ballmer told me. Ballmer responded that the area had long since been converted to vineyards and roads, and "the fly that you collected back in 1938 is probably gone by now." "Don't be so sure," Wilcox told him. Right on cue, another amateur entomologist—Rick Rogers—was collecting all of the flies that Cazier had described, and he found the elusive Delhi Sands flower-loving fly in a vacant lot in Colton. Ballmer visited the site and "by golly, they were there." Soon, they found flies in about a dozen discrete spots, often in vacant fields that had once been citrus orchards and were now surrounded by homes. They mapped the locations of the sightings and noticed that they all fell in the area of the Delhi Sands on the old Soil Conservation Service maps. But there were not that many of them, and they lived in just five locations within an eight-mile radius along the border of San Bernardino and Riverside counties. Ballmer also noted that "almost every place where Rick had found them had a for sale sign on the property," so he knew that the habitat was going to disappear quickly.[22]

Ballmer responded to the evidence of the fly's plight by doing what any concerned entomologist would do: he filed a petition with the FWS in October 1989 to list the fly as endangered under the ESA. I talked with Ballmer in his laboratory at the University of California–Riverside. It was a humble venue for the instigator of a lot of trouble and befitted a rather humble man. Ballmer was older than I had expected, perhaps in his fifties, with silver hair. He began our meeting by showing me some of the bugs that he was studying because of their effect on California's agricultural crops. For after all, Ballmer is an agricultural entomologist. His studies of the fly must be more of a hobby than a job. Ballmer viewed the fly as "spectacular," and he was concerned about its survival. After Ballmer's 1989 petition, he filed another petition in March 1992 asking the FWS to list the fly on an emergency basis because of the urgency of the development pressures on all of the fly's remaining habitat. He noted that three of the remaining six colonies of flies "remain north of the I-10 freeway in the City of Colton; all three are in poor condition due to illegal dumping, discing, weed invasion, and off-road vehicle use; they are also advertised for sale and are in rapidly developing residential and commercial/industrial areas." Ballmer added that "the best quality and greatest remaining quantity" of habitat for the fly "remains south of the I-10 freeway in the Cities of Colton and Rialto and unincorporated land in San Bernardino County."[23]

Ballmer was asking the FWS to invoke the protections of the ESA on behalf of a fly for the first time. In fact, the only time since then that the FWS has listed flies under the ESA occurred in 2006, when the agency found that eleven species of Hawaiian picture-wing flies are endangered or threatened. One of those flies is far more bizarre than the Delhi Sands flower-loving fly: its larvae develop in "the moldy slime flux (seep) that occasionally appears on certain trees with injured plant tissue and seeping sap," and it has been seen only once since 1972. The fact that the Delhi Sands flower-loving fly is a subspecies was controversial at that time, too. During 1995 congressional hearings on the ESA, opponents of the listing of subspecies argued that they need not be protected unless their survival was essential to the survival of the species as a whole. At a minimum, they argued, "the sub-species or sub-sub-species of kangaroo rat should not receive the same treatment as the California condor." Secretary of the Interior Bruce Babbitt answered that "should a subspecies begin to decline, this may be a warning that the species as a whole may be in danger" and that an early response to such a trend can improve the likelihood of success and decrease the cost of protection efforts. He added that the existence of genetically distinct subspecies "improve[s] the ability of the species as a whole to survive." The defenders of the status quo prevailed, so the ESA still defines "species" to include "any subspecies of fish or wildlife or plants."[24]

The ESA prescribes a timetable for decisions on listing petitions. The FWS has ninety days to determine whether a petition presents substantial evidence that listing is warranted. If so, then the agency has another twelve months to decide whether listing is warranted, unwarranted, or warranted but precluded by higher agency priorities. If the FWS proposes to list a species, then the public has sixty days to submit comments, and the agency must make a final decision within twelve months. Those dates are often missed, however, because the FWS lacks the funds—or sometimes the will—to act upon all petitions in a timely fashion. A petitioner's ordinary recourse is to file a lawsuit seeking the agency's action on the petition, and that lawsuit is often the vehicle for establishing a schedule that both the petitioner and the FWS find acceptable. After Ballmer's 1989 petition, he did not go to court on behalf of the fly, preferring instead to periodically file supplemental information advising the FWS of the fly's worsening prospects. The FWS concluded in October 1990 that listing may be warranted, and in November 1991 the fly was formally designated as a candidate for listing. In November 1992, the FWS issued a formal proposal to list the fly as endangered.[25]

Finally, the FWS issued the rule adding the fly to the list of endangered species on September 23, 1993. According to the ESA, a species must be listed if it is "endangered" (defined as in "danger of extinction within the foreseeable future throughout all or a significant portion of its range") or "threatened" (defined as "likely to become endangered within the foreseeable future throughout all or a significant portion of its range"). Of the five factors specified in the ESA for determining whether a species is endangered or threatened, two of the factors cut against listing the fly: the fly was not overutilized, nor was it subject to disease or predation. The three other factors, however, pointed toward listing. First, the small number of flies—probably numbering in the hundreds, though no one knows for sure—made the survival of the species susceptible to natural changes in its environment. Second, the FWS found that neither the fly nor its habitat was protected by federal, state, or local law. And third and most important, the FWS concluded that "the major threats to the Delhi Sands flower-loving fly are habitat loss and degradation." The FWS observed that "most of the former habitat for the Delhi Sands flower-loving fly was destroyed by agricultural conversion in the 1880s," with much of the remainder facing "rapid and intensive urbanization." An estimated 98 percent of the fly's original habitat had been destroyed, but a "significant amount" of its habitat was located south of I-10 in Colton. The agency worried that the Agua Mansa Enterprise Zone could attract industrial developments that would quickly eliminate the few remaining colonies of the fly. Those concerns did not persuade the 81 percent of the fifty-seven commentators who opposed the listing proposal because of its economic effects or its inadequate scientific grounding. The FWS responded that the ESA precluded it from considering the economic effects of listing a species, and although "more precise scientific information" would "benefit the fly's recovery," that was not "a legitimate basis for postponing a listing decision."[26]

FIGHTING THE FLY

The listing of a species triggers the ESA's impressive collection of legal duties. Upon listing, the FWS must designate the "critical habitat" of the species to the maximum extent that it can be determined or prudent to do so. The efficacy of critical habitat designations has been a source of considerable controversy in recent years; many environmentalists see critical habitat as a central part of the protection of a species while the FWS objects that it spends far too many of its limited resources on a determination that has little practical effect. In the case of the fly, the FWS circumvented this debate by finding that it would not be "prudent" to designate its critical habitat. "The precise pinpointing of localities that would result from publication of critical habitat descriptions and maps in the Federal Register would render the species more vulnerable to collecting," the agency warned. The FWS also cited "the threat of vandalism" of known fly habitats, a reasonable concern given the public's reaction to the fly's protection. These reasons might not survive judicial review after a 1997 federal court of appeals decision involving the coastal California gnatcatcher. In that case, the FWS had worried that the identification of critical habitat would prompt landowners to destroy that habitat, but the Court of Appeals for the Ninth Circuit responded that the agency failed to show why such critical habitat would not instead cause landowners to protect gnatcatcher sites. Despite this new precedent, no environmental group has asked the FWS to list the critical habitat of the Delhi Sands flower-loving fly. Instead, it is the City of Colton that has objected to the de facto selection of critical habitat without the formal administrative process afforded by the ESA.[27]

Next, the ESA instructs the FWS to prepare a "recovery plan" upon the listing of a species. Again, many species are still waiting for their plans, but the FWS completed the recovery plan for the fly in 1997. The goal of the plan is to downlist the fly from endangered to threatened.

This can be considered, says the plan, when "at least eight populations in the three Recovery Units (RUs)—Colton, Jurupa, and Ontario—are permanently protected." Four of those populations must be in the Colton recovery unit, and "the population that inhabits the largest remaining block of Colton Dunes (located east of Riverside Avenue, south of Interstate 10, north of the Santa Ana River, and west of the cement plant) must be protected." The preservation of the fly in those areas is to be accomplished by "actions by landowners that are either voluntary or mandated by law." The recovery plan endorses the development of a regional habitat conservation plan (HCP), the use of mitigation banking and conservation easements, the captive breeding of flies, and the implementation of cooperative agreements with state agencies. The plan recognizes the importance of the actions of private landowners whose property contains (or could support) flies, and to cultivate that support, the plan calls for a public outreach campaign. "A specific educational effort should be aimed at dispelling the public's automatic association with, and disdain for, house flies." The plan calls for the expenditure of $1.6 million to enable the fly to be downlisted by 2017. Even so, the recovery plan concludes that "the likelihood of extinction remains high unless the habitat protection and captive breeding and release programs are initiated without delay."[28]

Twelve years later, the recovery plan has not been fulfilled. No serious captive breeding efforts have been made, much to the chagrin of Colton's city leaders. Mayor Bennett complained "that habitat acquisition is the only strategy being pursued." Moreover, very little habitat has actually been "acquired." Instead, Section 9 of the ESA has been employed to regulate development in the fly's habitat. Section 9 prohibits the "take" of a protected species—defined by the ESA to include, among other things, "harm" to a species—by any party. In 1980, the FWS issued a regulation defining "harm" as including "significant habitat modification or degradation where it actually kills or injures wildlife by significantly impairing essential behavioral patterns, including breeding, feeding, or sheltering." Timber producers and Oregon communities affected by the application of the take prohibition to the northern spotted owl challenged the regulation, but the Supreme Court held in 1995 that the regulation represented a permissible interpretation of the statute.[29]

The take prohibition had an immediate effect in Colton. At the first meeting between local officials and the FWS, an agency employee surveyed the scene and suggested that I-10 would have to be closed for two months each summer when the fly was above ground. The FWS employee's supervisors quickly disavowed her idea, but another crisis loomed. The September 23, 1993, listing of the fly happened to be the day before construction was to begin on San Bernardino County's new Arrowhead Regional Medical Center project smack in the middle of some of the fly's prime habitat. Plans to replace San Bernardino's aging county medical center began in the late 1970s. Building a new hospital on the existing site in San Bernardino was ruled out because it would be "prohibitively expensive" and "create environmental problems," according to a history of the hospital. Another site was rejected because of its proximity to a school and because the neighboring residents "did not care to have their view of the mountains blocked by a multi-story building." A third possible site in Ontario was offered instead to "a large, tax-paying tenant." The hospital finally settled on a vacant tract of land just north of I-10 on the west side of Colton. Some critics of the site suggest that it was "all tied up in local politics" and that "somebody must have made a lot of money off that." Supporters respond that perhaps people in Loma Linda did not want a competing hospital.[30]

Local officials were stuck and tried to cut a deal with the FWS. At first, the parties agreed that the hospital could be built if it was moved three hundred feet to the north and if the county established a refuge for the fly. The "refuge" was vacant land adjacent to the hospital that was bordered by orange plastic fencing. Happily, the flies loved the fencing. Then the county realized that it would need to build a new electrical substation to power the hospital; that resulted in seven more acres for the refuge. But when the county sought permission to reconfigure the roads in the area surrounding the hospital, the FWS balked.

The county sued, joined by the cities of Colton and Fontana and by local developers, claiming that the ESA could not be constitutionally applied to regulate construction projects involving a species like the fly that lived in only one state and that was not involved in interstate commerce. They brought their lawsuit in the federal appeals court in Washington, D.C., presumably because of the liberal, pro-environmentalist reputation of the Ninth Circuit appeals court with jurisdiction over California. The

FWS's use of the ESA, the plaintiffs claimed, exceeded the power that the Constitution gives Congress to regulate "commerce . . . among the several states." The district court held that such an application of the ESA was constitutional, so the plaintiffs appealed. The three judges of the D.C. Circuit approached the problem in three different ways. Judge Patricia Wald found that there was a sufficient relationship between *all endangered species* and interstate commerce. By contrast, Judge David Sentelle concluded that there was no relationship between the *fly* and interstate commerce. Judge Karen Henderson cast the decisive vote upholding the application of the law, finding that there was a relationship between the *hospital* and interstate commerce. Any hope for a constitutional exit disappeared in June 1998 when the Supreme Court declined to hear the case. A few years later, the D.C. Circuit reached the same conclusion in another ESA case arising from San Diego over the dissent of Judge John Roberts, who complained that the use of the ESA to protect a "hapless frog" in the path of a planned development contradicted the Supreme Court's more recent interpretations of the commerce clause. Colton has declined to press its case again to the Supreme Court now headed by Chief Justice John Roberts.[31]

The fly, thanks to the ESA's take prohibition, now occupied a position of great strength in future discussions about the development of Colton. Because of their possible effect on the fly and its remaining habitat, a host of developments were challenged, including a 2.8-million-square-foot WalMart distribution facility; the proposal by Viny Industries, a paper products company, to build on sixty acres of land in southern Colton, thereby creating four hundred jobs; and the expansion of a truck manufacturing plant that would have added thirty jobs to the fifty workers already at the site. Furthermore, Stater Brothers Markets, one of Colton's largest employers, moved its corporate headquarters to the former Norton Air Force Base in nearby San Bernardino, saying it "could not find a place that would work" in Colton because of the fly.[32]

The hospital finally opened in March 1999 after the county set aside a total of twelve acres of land for a fly refuge. But the fly continued to block the proposed road construction projects that resulted in the commerce clause litigation. Colton officials and the FWS had not reached an agreement that would permit the realignment of roads near the new hospital despite meetings held throughout 1999. In 2003, the city had to

The defaced sign marking the fly refuge next to the hospital in Colton.

redesign the storm-drain system for the hospital because the original route ran through the fly's habitat. The county estimated that moving the site of the hospital, establishing the fly preserves, and otherwise accommodating the fly cost the county nearly $3 million. Altogether, city officials estimated in 2007 that Colton had lost $175 million in potential economic development since the fly's listing, though it is difficult to quantify that claim.[33]

The regulation of the fly's habitat has also affected ordinary citizens. The most poignant story involves Mel Pierson, whom his daughter described as "an endangered species of the human kind." He fought in World War II, was married for fifty-two years, raised four daughters, and "served his church and community his whole life." During the 1970s, Pierson and his wife purchased fourteen acres of land on Pepper Avenue in Colton as their "retirement plan for their golden years." He was unable to recoup their investment, though, because no one would buy the land while the ESA's regulations hovered over it. Hours before he died, his daughter "actually whispered in his ear, 'Dad, you can go now, it's okay. I have the Pepper Street in escrow, I'll take care of everything with mom.'" But the sale fell through, and Pierson's widow had to live on $800 per month in Social Security payments. Pierson's daughter later complained that "it's more important to preserve a sand fly than it was to have my parents live a comfortable retirement."[34]

The take prohibition regulated other activities besides proposed developments. For instance, the FWS's listing decision cited ORV use as one of the threats to the fly and its habitat. Greg Ballmer, however, is not so sure of the extent of the threat. "Some of that is very detrimental," he says, "but some of it may not be" because the flies are using the ORV trails as flyways. The vacant, sandy land favored by the fly and the ORV users is also an attractive spot for the illegal dumping of trash. I spotted abandoned appliances, old furniture, used diapers, and yard debris during a walk through the vacant land west of the hospital. City officials wanted to remove the trash, but the FWS insisted that it must be picked up by hand instead of by any heavy machinery that could disturb the fly larvae that are buried in the sand. Trash removal thus became a volunteer activity for Colton High School football players and for juvenile offenders, with an FWS biologist available to supervise their work. To prevent additional trash from being dumped in the area, Colton enacted an ordinance authorizing the forfeiture of any vehicle used to transport trash that is dumped in the sands. Other local towns are considering similar ordinances, in part because of concerns that they will become havens for trash dumpers who fear the more stringent sanctions imposed in neighboring communities.

Colton officials and residents vilified the fly. "To us and the majority of Americans with any common sense at all," protested Mayor Bennett, flies "are pests, nothing more, nothing less—pests we have historically grown up swatting." Julie Biggs, the Colton city attorney, characterized the fly's habitat as "a bunch of dirt and weeds." Local residents were quick to offer their own reactions to the predicament: one man claimed that the fly "larva is the same I've seen in tequila bottles being imported here from Mexico," and a woman worried that children and schools were "an endangered species that get no help." Joe Baca, who has represented Colton in the state assembly and in Congress, objected that the application of the ESA "cost the county more than half a million dollars per fly." Colton city officials also complained that the application of the ESA discriminated against its poor residents. "The community where the greatest amount of habitat is set aside has the lowest median income" in the region, Mayor Bennett told a task force organized by Secretary of the Interior Dirk Kempthorne in 2006. "This environmental injustice must stop." City historian Larry Sheffield observed that there really is not a controversy in Colton because the fly has no supporters there, noting that the "FWS hasn't been effective at all in communicating to the public just why the fly is important."[35]

One has to leave Colton to find defenders of the fly. The Xerces Society for Invertebrate Conservation singled out the fly as the insect most in need of saving in the world. Professor Rudy Mattoni at the University of California–Los Angeles described the fly as "a national treasure in the middle of junkyards. . . . It's a fly you can love. It's beautiful." An FWS official told CNN that the fly "isn't as charismatic as a panda bear or a sea otter, but that doesn't make it any less important." Another FWS official insisted that "the value of the fly to mankind is a very difficult thing to judge. It's much more of a moral issue. Do we have the right to destroy another creature when we, in our day-to-day activities, have the ability not to destroy a creature?" Environmentalists have emphasized the importance of the dune ecosystem rather than merely the fly. Greg Ballmer explained that the fly "is an umbrella species in that preserving its habitat preserves for posterity the entire community with which it lives." An FWS biologist pointed out that "every ecosystem has its intrinsic value, and maybe we can't quite put a dollar value on it. But every time one disappears, it's an indication that something else is wrong." Dan Silver, the head of the Endangered Habitats League, asserted that the ESA "is saving Riverside County from itself, its own short-sightedness. It is forcing people to take a longer view." Lindsey Groves of the Natural History Museum of Los Angeles County proclaimed: "kudos to everyone who favors the protection of creatures that have been driven to the brink of extinction in the name of development. Shame on the city of Colton.

Long live the Delhi Sands Flower-Loving Fly!" The local newspaper—Riverside's *Press-Enterprise*—editorialized in 2007 that "species such as the Delhi Sands flower-loving fly, which bedevils Inland developers, deserve preservation, too. It's simply good stewardship."[36]

The national media reported the story with a mixture of curiosity and disbelief. The CBS Evening News described it as "superfly, with the power to stop bulldozers." The *Los Angeles Times* reported that the fly could become "the snail darter of the 1990s." The *Washington Post* described the fly as "a creature that spends most of its life underground, living as a fat, clumsy, enigmatic maggot." The *Washington Times* editorialized that "one could build the flies their own mansion in Beverly Hills . . . fill it up from top to bottom with leftover potato salad and other fly delicacies, and it would still be cheaper than the royal estate Fish & Wildlife has in mind for them." NBC Nightly News discussed the controversy during its "Fleecing of America" segment. A book with the subtitle *100 Stories of Government Abuse* complained that the "endangered fly lives for two days, but curbs development for over a decade."[37]

For Colton, the application of the ESA was especially frustrating because many surrounding communities had already developed. "Colton was left holding the bag," admits Greg Ballmer, because it had a disproportionate amount of vacant land that was attractive to the fly. The problem only got worse for Colton when its neighbors solved it. The recovery plan anticipates that a population of flies will return to Ontario. But the fly's historic and potential habitat there was buried in the manure deposited by generations of dairy cattle, and the ESA was not employed to require the city to restore the land for the flies. By 2008, the FWS admitted that "habitat conditions have changed that preclude long-term conservation goals in the Ontario recovery unit." Or, "Ontario got out of jail," as one Colton leader put it. Next, Fontana reached an agreement with the FWS that allowed the city to develop a distribution center, though not the bigger retail and commercial development that the city had planned. (Fontana's elected mayor is Mark Nuaimi, who also served as Colton's assistant city manager—an arrangement that was approved in advance by the state attorney general's office.) Soon, Rialto resolved its differences with the FWS, too.[38]

That left Colton. City leaders were furious when developers sought to conserve land in Colton in order to develop land in nearby cities.

Mayor Bennett complained that "Colton properties are placed into a state of 'fly-induced blight' in disproportionate amounts so properties in surrounding communities can develop." So Colton fought the fly. Bennett admitted in 2006 that "for years our community response to the fly was to oppose conservation, fight the recovery plan, de-list the fly." The city blamed the FWS for insisting on "onerously high ratios" of conservation to developed lands. For example, when officials representing Colton, Fontana, Rialto, and other local cities met with the FWS in July 1999 to propose setting aside 850 acres of land for fly habitat in exchange for permission to develop throughout the area, they were told that FWS biologists were seeking 2,100 acres that could cost $220 million to purchase. And the FWS wanted a habitat-to-development ratio of three to one for the Big League Dreams park—a proposed small-scale replica of an historic major league sports complex—which the city says made the project economically unviable.[39]

The city also complained about the management of vacant land that was being de facto protected because development was prohibited. "Habitat conservation in Colton today looks like a dumping ground," according to Mayor Bennett, as "homeless encampments" and illegal dumps "rule the day." City Manager Daryl Parrish added that "habitat that is not properly managed leads to illegal dumping, homeless encampments, and invasive . . . non-native vegetation growth and reduction to the number of species." The FWS admitted in 2008 that even the land that had formally been set aside for the fly lacked the management needed to preserve individual flies and to ensure a perpetual supply of sand. A new threat—predatory Argentine ants that are invading the native ecosystem—is unchecked, too. Colton officials thus blame the FWS for creating an unfunded federal mandate by requiring the preservation of the fly's habitat without providing the funds to pay for it. "If the federal government is serious about species protection, then it should fund it," rather than merely listing and walking away, asserts Assistant City Manager Nuaimi. That's the opinion of the environmental community, too. A wildlife biologist told Senator Kempthorne's task force that "the agencies need much, much better funding to carry through these mandates" regarding the fly. Nuaimi thus pleads with the FWS to "stop the land grab. Stop acquiring more habitat and start focusing on restoring the habitat that you already have, which is south of the freeway."[40]

Colton next pushed to eliminate the ESA's protection of the fly altogether. The ESA requires the FWS to evaluate each listed species every five years. In 2003, the city petitioned the FWS to conduct the required review of the fly, but the FWS did not initiate that review until 2005. One year later, the city submitted a remarkable document articulating four reasons why the fly should be delisted. First, it argued that there is already sufficient habitat to protect the fly. It calculated that 627.3 acres had been preserved, 48 percent of which was in Colton. Second, Colton claimed that the FWS had improperly acted as if critical habitat had been designated for the fly without going through the formal designation process. That bothered the city because the FWS's alternative approach was "to set aside as much habitat as possible without any attempt to define how much is enough." By contrast, the ESA provides that critical habitat can be designated only after the economic effect of such a designation is considered, which Colton implied would result in a less ambitious understanding of protected habitat. Third, Colton objected to the fact that the recovery plan for the fly is ambiguous and not achievable. Fourth, and most striking, Colton insisted that the fly is in fact an invasive species that is not native to the area and actually threatens the native species. The city associated the fly's presence with the proximity of accumulations of water, which did not occur until after I-10 was built during the 1950s. The city suggested that the fly is better suited for the kind of coastal habitat occupied by its closest relative, the El Segundo flower-loving fly, instead of the hot, dry inland desert. Perhaps, the city said, the fly was "introduced accidentally by the early settlers" who arrived in the area at least a decade before the fly was first discovered in 1888. This claim that the fly is not native to Colton after all would seem farfetched except for two things: no one has looked for the fly outside of the places where it has already been found, and a newly discovered species is often later found in places where scientists did not expect to find it. The premise of the premier ESA case of *Tennessee Valley Authority v. Hill* was that the snail darter lived only in the Little Tennessee River, which was about to be impounded by the Tellico Dam, but a few years later the darters were found in multiple rivers in Alabama, Georgia, and Tennessee.[41]

The FWS rejected these arguments when it finally released its five-year review of the fly in May 2008. By its count, only 162 acres of the fly's habitat had been protected, as well as 150 acres in a new conservation bank (discussed below). Moreover, most of that land was too fragmented to sustain a permanent population of flies, so "additional lands will need to be acquired to ensure the long-term conservation" of the fly. Colton's argument that the fly was actually an invasive species failed, said the FWS, because "current scientific literature identifies the [fly] as a sub-species endemic to the Colton Dunes Ecosystem, and related taxa are similarly restricted to arid, often dune habitat." That scientific literature included only one paper published since the recovery plan was released in 1997, and the FWS repeatedly emphasized the "cryptic nature" of the fly. The FWS agreed with Colton that the recovery plan was inadequate, and it admitted that its efforts to educate the public about the value of the fly had failed and that support for conserving the fly's habitat was "limited."[42]

Colton's arguments failed in court and at the FWS, so the city turned to Congress. The city acknowledged that its arguments against the listing of the fly were really about the ESA instead of just the fly, which shifted the debate to "a different stage," as Daryl Parrish remarked to me. The drama on that stage has been equally unsuccessful from the perspective of Colton officials. Democratic state representative Joe Baca introduced a resolution in the California legislature calling upon Congress to remove the fly from the ESA's list of endangered species. The state legislature defeated the resolution, but the voters rewarded Baca by electing him to Congress in 1999. Colton then paid $48,000 for a Washington lobbyist to persuade Congress to remove the fly from the list of protected species. Again, Congress declined.

Colton's arguments merged with the national controversy surrounding the ESA. The first sustained effort to reform—or gut, depending on your perspective—the act occurred in 1994. Speaker of the House Newt Gingrich established an ESA task force that held hearings across the country in areas that had chafed under the restrictions of the law. Landowners and developers told horror stories of widows losing their life's savings when the presence of an endangered songbird prevented them from building on their land and of farmers facing federal prosecutions for attempting to prevent fires in a manner that harmed endangered kangaroo rats. Several bills were introduced to amend the ESA by requiring more rigorous scientific evidence before a species could be listed, helping private landowners who confront a listed species on their property, and speeding recovery efforts so that a species could be delisted. The bills stalled in the face of a certain presidential veto and pressure from environmentalists, religious leaders, moderate eastern politicians, and others who were intent on saving rare wildlife. The process repeated itself again in 2005, when the House of Representatives approved the Threatened and Endangered Species Act of 2005 (TESRA), which would overhaul the recovery planning process, repeal the ESA's critical habitat provisions, provide additional incentives for private actions to conserve protected species, and most controversially, mandate government compensation of landowners who are adversely affected by the ESA's land use regulations. Throughout the congressional debate, advocates for reform of the ESA seized on the controversy in Colton as an example of the kinds of problems that the law created, with the "people versus flies" argument being voiced frequently.

Both Colton's predicament and the broader attacks on the ESA were on display at a congressional hearing that Representative Richard Pombo held in Fontana in September 2004. Titled "Examining Impacts of the Endangered Species Act on Southern California's Inland Empire," the hearing featured attacks on the fly by Mayor Bennett, Mark Nuaimi (appearing as Fontana's mayor, not as Colton's assistant city manager), and Representative Joe Baca (whose congressional district includes Colton) while providing fodder for Pombo's broader efforts to revise the ESA. Representative Baca called the ESA "a broken law." "We need to protect endangered species," he agreed, "but not at the cost of thousands of jobs in our community." Mayor Bennett told the committee that the ESA "has been misapplied" and that the FWS had engaged in "legalized extortion," resulting in "a nightmare for the residents of the City of Colton without sufficient scientific data to support its [the fly's] listing." The four solutions Bennett proposed were to delist the fly, amend the ESA to prevent the listing of any insects, limit the powers of local FWS officials, and revise the ESA to require better scientific data. "People matter more than bugs," she concluded. Next, Nuaimi complained about "the lack of a recovery plan based upon financial constraints and reality," and he suggested that the fly might not be salvageable even with heroic efforts. He also asserted that the ESA's "original intent was to protect those species that held value to the history of the country and history of the region." That may have been what members of Congress were thinking about in 1973 when they voted for the ESA, but the courts had long since read the law's plain text as encompassing all species regardless of their apparent value. Nuaimi's advice was to convene the ESA's "God Squad" (a group of federal and state officials that has the statutory power to allow projects that endanger a protected species) to determine whether the fly was worth saving, to open an FWS office in the Inland Empire, and to make three revisions to the ESA: one to exempt property that "has had a substantial investment in infrastructure made prior to the listing of a species," a second to exempt property that no longer has the kind of ecosystem necessary to sustain a species, and a third "to create a binding arbitration process in lieu of lawsuits." Pombo built upon these stories to proclaim that although the ESA was "born of good intentions, it has failed to live up to its promises, and species are more threatened today because of its serious limitations." The only dissenting voice was sounded by Dan Silver of the Endangered Habitats League, who argued that the ESA was "not broken."[43]

Congress has not enacted any of the ideas that came up during the hearing. The House did approve the TESRA bill championed by Representative Pombo, though Colton officials were not really sure whether TESRA would solve their problems. In any event, the bill died in the Senate, and Pombo lost his bid for reelection in 2006 in part because of concern about his opposition to the ESA. Mark Nuaimi told me that he "would love for the Congress fairy godmother to come and wave her wand" to solve the problem, but he does not sound like he really expects that to happen.

LIVING WITH THE FLY

By 2006, Mayor Bennett told Secretary of the Interior Kempthorne's task force that Colton was done fighting the fly. Instead, the mayor described the city's commitment to "a proactive approach by crafting a cooperative strategy, a strategy whereby the possibility of the fly recovery could be maximized, while the city of Colton was also allowed to develop the economic base that we so rightly deserve." The tone of the discussions has changed, but one cannot neatly demarcate Colton's opposition to the listing of the fly and its embrace of a more cooperative strategy. Colton tried cooperation soon after the fly was listed; the city still resists conservation efforts that it deems unreasonable.[44]

In 1997, the FWS's regional director wrote to Colton's mayor that the agency "look[ed] forward to developing an HCP that conserves listed species while providing for the City's economic growth." The HCP, or habitat conservation plan, is a device that began to flourish during the 1990s as Secretary of the Interior Bruce Babbitt sought to deflect criticism of the ESA as hostile to private landowners. An HCP describes the commitments that a party makes to preserve the habitat of a listed species in exchange for an "incidental take permit" issued by the FWS. The idea, explains Alejandro Camacho, is to "rely on negotiated, collaborative decisionmaking and to focus on developing creative, flexible ways for managing uncertain, evolving ecosystems based on the best available science." The actors involved in listing the fly under the ESA expected that the fly would soon become encompassed by a regional HCP that protected multiple species. In 2003, Riverside County approved a multi-species HCP that is designed to protect more than 150 species and conserve more than five hundred thousand acres in the western part of the county. The fly is one of those species because there is an area south of Fontana that is fly habitat. The county boasts that its plan will "streamline regulatory review related to endangered species," "return local control to the county," and "conserve resources for future generations."[45]

Colton was among a dozen cities that signed a memorandum of understanding with county officials, the California Department of Fish and Game, and the FWS to produce a similar HCP for San Bernardino County. The anticipated plan would encompass more than three hundred thousand acres of land composed of eight different kinds of ecosystems in the southwestern part of the county, and it would protect about eighty species, including the fly, the San Bernardino kangaroo rat, and the Santa Ana River woolly-star, a flowering shrub. Colton later worked with a smaller group of cities to produce a smaller plan that would address the Colton Dunes ecosystem. But several years of negotiations failed to produce an agreeable plan. Rialto's mayor blamed the failure to develop a regional HCP on "a basic mistrust" of the FWS and the objections of Colton officials. Dan Silver noted that radical environmentalists opposed HCPs as insufficiently protective of habitat, and the county board simply decided that the effort was not worth the bother. Colton withdrew from its negotiations with the FWS in the summer of 2002, claiming that the anticipated $3 million cost of setting aside thirty-three acres as habitat for the fly amounted to "legalized extortion." An FWS spokesperson responded that the agency has worked with cities all across the country "in partnership to develop a plan that makes biological sense and balance the conservation needs of the species and opportunity for economic development." Rather than giving up, Silver has called for a renewed effort spearheaded by the San Bernardino Association of Governments that would include "a stakeholder advisory committee" composed of representatives of the "business community, conservation groups, [and] special districts." Silver recognizes that it is difficult to get all of the different interests in the same room and to agree to a mutually acceptable plan, but he adds that it happened in Riverside because one of the county supervisors took on the project as his personal mission and goal.[46]

Meanwhile, both economic development and protection of the fly proceeded on a piecemeal basis, thanks to more modest solutions offered by the ESA and the federal Clean Water Act. Section 7 of the ESA requires federal agencies to "consult" with the FWS in order to avoid jeopardizing the survival of a listed species. A housing project on the north side of Colton and the redesign of the I-10 interchange proceeded through the Section 7 review process. But Dan Silver complains that Section 7 "has become an end run around" the more onerous regulatory requirements contained in the take prohibition of ESA Section 9. "Section 7 doesn't drag on, there's a time limit, no public participation, and no actual [jeopardy findings] that would stop a project," Silver says. He believes that developers purposefully nick a fraction of an acre in order to trigger Section 7 and thus obtain a permit through that easier route. Section 404 of the Clean Water Act requires a permit before a developer can build on wetlands, and although the fly's habitat contains few wetlands, there have been some instances in which developers have obtained permits through a combined permit and consultation process.

If the Clean Water Act or ESA Section 7 is not available, then developers often turn to ESA's Section 10(a)(1)(B). Congress added that provision in 1982, and it authorizes the FWS to permit an incidental take of a listed species. An *incidental take* is an action that constitutes a take within ESA Section 9, but it is "incidental to, and not the purpose of, the carrying out of an otherwise lawful activity." Michael Bean and

Melanie Rowland assert that "this provision likely increased the Secretary's leverage over activities that incidentally take endangered species because it substituted a flexible regulatory authority for a threat of prosecution that few found credible." The FWS issued eleven such permits between 1995 and 2007 for activities affecting the fly. The typical approach involved landowners agreeing to set aside some of their property to serve as habitat for the fly in exchange for FWS permission to build on another part of the property. For example, in 1997, Colton and the FWS reached such an agreement to allow development on 80 acres within the Agua Mansa Enterprise Zone while setting aside 160 acres for the fly. This may not be the best example, though, for the original plan had been to sell all 240 acres to a company that would deed the 160 acres to the federal government while leasing the 80 acres to a developer. That, at least, was the hope of Mayor Gaytan (who would soon be convicted of bribery) as he negotiated such a deal with Enron (whose own difficulties soon became apparent as well).[47]

Nobody was really satisfied by such arrangements. Developers watched as their proposed building sites remained vacant as the economic boom of the 1990s ended. The city complained that the FWS demanded too much habitat preservation, as in the case of the Big League Dreams park. The city finally abandoned the park in 2006, complaining that the FWS "took a project and doubled it in price and shrunk it down over a fly." For their part, environmentalists worried that the haphazard patches of protected land would not sustain a healthy population of the fly. As Dan Silver summarized the problem, "developers in San Bernardino continue to face substantial uncertainty" while the fly is "slowly going extinct under current project-by-project permitting."[48]

The next idea involved the establishment of a *conservation bank*. "A conservation bank is like a biological bank account," explains the FWS, in which lands that are managed for endangered or otherwise rare species may be sold "to developers or others who need to compensate for the environmental impacts of their projects." The FWS contacted the California Portland Cement Company in 1996 "to discuss a potential conservation bank" for the fly. The FWS stated its position with surprising candor: "The properties owned by your company and CALMAT in the City of Colton contain the largest remaining block of habitat for the Delhi Sands flower-loving fly, as well as other plants and animals endemic to the Colton Dunes. Consequently, the assistance of your company will be critical in preventing its extinction." California Portland did not act, but soon CALMAT was acquired by the Vulcan Materials Company, the nation's largest producer of crushed stone, sand, gravel, and other construction aggregates. Vulcan thus became the owner of one of the largest blocks of fly habitat, located south of I-10 in Colton.[49]

In June 2005, Vulcan agreed to permanently preserve 150 acres of its land as part of a new conservation bank containing habitat for the fly. "The property we have has very little development potential," explained Vulcan's Michael Linton, "and we figured that the best thing we can do is participate in a market that allows development to go forward in the community." The conservation bank will be expanded as other businesses donate land that can serve as habitat for the fly in order to receive development credits from the FWS. The Riverside Habitat League (RHL) holds the conservation easement on the property and performs regular oversight to ensure that the property is being used appropriately by Vulcan and not harmed by trespassers. "Trespass and trash is always one of the biggest issues that we face" when preserving habitat, according to the RHL's Jane Block, because people take advantage of land when they don't see an active human use. The first sale from the conservation bank occurred in January 2006 when a commercial developer paid $300,000 for two credits, thus preserving two acres of habitat in order to obtain FWS approval to develop five acres of degraded habitat elsewhere in the area. San Bernardino County included an option to purchase five credits to mitigate a long-delayed road alignment near the hospital in Colton, and Union Pacific bought three credits (comprising three acres costing $200,000 per acre) to mitigate a railroad improvement project in Colton and unincorporated parts of the county. Governor Arnold Schwarzenegger awarded Vulcan and the RHL an Environmental and Economic Leadership Award because "the revolutionary concept provided a means for developers to mitigate the habitat impacts of their projects through immediate habitat conservation."[50]

Colton officials were unimpressed. They were upset that they had not been included in the negotiations that produced the conservation bank. And they were even more upset that land within Colton would now become the "dumping ground for habitat" needed to gain FWS approval of development activities elsewhere. In January 2006, the city council expressed its concern about the amount of lands set aside "by open space conservation agreements, easements, and other contractual mechanisms by their owners to insure that these properties will never be used for anything except open space conservation and Delhi Fly Habitat, despite the properties' current land use and zoning designations which may allow for some reasonable development." Accordingly, the city council passed an emergency ordinance requiring the rezoning of any protected land as "Open Space" and the receipt of a conditional use permit before any land within the city may be encumbered with an easement or other device to protect the fly. The city defended its ordinance as a means of generating funds—paid by permit applicants—that could be spent on managing the fly's habitat. The other view was that Colton was "trying to make conservation illegal," as Dan Silver complained. So Vulcan sued the city to invalidate the ordinance, arguing that it was preempted by federal and state law and that Colton had failed to comply with the review requirements of the California Environmental Quality Act. The court agreed with Vulcan that the act exemption cited by the city applied only to "regulatory actions that protect the environment. The Ordinance hampers the recordation of conservation easements and only favors development." The court did not reach Vulcan's alternative arguments that the city's ordinance was preempted by state and federal law.[51]

THE SURVIVAL OF THE FLY AND THE DEVELOPMENT OF COLTON

I wanted to see a Delhi Sands flower-loving fly. During his 2004 hearing, Representative Pombo asked the witnesses whether they had ever actually seen a fly. Mayor Bennett, Mark Nuaimi, Dan Silver, and Deputy Secretary of the Interior Julie McDonald (who later resigned amidst allegations of inappropriate interference with ESA decisions) had not. Jim Bartel, the field supervisor of the Carlsbad office of the FWS, once noted that he had never seen a fly either. But Colton officials told me that they knew people who had, including a man who watched one perch on his side-view mirror as he filled his car with gasoline.

So I set out to find the fly. I began looking in the vacant property across Pepper Avenue just west of the hospital. I learned later that the lot is known as the "King Is Coming" property because of the old, seemingly closed church on the northeast corner of the block. The sandy, rolling, and trash-filled property was hardly the kind of place where one would expect to find a rare animal, even a rare fly. Soon after I arrived, I saw a large, brownish insect perched on a buckwheat plant, but it flew away as I approached for a better look. It could have been a fly, but it probably was a grasshopper or another insect. Besides that, I saw a bunch of little lizards scurrying across the sand and into holes whenever I got too near, a few colorful butterflies, a couple of birds, and lots of honeybees buzzing around the flowers. I visited the site many times during my visits to Colton, and the scene was pretty much the same each time. I also visited the land owned by Vulcan for its fly conservation bank. It was a large, vacant patch of land with much less trash than the King Is Coming site, though you could still see the ORV trails. The area was fenced, but the barbed wire blocking the north side of the land along Slover Avenue was already buried by the shifting sand dunes just one year after it had been installed. There were some very sandy parts to the north part of the land where the dunes were obviously shifting, and the rest of the property was covered with scattered buckwheat and other plants. But no flies.

Will this land host the fly ten, twenty, or fifty years from now? Dan Silver says that "the fly is in terrible shape." He thinks that it could survive, though it is the Colton city government that is in the "godly position to determine what lives and what dies." Silver agrees with those biologists who recommend preserving the place where the fly has the most likelihood of long-term viability. That means Colton, which experiences the natural cycle of the sand blowing in to maintain the dunes. Silver's approach means that land should be saved for the fly in Colton and everything else should be let go. The alternative perspective heeds the maxim of not putting all of your eggs in one basket. You protect the fly wherever you find it. The FWS straddles both approaches, seeking to identify sites to support multiple populations of the fly while emphasizing the importance of preserving the fly's best habitat in Colton. The FWS still "believe[s] that sufficient Delhi Sands flower-loving fly habitat remains to establish Delhi Sands flower-loving fly reserves that will support the long-term conservation of the species."[52]

Colton officials remain cautiously optimistic, too. They see only two options. One is the status quo, where the species will eventually die. Mayor Chastain insists that "we must be allowed to develop in order for the fly to have any chance at recovery," for the survival of the fly depends on the habitat that is preserved as a result of the development approval process. The second option is some kind of deal with the FWS. City Manager Daryl Parrish told me in August 2007 that he was hopeful of having a comprehensive solution to the problem "in a few months." Of course, that was eight months after Mark Nuaimi stated that "we are as close as we have ever been to the city being able to develop its economy while the fly is conserved" and more than two years after Mayor Bennett said in April 2005 that "today was actually the first time I felt there could be a solution coming down in the near future." Parrish left Colton to become the city manager of Covina in May 2009, and the problem still was not resolved. Even so, Greg Ballmer denies that the habitat efforts have stalled. "They move along slowly," he says. "There's an incremental change now and then. It's like watching the grass grow." So the parties continue to explore new ideas. One frustrated letter writer suggested that "Greg Ballmer, who is most responsible for this insect's protected status, should purchase all the privately owned properties declared to be fly habitat." A more intriguing, though equally novel idea would be to establish some kind of revenue sharing scheme in which Colton provides the land for the fly while it shares in the tax revenue generated by development in neighboring cities. Revenue sharing has not happened in habitat conservation efforts before, there is no existing legal vehicle to facilitate it, and it would require unprecedented cooperation between often competing jurisdictions. But it still may be an idea worth pursuing.[53]

Surprisingly, Colton recognized that its extended struggle with the fly's habitat "could end up being a plus," as Mark Nuaimi put it. The economic wave that swept through the Inland Empire left Colton with the largest tract of undeveloped land along I-10. The fact that development has been held up for so long as the economy has changed could mean that a better project will be pursued than would have gone in before. Thus Colton is promoting the "Super Block": 285 acres of restaurants, townhouses, a business park, a movie theater complex, and parks that mimics the new Victoria Gardens Mall in Rancho Cucamonga—albeit with "a Target or something of that nature" as an anchor store instead of the more upscale shops at Victoria Gardens. The Super Block would be located just west of the hospital on the vacant King Is Coming site. The city would try to entice developers to come in and make it happen. And the city recognizes that it has one last chance to succeed because there are no other spots like it. Yet even the Super Block has its opponents. Existing businesses feel left out by the city's emphasis on more expensive developments. The city wants to avoid piecemeal development of the property in twenty-acre chunks, so it enacted a temporary moratorium on construction there while the Super Block idea is pursued. Colton also engaged in a battle with an historic cemetery that opened in 1887 and now wants to expand on its property located just east of the hospital. The cemetery accused the city of wanting to set aside some of that land in order to gain FWS permission to develop the Super Block on the other side of the hospital. The city and the cemetery reached an agreement in June 2009 that would allow the cemetery to develop eighteen acres of land while leaving the remaining eleven acres for conservation of the fly's habitat. Meanwhile, frustration with the Super Block plan helped fuel the recall challenge to Mayor Chastain in June 2008, with opponents saying that the city has been "spending a lot of money on something that's probably a long shot, and they've alienated almost everyone with a lack of communication." The pending environmental study of the project should address many of the questions that the Super Block raises.[54]

The Super Block is a reminder that Colton's battle against the fly is a battle between tax revenues and open space, as the fly's habitat in Colton is one of the last vestiges of open space in the area. By 1990, Colton's land use plan acknowledged that the city was almost all built out. Now, many environmentalists extol the value of open spaces, especially as they disappear amidst the sea of development in the Inland Empire. "Open space becomes more precious as you lose it," observes Greg Ballmer. He imagines Colton transforming the fly's habitat into a city park where people walk, jog, and fly kites—except during the fly's flight season in the summer when the heat makes outdoor recreation less enticing anyway. Even those outside the environmental community acknowledge the problems that Colton will face if it surrenders all of its open space. Colton's city leaders, by contrast, see open spaces as opportunities for generating tax receipts from expensive new developments to pay for much needed municipal services. Twenty percent of the city's revenues come from sales taxes. City Manager Parrish told me in August 2006 that the city's economic condition will be fine as long as the sales of recreational vehicles (RVs) hold up. Colton is home to lots of RV dealers whose sales taxes contribute to a substantial portion of the city's budget. But alas, RV sales have been tanking since gas prices rose in the summer of 2008 and the whole economy plummeted soon thereafter. By January 2009, Colton had lost 30 percent of its tax revenue as RV dealers and other businesses closed.

Whatever its budgetary situation, and whatever the fate of the Delhi Sands flower-loving fly, Colton will continue to face numerous environmental problems. Conspiracy theorists murmur that the next insect, plant, fish, or other species will show up as soon as the fly dispute is resolved. A reference to the "possibility that the Coast Horned Lizard, a Candidate I for federal listing for protection, inhabits the Santa Ana River floodplain river area" is buried within the 1985 environmental impact report on the Agua Mansa Enterprise Zone. Further detail appears in the 2008 draft report for the proposed Agua Mansa Commerce Center, which found that the project could affect the burrowing owl and the Los Angeles pocket mouse—both species of special concern under California state law. The same report found no evidence of two plants, two birds, and two rats that live in the area and are listed under the federal ESA, but the fact that the biologists thought that the species were worth investigating could be telling. And even if another endangered species does not surface, Colton will still confront some of the nation's worst air pollution, contaminated groundwater, and dozens of brownfield sites.[55]

So the beginning of the twenty-first century finds government officials, developers, environmentalists, and other interested parties still debating the needs of the fly, the dunes, and the people who live there. Nonetheless, scientists and federal officials still fear that the fly will become extinct early in this century despite all of the efforts to save it. Colton also continues to struggle with the pollution that is the legacy of its industrial history and of its location along I-10. Yet few people in Colton seem to care. Documentarian Robert Gonzales showed "Living on the Dime," his multimedia production examining life in the Mexican communities along I-10, to numerous local audiences over a three-year period, but no one asked him about the environmental issues in the area. Instead, they asked "why should we care about a bug when we need jobs?" A rare, recent complaint about Colton's environment appeared in a flyer protesting that the city had welcomed "a pollution monster" that had been kicked out of another city, but the only litigation this situation produced involved the alleged defamation of the business and an anti-SLAPP (Strategic Lawsuit against Public Participation) claim filed by the flyer's author. Both lawsuits failed. Gonzales further laments that "the area has been avoided by most of the more traditional organizing groups." That leaves the people of Colton to struggle with their natural environment without much help from those who care about that environment, or from the provisions of environmental law.[56]

CHAPTER THREE

Heaven or Hell?

THE BADLANDS OF WESTERN NORTH DAKOTA

GENERAL ALFRED SULLY WAS A PROTÉGÉ of General George Mc-
Clellan during the Civil War. And so when President Abraham Lincoln
dismissed McClellan in 1862 for failing to aggressively prosecute the war,
Sully found himself reassigned to the remote Dakota Territory. He spent
the next decade traversing uncharted land as he fought the Sioux Indians.
During one of those trips he quipped that the badlands of what is now
western North Dakota looked like "hell with the fires burned out."[1]

A few years later, in September 1883, a twenty-five-year-old New
Yorker named Theodore Roosevelt arrived in the badlands to hunt a buffalo. It took ten days for him to get his buffalo, which by then had been
nearly exterminated. But Roosevelt developed a genuine affection for the
land. Five months later, Valentine's Day of 1884 was very unkind to him.
He had rushed to his Oyster Bay home from New York City just in time
for his mother to die that morning, and then he moved upstairs and held
his wife in his arms as she died in the afternoon from complications of
childbirth. Stricken by grief, the future president indulged the under-
standable impulse to flee far from the home that now held such tragic
memories for him. Where he fled demonstrates his peculiar character:
he spent much of the next few years in the Dakota Territory.

Roosevelt's destination had only recently been settled by whites.
Meriwether Lewis and William Clark followed the Missouri River during

their expedition in the early nineteenth century, so they passed north of the badlands. Various native peoples had lived in the region for millennia, culminating in the Mandan culture and nomadic visits by Arikara, Assiniboine, Cheyenne, Crow, Gros Ventre, Hidatsa, Lakota, and Sioux who hunted the millions of buffalo that lived throughout the Great Plains. General Sully and his twenty-five hundred troops drove the Sioux out of the area in 1864, but the Indians returned as soon as Sully left. General George Custer followed Sully's route through the badlands into Montana, only to meet his demise at Little Bighorn. The military finally evicted the natives, and the Northern Pacific Railroad followed as soon as the land was deemed to be safe. The railroad reached the southern end of the badlands by 1880. A young French adventurer named Marquis de Mores arrived there in early 1883 and planned to operate a meat-packing business. The Marquis named the new town after his wife Medora, and he built an extravagant mansion just outside of town overlooking the Little Missouri River. In September, Roosevelt took the five-day train trip from New York to Medora to hunt buffalo. He arrived "wearing a designer suit of cowboy duds, a knife purchased at Tiffany's, and monogrammed spurs."[2]

Roosevelt loved his time in the Dakota Territory and became a partner in the Maltese Cross Ranch, seven miles south of Medora, during his first visit. He built his own, larger Elkhorn Ranch thirty-five miles north of town when he returned in June 1884 after the death of his wife and mother. His exploits became legendary. He once spent forty consecutive hours on horseback watching his herd, earned the respect of the locals by slugging a man who had the temerity to call him "four-eyes," organized the area's first grazing association, and spent three days chasing the three men who stole his boat and then marched them fifty miles to the nearest sheriff in Dickinson. According to Clay Jenkinson, the Theodore Roosevelt Scholar-in-Residence at Dickinson State University, "T.R." "preferred to spend his time in the badlands either hunting or writing books." Of course, T.R. combined his interests by writing about hunting and his other adventures. "I heartily enjoy this life," T.R. exclaimed, "with its perfect freedom, for I am very fond of hunting, and there are few sensations I prefer to that of galloping over these rolling limitless prairies, with rifle in hand, or winding my way among the barren, fantastic and grimly picturesque deserts of the so-called Bad Lands."[3]

The brutal winter of 1886 ended this idyllic life. Bison had survived the western North Dakota climate for centuries, but the influx of too many cattle overgrazing the prairie provided a literal demonstration of the tragedy of the commons. T.R. had warned his fellow ranchers that their days of inexhaustible grazing were limited, to no avail. Nearly all of the cattle died, including most of T.R.'s herd, which had once numbered nearly five thousand. The Marquis returned to France, led an anti-Semitic political party, and was killed in Africa in 1896 while resisting British expansion there. North Dakota became a state in 1889, and there had been speculation as statehood approached that T.R. would represent the new state in the U.S. Senate. But instead, he also left. He sold his holdings, returned to New York with the buffalo that he had shot on his arrival in the Dakotas (which is still on display at his home in Sagamore Hill today), and continued the political career that culminated in his earning the reputation as the first great conservationist in the White House. Altogether, he spent only about 359 days in the Dakotas between 1883 and 1887. Even so, T.R. later told a North Dakota audience that he would not have become president but for his experiences in the state's badlands.

Today, the most notable feature of the North Dakota badlands is the Theodore Roosevelt National Park (TRNP). Established as a "national memorial park" in 1947 and promoted to a full-fledged national park in 1978, TRNP is one of only fifty-eight places that Congress has preserved as a national park. It is also the leading tourist destination in North Dakota. The state's tourist agency triumphantly proclaims that the area is "heaven" on earth.

Which is it: heaven or hell? The object of these conflicting accounts is ill-defined.

Generally, North Dakota's badlands extend along the Little Missouri River, which flows northeast for 560 miles from northeastern Wyoming until it reaches the main Missouri River at the Sakakawea Reservoir. The unique features of the badlands evolved during numerous geological epochs. Sedimentation and volcanic activity produced the rainbow of colors in the rocks, then the Little Missouri River carved "the fantastically

broken topography that is today's badlands." The processes continue today and could eventually flatten the landscape to make it indistinguish-
able from the rest of the Great Plains. But that will take a long time.[4]

The badlands are concentrated in Billings and McKenzie counties,
which had a combined population of 6,415 in 2005. The national park is
split into three sections: the South Unit is in Billings County, the North
Unit is seventy miles away in McKenzie County, and the tiny Elkhorn
Ranch site straddles the Little Missouri River in between. The park's headquarters are located in Medora, which has a population of fewer than one
hundred—fewer than the number of people who lived there with T.R. Medora is so small that one has no idea that it exists as one travels along Interstate 94 save for the exit signs announcing its presence. Medora hosts
more tourists during the summer, but by the time I arrived at the end of
September, nearly all of the handful of restaurants and shops had shut
down for the season. The largest "city" in the area is Watford City, a town
of about two thousand that serves as the seat of McKenzie County and the
gateway to the North Unit of the national park fifteen miles to the town's
south. Unlike Medora, Watford City is open year-round, with several small
stores of the sort that one expects to find in a small town as opposed to a
mere tourist destination, such as a hardware store, a card shop, a grocery
store, some banks, and numerous cafes and restaurants.

The human communities in the badlands are supported by several
activities. Hunting came first, as witnessed by T.R., and it continues to
provide a modest amount of income for the area today. Grazing quickly
followed, again with T.R., and cattle provided the backbone of the economy for decades. Oil production began in the 1950s and today generates
more revenue than any other enterprise in the region. Thus, the logo of
the McKenzie County Bank features an oil rig and a cow's head, and the
bank has surely supported both activities for generations. Most recently,
tourism and recreational activities have attracted more residents and
visitors to the badlands and have begun to disrupt the expectations that
nearly a century of locals had for the use of the land.

Despite the rise in tourism, TRNP is still one of the least visited of
the national parks, attracting not quite half a million people in 2007,
compared with the 9.4 million who visited the Great Smoky Mountains
National Park and the 4.4 million who visited the Grand Canyon. Even
that half million number is misleading, however, for the Painted Canyon

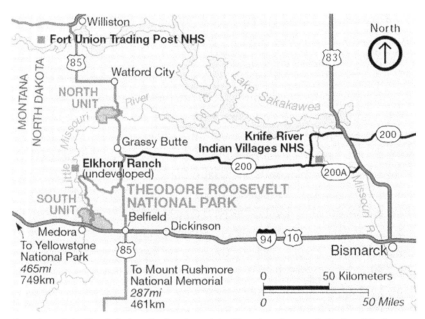

Location of the North Dakota badlands and the Theodore Roosevelt National Park. Courtesy of the National Park Service (http://www.nps.gov).

Visitor Center registered nearly half of those visitors to the park. Painted Canyon offers a spectacular vista of the badlands, but it is little more than a glorified rest stop along I-94 where travelers can get out of their cars for a minute to gaze at the scenery and buy a souvenir before returning to the highway. Well, not literally a minute, but fourteen minutes—according to the average visit time found in a 1989 report—which is less than a quarter of the eighty-two minutes that the average customer spends in a shopping mall. The same report explained that Sunday is the busiest time in the park's North Unit "when there is heavy use of the unit's campground and picnic areas by local residents." In other words, it is not the prototypical national park experience, nor is it a reminder of T.R.'s own time in the badlands. And, according to a 1992 book published by the National Geographic Society titled *America's Hidden Treasures: Exploring Our Little-Known National Parks:* "though the park is located at the edge of an interstate, the highway is not heavily traveled. A lot of people don't stop at the park. 'Most,' one observer said, 'are passing through on their way to somewhere else—the general fate of all North Dakota.'"[5]

This chapter considers five questions about how the law governs North Dakota's badlands. First, do the badlands deserve the legal protections provided to a national park? Not according to President Truman, who vetoed the initial bill to establish a national park there because he felt the area was not scenic enough. The standards for identifying which places should be afforded national park status have troubled Congress, the National Park Service (NPS), and interested observers ever since the first national park was established in 1872. Second, how should the land within the park be managed? Nationally, Congress and the NPS are overseeing a debate over the relative importance of the preservation versus the use of national parks. The TRNP's signature contribution to that debate involves the management of elk, with the park's staff, Senator Byron Dorgan, and the North Dakota Game and Fish Department favoring competing plans. The resolution of that dispute will turn on what we expect to happen within a national park and could affect other management issues at TRNP involving wildlife and oil production. Third, how is the land outside the park affected by the national park nearby?—in particular the Clean Air Act restrictions imposed on air pollution that drifts over a national park. The TRNP demonstrates the irony of seeking national park status. Local North Dakotans were the biggest boosters of the idea of the park during the 1930s, presuming that the presence of a national park would be a boon to the area's economy. Instead, the designation of the national park means that energy development outside of the park is constrained by the especially stringent Clean Air Act regulations applicable to lands near national parks. Fourth, how is the Little Missouri National Grassland—which surrounds the park—managed? Recreational interests and biodiversity conservation now compete with grazing for priority on the national grassland, and their claims rely on the unique twist that the history of the national grassland provides for the common debates about who should control the use of federal public lands. Finally, how will environmental law shape the future of North Dakota's badlands?

THE NATIONAL PARK

The author Wallace Stegner once wrote that "national parks are the best idea we ever had." National parks were an American idea, beginning with President Ulysses S. Grant's approval of legislation to establish Yel-

lowstone National Park in 1872. Historians still debate the precise ratio-
nale for the unprecedented act of taking federal land out of the general
public domain and denominating it a national park. Nineteenth-century
landscape painters such as Albert Bierstadt gave Americans a sense of
the hidden wonders of the western United States, which prompted many
people to want to preserve them. The landscape designer Frederick Law
Olmsted played an important role in galvanizing support for the new
idea of national parks, too. At the least, public preservation of spectacular areas was a reaction against the crass commercialization of Niagara
Falls by private interests earlier in the nineteenth century. Whatever the
motivation, the national park idea proved to be immensely popular. The
national park system now includes 391 units; along with the fifty-eight
national parks, there are national monuments, preserves, historic parks,
historic sites, battlefield parks, military parks, battlefields, memorials,
recreation areas, seashores, lakeshores, rivers, reserves, historic and scenic trails, cemeteries, and heritage areas. More than one hundred foreign
nations have imitated the idea and established more than twelve hundred
national parks and conservation areas of their own.

But not every idea for a national park has been a good one, and several places—especially the Cuyahoga Valley in Ohio, established as a
national park in 2000—have been the subject of intense debate concerning their national parkworthiness. By contrast, dozens of proposed
national parks were never approved, and six national parks even had
their park status revoked. The debate concerning the qualifications of
North Dakota's badlands for a national park has occurred within this
context.

National parks have what I'll call a Lefty O'Doul problem. O'Doul is
my favorite baseball player, even though he played decades before my
childhood. His 254 hits while playing for the Philadelphia Phillies in
1929 are still tied for the National League record. But O'Doul played
only seven seasons as an outfielder in the National League, having spent
the previous decade as an unsuccessful pitcher and as a minor leaguer.
His fans insist that his hitting accomplishments, his role in introducing
baseball to Japan, and his longtime service as a manager in the Pacific
Coast League justify O'Doul's election to the Baseball Hall of Fame.
Thus far, the campaign has been unsuccessful, garnering only fifteen of
the necessary sixty-two votes in the 2007 balloting by the Veteran's

Committee that considers players from generations gone by. The argument against O'Doul insists that his record, although impressive, does not meet the lofty standards necessary to preserve the integrity of the Hall of Fame.

Innumerable places are championed as potential national parks, but their opponents respond that the stature of the existing national parks would be diminished by lesser additions. The question of what deserves to be a national park was debated throughout the first several decades of the twentieth century when many new national parks were created, many proposed national parks were rejected, and the newly created NPS was thrust into the debate. For example, in a famous 1918 letter, Secretary of the Interior Franklin Lane advised NPS director Stephen Mather, "In studying new park projects, you should seek to find scenery of supreme and distinctive quality or some natural feature so extraordinary or unique as to be of national interest and importance." Lane further warned, "The national park system as now constituted should not be lowered in standard, dignity, and prestige by the inclusion of areas which express in less than the highest terms the particular class or kind of exhibit which they represent." The most recent expression of these standards appears in the 2006 NPS Management Policies, which identify national significance, the absence of similar resources in existing national parks, the size and feasibility of managing the area, and the necessity of NPS management as the four required criteria for inclusion in the national park system. Not surprisingly, these standards yield different responses when applied to particular places, and in any event, Congress always retains the final word about what should be a national park. And in 1998, Congress included a provision in the National Parks Omnibus Management Act that prohibits the NPS from studying the addition of new park service units without prior congressional approval.[6]

Whether there should be a national park in western North Dakota depends in part on how the area compares both to other places that have been awarded park status and to those that have not. Few people would argue that the badlands are the equal of the most renowned national parks: Yellowstone, Yosemite, Glacier, Denali, and the Grand Canyon. The next tier of national parks is almost as impressive: Rocky Mountain, Zion, Bryce Canyon, the Everglades, Mount Rainier, Glacier Bay, Crater

Lake, and Acadia. On the other hand, some national parks are more questionable and are little known outside their local areas.

Then there are those places that have not been designated national parks. My Uncle Don, a retired coal miner, has visited most of the country's national parks and still insists that the scenery near his southwestern Pennsylvania home is the most impressive of all. Of perhaps greater significance, the NPS continues to consider whether there are more places worthy of being designated a national park. The NPS studied whether to recommend a national park along the Niobrara River valley in western Nebraska, but in 1995 it decided against doing so. And dozens of national parks were proposed and rejected during the 1920s, including national parks to be located at Lake Tahoe, Utah's Wasatch Mountains, the Sawtooth Mountains of Idaho, Mount St. Helens, and the Sacramento Mountains and White Sands of southern New Mexico (see Chapter 5).

The proposal that came closest without succeeding was Ouachita National Park. The Ouachita Mountains are a heavily forested area in western Arkansas where T.R. established the Ouachita National Forest in 1907. Congress first considered a bill to establish the Ouachita National Park in 1927. Most local residents supported the national park proposal, citing both the area's superlative scenery and the economic benefits that would flow from a park designation. But an NPS study concluded that "the Ouachita area does not contain features nor scenery on a scale equal to, nor even approaching, the majority of the national parks that have been established by Congress." More specifically, the Ouachita Mountains were "beautiful, attractive, luxuriant, verdant, friendly, [and] peaceful," but they were "not grand, spectacular, unique, nor superlative." This battle of adjectives shifted to the floor of the House of Representatives during the lame-duck session of February 1929. One member proclaimed that "this is one of the most scenically beautiful spots in all of America." Representative Louis Cramton of Michigan rebutted that claim by quoting a letter from the American Civic Association which advised that "even as a forest it is far less impressive than many of the forests in the White and Green Mountains in New England, the Adirondacks and Catskills of New York, the Blue Ridge in Pennsylvania, Maryland, and Virginia, the Appalachians in North Carolina and Tennessee, the Rocky Mountains in Colorado, and the Cascade and Coast Range in

Washington, Oregon, and California." Much of the debate considered the broader implications for national parks throughout the nation. "We have proceeded on the theory that we would have something inspirational, distinctive, or outstanding," explained Utah's representative Don Colton. "If you are going to pass this bill because it means something commercially to a community," warned Representative Cramton, "that is unfair to the lovers of nature who cherish the name 'national park.'" Another representative feared that every state would soon want its own national park. Supporters of the proposal suggested that the mere inability to match the scenery of the most famous parks in the West should not disqualify other areas and that "a national park standard in one part of the country is not at all the standard in another." Representative Otis Wingo of Arkansas uttered the most memorable argument when he said that "parks are just like women—they are of different types; no two of them exactly alike; but they are all beautiful. This may not be a Rocky Mountain brunette, but it is a Mississippi Valley blonde." His colleagues applauded. Then the House approved the creation of Ouachita National Park by a vote of 164 to 71, joining the Senate's unanimous vote ten days before. But President Calvin Coolidge vetoed the bill as one of his last acts in office. He never explained his decision, and the national park proposal soon disappeared with the onset of the Great Depression. Ouachita remains a national forest to this day.[7]

Then there are the places that were once designated as national parks but had that honor revoked. The best example is offered by Theodore Roosevelt—the man, not the park. As president, Roosevelt approved five new national parks, only three of which survive today: Crater Lake in Oregon, Wind Cave in South Dakota, and Mesa Verde in Colorado. Roosevelt also designated Platt National Park in Oklahoma, which is now part of the Chickasaw National Recreation Area. And in 1906, he approved the creation of Sullys Hill National Park. Sully, you will recall, was the army general who disdained the badlands during his travels in western North Dakota during the 1870s. Earlier, an army cavalry unit had awaited a visit from the general at a hill in the northeastern part of the state. Sully never showed up, but the hill became known as Sullys Hill nonetheless. In 1904, as part of a settlement of the land claims of the residents of the nearby Devil's Lake Indian Reservation, Congress empowered the president to keep Sullys Hill "as a public park." Roosevelt agreed to set aside 780 acres—in other words, about one square mile—"for public use as a park to be known as Sullys Hill Park." The property soon became known as Sullys Hill National Park because it was within the jurisdiction of the Department of the Interior (thanks to the involvement of the Bureau of Indian Affairs) and, in the words of one historian, "simply because it was not otherwise classified as a state or local park." Sullys Hill thus became a national park before such iconic areas as the Grand Canyon, the Grand Tetons, Bryce Canyon, Zion, the Everglades, and Glacier Bay. By the late 1920s, Sullys Hill National Park even attracted more visitors than Mesa Verde and about the same number as Zion. But the NPS was embarrassed by what it characterized "as merely a deserted bit of wilderness" that complicated the agency's efforts to develop a more stringent set of criteria for what should constitute a national park. Stephen Mather, the first director of the NPS, insisted that Sullys Hill was "not of national park caliber." Finally, in 1931 Representative Cramton—fresh from his successful fight against Ouachita National Park—sponsored legislation to recharacterize Sullys Hill as a national game preserve. As Cramton explained, "Tourists who see it listed as a national park sometimes travel quite a distance to see the park and when they get there they are disappointed because it is not up to the standard of scenery that they anticipated because of the name 'national park.'" Congress agreed, and Sullys Hill has been a game preserve ever since. National park histories explain the episode by stating that Sullys Hill lacked the requisite qualities for a national park. John Ise, a historian of the national parks, called Sullys Hill "the most unworthy national park ever created." The irony is that Roosevelt accepted Sullys Hill for national park status instead of his beloved badlands. Apparently, TRNP honors T.R. for things other than his judgment in creating national parks.[8]

The controversy regarding Sullys Hill occurred while the NPS began to struggle to figure out what, exactly, a national park is. Its first publicity chief, Robert Sterling Yard, stated the concern well when he compared national parks to a trademark that could be diluted by inferior parks. "The trade-mark 'National Parks of America' has been soundly established," Yard wrote in 1923. The trademark analogy is useful. Trademark law protects the holder of a trademark from dilution by other users. The federal Trademark Dilution Act allows "the owner of a famous mark" to block "another person's commercial use in commerce of a mark or trade name, if such use begins after the mark has become famous and causes dilution of the distinctive quality of the mark." The law defines *dilution* as "the lessening of the capacity of a famous mark to identify and distinguish goods or services." Yard expressed a similar fear that the national park trademark would be diluted by inferior products. "When Zion National Park was created in 1919," he wrote, "the whole world knew from the simple announcement of the fact that another stupendous scenic wonderland had been discovered. But when pleasant wooded summits, limestone caves, pretty local ravines, local mountains and gaps between mountains become National Parks, the name 'Zion National Park' will mean nothing at home or abroad to those who have not already seen it." There was sure to be congressional pressure to designate the "pretty local ravines" and their ilk as national parks. "Open the door of the System to just one National Park of inferior standards, and local pride in competition will do the rest. Every Congressional District will also want its own, and Congress cannot then refuse."[9]

North Dakota's congressional delegation did everything that it could to prove Yard right. "For some in North Dakota," begins David Harmon's history of TRNP, "the national park idea was nothing more than a money idea." The state legislature made the first proposal to establish a national park in the badlands in 1921, only two years after T.R. had died and only five years after the establishment of the NPS. The Roosevelt Memorial National Park Association emerged from a 1924 visit by forty civic leaders to the badlands, and a group of cowboys, members of Congress, and other government officials approved of a national park upon visiting the area one year later. The park's boosters argued that national parks "are for all the people, not alone for those who have the time and means to travel far." They envisioned a national park in North Dakota as necessary "to provide health facilities," anticipating the idea of national parks as places for exercise and recreation. But the NPS opposed the establishment of a national park in North Dakota's badlands, and local ranchers were skeptical of the effect of a park on their grazing rights. The dynamics soon changed with the onset of the Great Depression, which reduced many North Dakota ranchers to poverty. The federal government bailed out many ranchers by repurchasing their land (discussed in greater detail below), and much of the property that was returned to the federal government was slated for a park. The contested question was what kind of park.[10]

In Congress, North Dakota's senator Gerald Nye was the initial champion of the national park idea. Nye had owned a newspaper in Billings County, where T.R. had lived only a few decades before, until he was appointed to fill a vacancy in the Senate in 1925. Nye was placed on the Senate's Public Lands Committee, where he immediately gained national attention for suggesting that capital punishment might be appropriate for the two oil industry barons who instigated the Teapot Dome scandal in which Secretary of the Interior Albert Fall (the pride of Alamogordo, New Mexico; see Chapter 5) had leased public lands containing lucrative oilfields in exchange for contributions to the Republican National Committee. Less dramatically, Nye's committee had jurisdiction over national parks, which gave him significant power over the NPS. In 1928, Nye brought some of his colleagues to the badlands for a fact-finding tour that concluded with a recommendation for a national park. But Nye's primary reputation was as an isolationist in foreign affairs, and his lack of interest in North Dakota's affairs contributed to his reelection defeat in 1944.

Instead, it was William Lemke, one of North Dakota's two members of the House of Representatives, who was the leading force behind the establishment of the national park. A populist Republican who fought for distressed North Dakota ranchers and farmers during the Depression, Lemke was an unlikely champion. He was no fan of Theodore Roosevelt. Indeed, Lemke viewed T.R.'s nephew, President Franklin D. Roosevelt, as an unreconstructed conservative who refused to take the radical actions necessary to save farmers suffering from the "Three D's": drought, depression, and dust. Lemke's biographer relates that the New Deal bureaucrats of FDR's administration viewed Lemke "as a 'madman from the sticks,' one whom the excesses of democracy compelled more urban public servants to endure." Lemke even attempted to defeat FDR in the 1936 presidential election, and his miserable failure cast Lemke into political exile even though he continued to serve in the House until his death in 1950.[11]

Lemke took up the cause for a national park after his ill-fated presidential campaign. Beginning in the early 1940s, he promoted the national park proposal and fought with the NPS over the idea. The land had been called Roosevelt Regional Park when the federal government reacquired it in 1934 and combined it with some original public domain lands and state school lands; one year later it was redesignated a recreational demonstration area. The NPS favored the creation of a state park in the badlands, or failing that, a national wildlife refuge. North Dakota has more national wildlife refuges than any other state, so the move for another one seemed logical even though much of the wildlife that had greeted T.R. had long since disappeared.

The congressional hearings regarding the national park proposal generated several familiar arguments. J. Hardin Peterson, who chaired the House Committee on Public Lands and had visited the area with Lemke, said that North Dakota's badlands reminded him of Bryce Canyon. Lemke compared the badlands to other western national parks, insisting that "the big things do not always contain all of the beauty." In particular, Lemke told the NPS that the badlands were "a whole lot more picturesque than that Jackson Hole," the site of a contemporary dispute that was the opposite of what was occurring in North Dakota's badlands: the NPS wanted to establish Grand Teton National Park over the objections of the local residents in Wyoming. Lemke further boasted that the Marquis de Mores's home in Medora "is more interesting than Mount Vernon." But Ira Gabrielson, who headed the FWS within the Department of the Interior and later helped to found the World Wildlife Fund, responded that the "area does not possess the qualities, the outstanding qualities, of scenic or scientific or historic interest that would justify pressing the matter of its being included in the National Park system." Acting Secretary of the Interior Oscar Chapman echoed that view and stated his preference for making the area a national wildlife refuge.[12]

Lemke succeeded in pushing a national park bill through Congress in 1946. To do so, however, he emphasized the area's scenic qualifications and downplayed both the historical association with T.R. (which could have resulted in a less desirable national *historic* park designation) and the area's wildlife (which could have supported the national wildlife refuge plan). Lemke's strategy backfired when President Truman pocket-vetoed the bill in August 1946 because of the insufficiency of the scenery argument. Truman explained that "the area to be established by this bill as the Theodore Roosevelt National Park does not possess those outstanding natural features or scenic qualities that would justify its establishment as a national park," echoing the advice that he received from the Interior Department and prominent conservationists. Truman's veto message also elaborated his understanding of the standards for establishing a national park, observing that national parks should "contain or relate to areas that possess scenic, scientific, or historic features of outstanding national significance." To add insult to North Dakota's injury, Secretary of the Interior Chapman redesignated the property as the Theodore Roosevelt National Wildlife Refuge in November 1946.[13]

The feuding parties reached a compromise in 1947. The new park would be called the Theodore Roosevelt National *Memorial* Park. The NPS acquiesced, and Lemke spun the deal by claiming that the additional word "memorial" connoted "something more, not less, than a national park in the ordinary usage." The House Committee on Public Lands reported that "there is a Nation-wide desire that the unique scenery of the Badlands be set apart for posterity." Warming to the task, the committee report added: "This area is about midway between the heavily populated sections in the Great Lakes region and the Yellowstone and other national parks. Its scenery is different from that of any other national park. Many tourists have pronounced it as more interesting than any other national park they have visited." This time President Truman approved, too. Not to be outdone, Watford City's leaders now wanted their share of a national park, reasoning that the badlands near them were "of little practical use to mankind," so why not make them a national park? Again, local residents compared the area to Yellowstone and Glacier national parks. "They do not have the geysers or the freaks of nature there, but from a scenic standpoint I think it as beautiful as anything I have seen," testified a longtime North Dakota resident and Izaak Walton League member. Congress quickly added the North Unit to the national park in 1948. Nearly forty thousand spectators from North Dakota and beyond attended the dedication ceremony for the national park in June 1949.[14]

The national memorial park compromise proved to be unstable. The NPS didn't know what to make of this new kind of entity for which it was suddenly responsible. The memorial label seemed to invoke the history of T.R.'s time in the area, but "the only historical resource directly connecting the park to the man it was memorializing was a detached 218-acre tract of badlands, thirty miles from any decent road and more than twenty from the main units of the park." That resource—T.R.'s Elkhorn Ranch—played a central role in the NPS's early years of managing the new national park, despite the ranch's remote location. The North and South units took a back seat, thus minimizing the expected economic boon for Watford City and Medora, respectively. And North Dakota's boosters longed to shed the memorial label, which they blamed for the park's second-class status. Years of efforts to transform the park into an unqualified national park culminated in 1978, when Congress enacted sweeping legislation addressed to a host of national park issues. For nearly a decade, North Dakota's senator Quentin Burdick had introduced bills to delete "memorial" from the park's name. In July 1978, he wrote the Senate Parks and Recreation Subcommittee that it was "unclear" why the area had become a national memorial park in the first place and that the unique qualifier gave the park a "dubious distinction." Senator Burdick's affirmative arguments for the change were rather modest: it would help with administration, it would ensure that the park was included in appropriate publications, and it would "provide relief to the overcrowded parks of Yellowstone, Glacier, and Grand Teton." It is hard to imagine that his colleagues were swayed by such reasoning, but by this time the opponents to national park status—including the Interior Department itself—had relented. The deal was sweetened by the willingness of North Dakota's congressional delegation to support the simultaneous redesignation of Badlands National Monument in South Dakota to Badlands National Park. And so TRNP emerged from the National Parks and Recreation Act of 1978, a statute that was so laden with special provisions that critics demeaned it as pork barrel legislation for the national parks.[15]

Still, the question remains: should any of North Dakota's badlands be preserved as a national park? As already noted, President Truman thought that the area didn't have "those outstanding features or scenic qualities" that would justify its becoming a national park. John Burroughs, a naturalist writer who visited the region early in the twentieth century, described it as "utterly demoralized and gone to the bad." A *New York Times* reporter wrote around 1880 that "the lands are sterile, the hills bleak and without verdure, and the buttes fantastic and curious in shape." General William Tecumseh Sherman described the area between the Red and Missouri rivers as "barren and worthless" and as "bad as God ever made, or anyone could scare up this side of Africa." And then there was General Sully's description of "hell with the fires burned out." Sully, like T.R., arrived in North Dakota's badlands after the tragic death of his young wife. He was an embittered man, and his time there did not change him. Yet despite his description of "hell," he also praised the landscape in his official military reports. "I have not sufficient power of language to describe the country in front of us," he wrote, settling for "grand, dismal and majestic" and "a wonderful and most interesting country." T.R. credited the badlands with reviving him and equipping him for the more famous years that he had ahead of him. His many writings about western North Dakota extol the region's beauty: "The scenery is often exceedingly striking in character, especially in the Bad Lands, with their queer fantastic formations." The editor of the *Bismarck Weekly Tribune* sought to change the region's name from badlands to Pyramid Park because of the ubiquitous "mounds of clay presenting the appearance of deserted castles or grand old pyramids." The website of the City of Medora makes similar claims about the land's charms today. (The website doesn't mention that T.R. described Medora as "an excessively unattractive little hamlet.")[16]

The champions of the establishment of a national park won little favor in my eyes by exaggerating their case. Grand Teton is my favorite national park—indeed, I spent four months in Jackson Hole for my sabbatical writing this book—so Representative Lemke's insistence that the North Dakota badlands were far more scenic and deserving of national park status than the Tetons made me question the parkworthiness of North Dakota's badlands. But although I didn't trust Lemke, I didn't know whether to believe General Sully or T.R. So I arrived in the badlands with skepticism, but an open mind. And I was immediately impressed. The scenery *is* spectacular. I drove the thirty-six-mile scenic loop through the South Unit in the morning and again in the afternoon. The colors, shapes, and strangeness of the topography were unlike anything I had ever seen. The wildlife was similarly appealing; I spotted bison, several large colonies of prairie dogs, a group of wild horses, a few deer, some turkeys, and a coyote that trotted up a rocky area before it disappeared behind a larger mound. I spent a night camping in the

The grasslands amid the badlands in TRNP's North Unit.

North Unit's nearly vacant campground, and for a while I felt as if I were sharing the same kind of experience that T.R. had enjoyed 120 years before.

The standards for a national park are famously elusive, so I would not want to rely on my own visit alone to make a judgment of parkworthiness. Thankfully, the park's official newspaper, which the ranger handed me when I entered the park, states the case for a national park especially well. The park lists seven reasons why "Theodore Roosevelt National Park is preserved for the public." Let me list and critique each of them in reverse order of their persuasiveness:[17]

- *"The colorful North Dakota badlands provide the scenic backdrop to the park which memorializes the 26th president for his enduring contributions to the conservation of our nation's resources."* T.R. was an integral figure in the history of conservation in the United States, if not the history of national parks themselves. The TRNP's management plan correctly observes that "without Roosevelt's experiences and perceptions gained here in his formative years between 1883 and

1898, the development of America's forest and park conservation programs might have been much different." But national parks don't exist to honor individuals. Other units of the national park system serve that purpose, and T.R. is well represented in those units. Ulysses S. Grant was the only other individual for whom a park was named, thanks to the 1890 establishment of tiny General Grant National Park in California. But in 1940 Congress incorporated that park into the newly created Kings Canyon National Park. Grant's name is still attached to a small grove of giant sequoia trees, but not to an entire park.[18]

- *"The park is designated as a Class I air quality area providing for clean air, brilliant, clear day and night skies and outstanding examples of a relatively unpolluted environment."* The air *is* clear, the skies *are* amazingly dark at night, and the park *is* generally unpolluted. We have come to a sorry point, though, if the mere fact that a place is not polluted qualifies it as a national park. The Class I air-quality area is important for the region's clean air, as I will discuss further below, but any argument for a national park based on that designation is backwards. The Clean Air Act protects the air in Class I areas because of the importance of national parks; national parks are not established simply to collect the benefits of the Clean Air Act.

- *"The park contains one of the few islands of designated wilderness in the Northern Great Plains."* The designation of much of the park pursuant to the Wilderness Act adds further legal protections to the area, again as I will detail below. The fact of that designation, however, does not justify the creation of a national park. Indeed, wilderness designations have been contested in other national parks precisely because the strictures of the Wilderness Act can interfere with some of the preferred methods of enjoying national parks.

- *"The park has one of the largest petrified forests in the U.S. and extensive paleontological deposits from the Paleocene era that provide outstanding examples for visitor viewing."* This begins to hint toward the unique landscape that often justifies the establishment of a national park. But these features are absent from much of the promotional literature for the park. I didn't even know about the petrified forest and paleontological deposits until I visited the park, and I never did see them while I was there because they are a three-mile round-trip hike away from the park's solitary road. T.R. scholar Clay Jenkinson likened the petrified forest to "the ruins of an ancient temple" and marveled that it was "one of the most amazing places I have ever seen."[19]

- *"On-going geological activities create spectacular examples of badlands and provide opportunities for visual interpretation of erosional processes."* The badlands scenery is truly remarkable. I don't know how well I interpreted the erosional processes, but I certainly enjoyed the sights.

- *"The Little Missouri River has shaped the land which is home to a variety of prairie plants and animals including bison, elk and feral (wild) horses. A park experience is created by the interplay of natural forces including weather, vegetation, wildlife, vistas, smells, colors and shape of landforms, air quality, natural science, varied light and seasons."* The river runs through the park with dramatic effect, and the park's wildlife is fascinating. The colors, shapes, and magnitude of the landscape were quite unlike anything I had ever seen. The badlands are especially notable because they are so out of character for the rest of the northern Great Plains in which they are situated.

- *"The park allows people to enjoy panoramic vistas and a sense of the solitude, inspiration, and timelessness of Theodore Roosevelt's experience in Dakota Territory in the 1880s. The area provides an opportunity to learn about an environment and way of life that helped shape Theodore Roosevelt's attitudes and philosophy regarding conservation."* This is what is most special about the park: the interaction of the natural landscape and ecosystem with the effort to mimic the experience of an extraordinary human resident. That is why there is, and should be, a Theodore Roosevelt National Park.

My visit convinced me of the worthiness of a national park in North Dakota's badlands. My conclusion was bolstered by Dan Kaercher, who cited TRNP as his favorite park after visiting 130 national and state parks throughout the Midwest. "Surely this must be what captivated Theodore Roosevelt as well," Kaercher wrote in his book *Parklands of the Midwest: Celebrating the Natural Wonders of America's Heartland.* Still, I was curious how others would evaluate the same evidence. So I asked my students for their perspectives after they had read about the area and its history. The few students who had visited TRNP enthusiastically agreed that it deserves to be a national park; but several others dissented. One opined that North Dakota's landscape does not appeal to the national consensus in the same way as Glacier or Yosemite national parks. Another student concluded that the small number of visitors should serve as a proxy for the elusive judgment about the quality of the scenery. Or, said a student, everyone should agree that a particular place deserves to be a national park. A fourth student was more concerned about the management of the entire badlands, preferring to govern the ecosystem as a whole instead of dividing it between different federal agencies and private owners. These comments each suggested the difficulty in evaluating the role of national parks, but they may also show that the real value of TRNP is understood only by those who have seen it.[20]

THE LAW OF NATIONAL PARKS

And so, for better or worse, North Dakota's badlands contain a national park. Now what happens? What difference does it make that these three bits of land constitute a national park?

Congress has been surprisingly brief in describing the rules governing national parks. As Joseph Sax has observed, "the governing statutes speak in very general and unrevealing language." The 1872 statute establishing Yellowstone National Park directed that the area was to be "reserved . . . dedicated, and set apart as a public park or pleasuring-ground for the benefit and enjoyment of the people," adding that the park should be managed "for the preservation, from injury or spoliation, of all timber, mineral deposits, natural curiosities, or wonders within . . . and their retention in their natural condition." Forty-four years later, the Organic Act of 1916 established the NPS and stated the rules for managing national parks. According to the act, the "fundamental purpose" of national parks "is to conserve the scenery and natural and historic objects and the wild life therein and to provide for the enjoyment of the same in such manner and by such means as will leave them unimpaired for the enjoyment of future generations." Around the same time, Secretary of the Interior Franklin Lane's 1918 letter to Stephen Mather articulated "three broad principles" for the management of national parks: "First that the national parks must be maintained in absolutely unimpaired form for the use of future generations as well as those in our own time;

second, that they are set apart for the use, observation, health, and plea-sure of the people; and third, that the national interest must dictate all decisions affecting public or private enterprise in the parks." In other words, each national park should be managed according to two general purposes: conservation and enjoyment. The law thus provides more pro-tection to national parks than to national forests, which are governed by a multiple-use standard that allows logging and other extractive activi-ties, but the law does not afford national parks as much protection as wilderness areas, where motor vehicles and commercial activities are prohibited.[21]

Most of the conflicts in national parks today involve the competing demands of conservation and enjoyment. Hundreds of visitors seek to enjoy Yellowstone National Park on snowmobiles each winter, but the preservation of the park's wildlife, air quality, and soundscape would benefit from their exclusion. Visitors to Yosemite National Park want to enjoy the park through the convenience of their own cars, but shuttle buses and caps on the numbers of visitors would help conserve the park. The demand for cruises to Glacier Bay National Park has steadily in-creased, but the cumulative effects of more cruises may adversely affect the park's famous wildlife. The contrasting perspectives are illustrated by a 2006 federal court decision overturning a series of proposed con-struction plans for Yosemite. "These are the projects the public has told us they want," the NPS insisted, blaming "fringe" groups for instigating the litigation. The representative of one of those groups responded: "We hope for a park that has meaningful environmental protection and equi-table social access. What we've seen instead is this pandering to commercialism, this rush to do construction and this shortchanging of environmental laws."[22]

This debate has influenced the NPS's most recent effort to rewrite its general management standards for national parks. Those standards are gleaned from statutes, regulations, executive orders, proclamations, departmental policies, and longstanding NPS practices. The NPS com-pleted one revision of the management standards at the very end of the Clinton administration in January 2001, and then it almost immedi-ately began considering further revisions once President George W. Bush took office. An initial draft would have worked significant changes in those standards, usually to favor visitor use rather than preservation.

The uproar surrounding that leaked draft spilled over into Congress. During congressional hearings in 2005, NPS officials embraced "the fundamental concept that when there is a conflict between use and conservation, conservation of the resources will be predominant." Several senators, including Colorado's Kenneth Salazar, quoted T.R., who once said, "Our duty to the whole, including the unborn generations, bids us to restrain an unprincipled present-day minority from wasting the heritage of these unborn generations." (President Barack Obama later tapped Salazar to serve as secretary of the interior with jurisdiction over the NPS.) Senator Lamar Alexander from Tennessee likened the redrafted policies to "sending out a warm-up singer to the Grand Ole Opry that was so off key that it ruined the rest of the night." But one witness warned that the Organic Act should not be viewed "as Congress' attempt to preserve parks from Americans," while an advocate for the owners of private property within national parks claimed that "for 40 years the preservationists have infiltrated the National Park Service." The effect, the witness added, is a "cloistered, cult like multigenerational culture in the agency where son follows father who follows grandfather into the work, and the agency becomes more and more isolated from anyone who disagrees with them. Park personnel often do not own private homes, live off a government paycheck in government housing most of their lives, and as a result have little in the way of a feel [for] or relationship with local communities, private business or the needs of many private citizens." Other witnesses distinguished between the conservation favored by T.R., which allowed for many active uses, and the preservationist ethic that resists many visitor activities. The NPS responded with a new, less provocative draft in 2006 that speaks of a duty to "always seek ways to avoid, or to minimize to the greatest extent practicable, unacceptable impacts on park resources and values" while embracing a broad understanding of "enjoyment" that "includes enjoyment both by people who visit parks and by those who appreciate them from afar."[23]

Part of the problem arises from the nature of *national* parks. The federal government owns the land that comprises each national park, but that land is located in different communities throughout the United States. Stephen Mather, the first director of the NPS, once remarked that "the parks do not belong to one state or to one section. [T]hey are national properties in which every citizen has a vested interest." These national constituencies often promote interests that are different from—and often conflict with—the local communities near national parks. And so it is with TRNP.[24]

Section 5 of the 1947 statute that established the park simply directed that it should be managed by the NPS pursuant to the provisions of the 1916 Organic Act. Of course, numerous other laws affect the management of the park, including the Environmental Protection Act, the Clean Air Act, the Clean Water Act, the Migratory Bird Treaty Act, the ESA, the National Historic Preservation Act, the Federal Noxious Weed Act of 1974, and the Farmland Protection Policy Act. A similar collection of executive orders guides the park's management, addressing such topics as floodplain management, wetlands protection, ORV use, invasive species, environmental justice, and the protection of children from environmental health and safety risks. The TRNP has identified four purposes to "reflect what we believe is the legislative intent" for the park: (1) to "memorialize and preserve the life, times and philosophy of Theodore Roosevelt in the North Dakota Badlands," (2) to "conserve unimpaired the scenery and the natural and cultural resources and facilitate the scientific interests in the Theodore Roosevelt National Park," (3) to "provide for the benefit, use, and enjoyment of the people," and (4) to "manage the Theodore Roosevelt wilderness as part of the National Wilderness Preservation System." The TRNP seeks to implement these legal norms via its general management plan, which dates from 1987 and replaced a 1973 plan that the park said had "become obsolete and no longer applicable for resolution of current issues involving the park."[25]

The goal of the national park is to re-create the ecosystem that T.R. encountered in the late nineteenth century. "In its prime," write TRNP employees Bruce Kaye and Henry Schoch, "the vast expanse of the unspoiled Great Plains supported a diverse fauna whose sheer numbers were rivaled only by the legendary game herds of pre-colonial Africa." The native grasses made it possible for a multitude of creatures to thrive in a hospitable environment. But the grasslands ecosystem has changed dramatically since T.R. and other hunters and ranchers waged war on the native animals and plants. The park's management plan notes another obstacle to ecosystem management in TRNP: "the park's separation into three distinct units makes it quite impossible to manage the area as an ecological system." The plan adds that "because the park is not free from man-made influences affecting ecosystems and their processes, some active manipulation (e.g., exotic plant control, prescribed burning, and wildlife population reductions) will be necessary to meet resource management objectives. Also, because the park does not include a complete ecosystem with its many components, some of the activities may need to be continued indefinitely." So although Kaye and Schoch admit that "the glory of the living past will never be fully regained," they nonetheless hope that "in protected areas careful management can help restore wild populations to a safe and balanced level."[26]

The park's management begins with the seven species of plains game that Roosevelt described during his time in the badlands: bear, bison, elk, bighorn sheep, antelope, and blacktail and whitetail deer. Bison are the signature animal of the park, and they are why T.R. visited the badlands for the first time in 1883. In fact, he arrived just in time, for that was the year of the last big buffalo hunt. Perhaps sixty million bison lived in the Great Plains in the middle of the nineteenth century, including herds of five million or more in the western Dakota area alone. But by 1883, only ten thousand were left; by September, T.R. had difficulty finding even one to shoot. Thousands of bison were slaughtered during the first nine months of that year. They almost became extinct until federal law intervened at just the last minute to save the bison from extinction. They recovered slowly, and once Congress created TRNP, the park's management moved to reintroduce a herd into the park. Bison were returned to the South Unit in 1956 and to the North Unit in 1962. The herd has thrived throughout the park, numbering between three hundred and four hundred animals. The bison attract visitors to the area, just as they lured T.R. there more than a century ago (albeit for a different purpose). Excess bison are sent elsewhere if the herd gets too large, which has happened as recently as November 2008 when 108 were rounded up and shipped to various foundations, tribes, and zoos. The only management challenge occurs if bison move outside the park, in which case they are treated as livestock under state law and thus the property of their owner rather than wild animals that may be hunted. The park pays a few thousand dollars every now and then to neighboring ranchers who bring suit in state small claims court for damages to fences or forage caused by wandering bison.[27]

Bison along the road through TRNP's South Unit.

Elk are a different story. T.R. named his ranch, Elkhorn, after the local animals that he described as "the most stately and beautiful animal of the chase to be found in America." But he also observed that the elk "is unfortunately one of those animals seemingly doomed to total destruction at no distant date," and the species avoided extinction only by moving to inaccessible parts of the Rocky Mountains to the southwest. The park reintroduced elk into the South Unit in 1985, brought from Wind Cave National Park in South Dakota (one of the national parks that T.R. approved), and they have thrived there. Too much so, in fact. Today, the park's biggest management problem is elk. Nearly 1,000 lived within the park as of 2008, far greater than the optimal number of 360, and the population is growing at 22 percent annually. The elk have not yet adversely affected the local plant communities, as they have already done in Rocky Mountain National Park and in the National Elk Refuge immediately south of Grand Teton National Park. The park managers are concerned, however, that the rising number of elk could hinder the efforts to preserve the ecological conditions of the area that existed at the time of T.R.'s arrival. There are no natural predators within TRNP. Elk are shot by hunters when they wander outside the park's boundaries, with 178 successful hunts in 2007. But hunting is prohibited in national parks; areas in which hunting is allowed are called national preserves instead of national parks. The park had simply moved excess elk to other locations until the threat of chronic wasting disease, a neurological disease that affects elk and deer, resulted in a national moratorium on moving live elk. So the park began to consider a number of options for culling the herd, including testing for the disease, implanting birth control devices, reintroducing gray wolves to prey upon the elk, and corralling and killing the elk for meat.[28]

In early 2007, the park announced that it preferred to employ sharpshooters to hunt elk from helicopters. Senator Byron Dorgan, who has represented North Dakota since 1992, objected to that plan in rather caustic language: "All you need are hunters with a pickup truck or two, and you'll be fine." Senator Dorgan also described the NPS as "completely devoid of common sense" in preferring the sharpshooter and helicopter alternative. So Dorgan introduced legislation that would authorize the NPS to allow hunters to shoot the elk in the park. The Elk Population Management Act of 2007 would have lifted the prohibition on hunting by an "authorized individual" who possesses "a valid resident big-game hunting license issued by the appropriate agency of the State," provided that the hunting is "in accordance with the elk management plan." Dorgan pressed his case when Secretary of the Interior Kenneth Salazar returned to the Senate to support the Department of the Interior's 2010 appropriations requests, prompting Salazar to agree that TRNP's elk issue "calls out for common sense solutions." And there is something fitting about allowing hunting in a park that seeks to reflect the landscape and lifestyle of Teddy Roosevelt's time.[29]

In response, Clay Jenkinson emphasized that "one of the core traditions of America's national park system—the glory and envy of the world—is that hunting is prohibited within its boundaries. . . . The no-hunting rule in national parks is so deeply ingrained into our national consciousness (not to mention American law) that to permit it now would be like allowing 10 men on a professional baseball team, or redefining the marathon as a 42-mile race." Jenkinson worried that a decision to allowing hunting in TRNP would inevitably serve as a precedent elsewhere, perhaps including Rocky Mountain National Park, which faces its own elk overpopulation problem. In fact, however, there already is an exception: the 1950 law that created Grand Teton National Park allowed elk hunting there. Yet Jenkinson admitted that there was "no easy answer to the problem." His tentative proposal was for "a volunteer 'Roosevelt Brigade' of national park hunters, who have spent months or years studying the history, ecology, geology, literature and philosophy of the national parks" who "could be permitted, under exceedingly careful supervision, to play a role in the future game management of the entire system." Presumably, that would rule out the hunter who posted an online comment to the *Bismarck Tribune*'s story about the controversy advising, "I have two boxes of good old 3006 shells just waiting."[30]

The NPS responded to the controversy by preparing an Elk Management Plan and Draft Environmental Impact Statement in December 2008. The plan recited an earlier court decision that emphasized that the NPS "need not wait until the damage through overbrowsing has taken its toll on park plant life . . . before taking preventative action." It also relied on the provision in the 2006 NPS Management Policies that authorizes wildlife management when "a population occurs in an unnaturally high . . . concentration" and when other species will not suffer from human management. The plan considers five alternative management strategies: hunting "by qualified federal employees and authorized agents," rounding up elk and euthanizing them elsewhere, testing the elk for the diseases of greatest concern, increasing hunting outside the park, and employing fertility control on female elk. Each of the alternatives would avoid the negative ecological consequences of doing nothing, and they would each encourage further research and testing, provide meat to nonprofit organizations, and enhance hunting outside the park. But the plan rejects several other alternatives, including the removal of all elk from TRNP, moving some elk to the park's North Unit, removing the feral horses, or reintroducing gray wolves or grizzly bears as natural predators. Most controversially, the plan rejected any public hunting within the national park as contrary to existing laws. That omission prompted the state to oppose the entire plan, and the state legislature approved a resolution urging Congress to amend federal law to "allow North Dakota resident sharpshooters to take elk" in the park. In February 2009, the NPS held several public hearings on the plan throughout the state, and it hoped to reach a decision on its preferred approach soon.

Then Senator Dorgan succeeded in attaching a rider to the Department of the Interior's appropriations bill that would direct the NPS to use volunteer sharpshooters to thin TRNP's elk herd. The issue soon gained the attention of the *New York Times*, which editorialized that Dorgan's proposal "violates both common sense and the very idea of a national park." Dorgan responded that he proposed "exactly the kind of solution Teddy Roosevelt would have wanted." The NPS finally relented in August 2009 when it wrote to Senator Dorgan approving the use of supervised volunteer hunters to cull 275 elk from TRNP per year for two years. TRNP superintendent Valerie Naylor emphasized the importance of public participation in reaching the decision, and another TRNP official insisted that Dorgan's "opinion was treated like all the other [285] people who took the time to comment."[31]

Bighorn sheep were nearly gone by the time T.R. arrived in the badlands. Lewis and Clark had observed the animals during their trip in the early 1800s, and John James Audubon hunted them when he retraced Lewis and Clark's trail in 1843. For many years, the bighorns in the area were known as Audubon bighorn sheep, one of seven subspecies of bighorn sheep. Hunting wiped them out, with the last bighorn in North Dakota spotted near the Elkhorn Ranch in 1906, and the subspecies was judged extinct around 1920. That, at least, was the conventional wisdom until recent studies demonstrated that the sheep that Lewis and Clark, Audubon, and T.R. saw were not really a distinct subspecies, but rather another population of Rocky Mountain bighorns. Scientists now recognize three subspecies of bighorn—Rocky Mountain, Sierra Nevada (formerly known as California), and Desert—with the Sierra Nevada subspecies and the Peninsular "distinct population segment" of the Desert subspecies listed as endangered under the ESA. In any event, the NPS reintroduced California bighorn sheep to the South Unit in the 1990s, but the population of those sheep dropped to four. Today, between 200 and 250 sheep live in the badlands outside the national park.

Pronghorn antelope have followed a similar pattern. Hunting and fencing resulted in fewer than five hundred pronghorns by 1913. In 1964, the North Dakota Supreme Court quoted T.R.'s 1898 observation that "pronghorns were formerly found all over the great plains of western North America . . . Like all other big game, their numbers have been greatly reduced." But the pronghorn population rebounded to more than one million, save for the endangered Sonoran subspecies in Arizona. Blacktail deer, whitetail deer, and pronghorn populations have remained stable within TRNP, albeit near the park's carrying capacity for the deer.[32]

The native predators are mostly gone; a few wolves have been sighted in and around the park in recent years. T.R. did not mention mountain lions, but they have returned to the badlands on their own. Mountain lions were always rare on the open prairie, and the few animals that once lived in the badlands were exterminated by the time the last lion was killed in 1902. They, too, have since returned to TRNP, and biologists estimate that North Dakota's badlands could support up to seventy-four mountain lions. Of T.R.'s list of seven game species, only bear are still missing from TRNP, and no one has seriously recommended reintroducing them. Of course, a far more ambitious proposal would introduce lions from Africa in an effort to "rewild" the Great Plains, but that remains even less likely than returning bear to the park.[33]

Several smaller animals present greater management challenges for the NPS than most of T.R.'s seven game species. "Prairie dogs are an important component of the prairie environment," reports the park's management plan, "and so are necessary in ecosystem management." T.R. described prairie dogs as "bothersome little fellows, and most prolific, increasing in spite of the perpetual war made on them by every carnivorous bird and beast." Senator Dorgan has an opinion about them, too. "We have far more prairie dogs than we know what to do with," he told his Senate colleagues when introducing his proposed elk hunting bill. "The prairie dogs were born—I should say luckily for them—with a button nose and fur on their tail. Otherwise, they would essentially look like a rat." I was not surprised, therefore, to collect a *North Dakota Prairie Dog Hunters Guide Book*—complete with a cover drawing of a rifle's crosshairs trained on a prairie dog's head—during my visit to the area. Prairie dogs inhabit about 350 acres within TRNP, where they are tourist favorites. A travel writer who listed his favorite recollections from visiting each of the fifty states rhapsodized about finding himself "among thousands of golden-coated prairie dogs, many staring at me, as they popped out from an underground 'city' that stretched for hundreds of yards." But they have created problems within the park, too. Prairie dogs dig through nearly anything, including road material, and the excrement produced by large prairie dog towns can threaten nearby water supplies. The park moved an entire campground in the South Unit, at the expense of millions of dollars, once the proximity of a prairie dog town compromised public health. In his 2007 speech, Senator Dorgan recalled that he had spoken about that issue at the time, too, and again preferred to "hire a couple of 16-year-old kids to tell the prairie dogs they have to be elsewhere."[34]

The black-tailed prairie dogs that inhabit TRNP are one of five species of prairie dog native to North America. They are the most abundant of the five species, but in 1997 the National Wildlife Federation petitioned to list them as threatened under the ESA. There are still millions of black-tailed prairie dogs, but their numbers have dropped precipitously because of relentless efforts to exterminate them. Prairie dogs have been shot, poisoned, and otherwise eradicated by the millions by ranchers who feared competition for forage and by hunters who shot the animals for sport. The federal FWS determined in 2000 that the listing was "warranted but precluded" by limited resources and higher priorities, but in 2004 the agency concluded that the species is no longer a candidate for listing. Nonetheless, the NPS now treats the black-tailed prairie dog as "a keystone species worth saving," echoing the studies of scientists who cite the dozens of other native species that depend on the activities of prairie dogs for food, shelter, and vegetation. But don't tell that to Senator Dorgan.[35]

And don't mention black-footed ferrets to Senator Dorgan, who once said, "The last person to spot a black-footed ferret in my State allegedly spotted a black-footed ferret some 20 years ago and was widely thought, according to local folklore, to have been drinking at the time." The only black-footed ferret in the park today is on display in a glass case in the visitor's center at the South Unit. John James Audubon first reported the existence of the black-footed ferret in 1851. T.R. viewed the animal both as "a handsome, rather rare animal" and as "a most bloodthirsty little brute." They became even rarer during the twentieth century because of the conversion of grasslands to agricultural uses, the reduction in prairie dog populations (a ferret eats one hundred prairie dogs each year), and sylvatic plague. Senator Dorgan, by contrast, suggested that the real reason for the disappearance of the ferrets was that "they apparently went to warmer climates in the South some long time ago." (Dorgan has not opined on whether he would welcome any ferrets that returned to North Dakota as a result of climate change.) The species was even thought to be extinct until a remnant population was discovered in Meeteetse, Wyoming, in 1981, thanks to a local rancher's dog. Since then, more than twenty-six hundred black-footed ferrets have been raised in captivity, and they have been reintroduced to Badlands National Park in South Dakota, as well as sites in Arizona, Colorado, Montana, Utah, and Mexico. There were four hundred wild ferrets in 2005, and the ESA recovery plan aims for ten or more separate, self-sustaining wild populations totaling fifteen hundred ferrets. They probably will not be reintroduced into TRNP, though, because the park doesn't have a large enough area for them and the prairie dogs that they prey upon.[36]

The TRNP preserves a remnant of the grasslands that once filled the Great Plains. "The thing that's nice," remarked a Dickinson State University naturalist, "is that these are all native plants. It's just like the native environment you might have seen 100 or 200 years ago." Well, almost. I was surprised to see helicopters buzzing the park during my visit. Later, I learned that they were spraying pesticides aimed at leafy spurge, a plant that the Montana Supreme Court recently described as "a controllable but virtually ineradicable noxious weed." Leafy spurge is a deep-rooted, perennial flowering plant that arrived in the United States in 1827 thanks to a seed impurity brought from Europe. It reached North Dakota early in the twentieth century and today has become the dominant vegetation on rangelands and pastures throughout much of the United States. It both outcompetes native plant species and lacks any natural means of control in this country, so it has spread to epidemic proportions throughout the Great Plains, and in TRNP in particular. The chemical spraying that I observed is just one technique for trying to control leafy spurge; biologists are experimenting with the introduction of sheep, goats, and especially beetles that eat the plant. (Traditional grazing won't help because leafy spurge is mildly poisonous to cattle.) Leafy spurge is just one of more than twenty invasive plants that have been found within the park, with six causing particular concern and demanding active management by the NPS. But most of the more than eight hundred vascular plants in the park are part of the natural grasslands ecosystem. Those plants benefit from the fact that the soils within the park are much healthier than they were after the severe erosion caused by drought and overgrazing during the 1930s.[37]

The NPS managed the park more for its cultural resources than for its natural ecosystem for several decades after Congress established the national memorial park in 1947. That has changed in recent years, but the TRNP still emphasizes the cultural importance of the land. The park's management goal is to re-create the experience that T.R. enjoyed in the area during the 1880s. The management plan states that the Elkhorn Ranch site "is the most important in the park for understanding the significance of Theodore Roosevelt's experiences in the badlands." But it is difficult to reach. My two options were to ford the Little Missouri River or drive nearly one hundred miles to approach the ranch by car from the other side of the river; I declined them both. I'm not alone, for only a few people visit there every year. T.R.'s original Maltese Cross Cabin is much more accessible as it stands just a few yards away from the park's headquarters building, having arrived there in 1959 via a circuitous route that took it from its original site seven miles south of Medora to an exhibit that traveled across the country during T.R.'s presidency, and then to the grounds of the state capitol in Bismarck. Even so, the connection between T.R., his conservationist actions as president, and the current park should not be exaggerated. T.R. visited the North Unit perhaps once, and the park's historian concludes that "there is no convincing evidence that the conservation ethic Roosevelt displayed as president was shaped entirely, or even primarily, by his time in Dakota Territory."[38]

The Organic Act expects that TRNP, like every other national park, will be both conserved and enjoyed. Visitors to the park view wildlife, enjoy scenic vistas, ride horses, camp, visit the museum, and participate in interpretive programs. The NPS reports that "the principal visitor activity is sightseeing from motor vehicles." Snowmobiling is permitted on and along the river but prohibited elsewhere, and that policy has avoided the snowmobiling controversy that has plagued Yellowstone and Voyageurs national parks. But the number of visitors has never reached the optimistic expectations of the local boosters who pressed for national park status. The visitor total reached 260,848 in 1965, jumped to 500,338 with the opening of I-94 one year later, peaked at 1,001,957 in 1972, and dropped as low as 386,615 in 1984. The drop during the 1970s and early

1980s resulted from the NPS's complaint that "interstate signs identify Painted Canyon as a rest area and visitor center only," and "travelers do not readily recognize this as a national park." The park closed the visitor center at Painted Canyon during the off-season because of cost concerns, thus affecting the place that attracts nearly half of TRNP's visitors (albeit for only fourteen minutes each, as noted above). Visits to the North Unit dropped 30 percent during the summer of 2008 as high gasoline prices discouraged travel to the more remote part of the park. And those who visit the South and North units do not stay long. A 1988 study found that the average visitor stay was 2.2 hours at the South Unit and 2.0 hours at the North Unit.[39]

No place in North Dakota's badlands satisfies the Wilderness Act's definition of wilderness as land "untrammeled by man," for there was lots of trammeling during the century after T.R. arrived. Nonetheless, Congress designated nearly thirty thousand acres—or 42 percent of TRNP—as wilderness in the same 1978 bill in which it changed the memorial park to the national park. The wilderness lands are subject to the limits of the Wilderness Act, which among other things prohibits any motor vehicles or commercial activities on those lands. Some environmental groups have pushed for further wilderness designations, but North Dakota's congressional delegation has not evidenced any interest in that idea.

The Wilderness Act also prohibits mineral development. Ordinarily, that would be a redundant legal prohibition within a national park, but TRNP is the only national park in which oil is produced. In 1948, Representative Lemke assured his colleagues that there was "no chance" of oil being discovered in the area. He was wrong. North Dakota's badlands, including TRNP, are located within the Williston Basin, home to vast amounts of hydrocarbons. The same geological processes that formed the badlands also trapped organic material in sandstone and other sediments, eventually yielding oil, natural gas, and coal. The first commercial drilling in the basin began in 1950, and oil booms occurred in the state in the 1950s and again in the 1970s. Many state law claims exist for the mineral rights below the national park, but actual oil production activities are prohibited inside the park. Undaunted, several oil producers have tried slant drilling, which angles into petroleum underneath the park from a hole outside the park's boundaries. Tenneco received permission for such a plan from the state's Industrial Commission in the 1950s, and Amerada Hess pressed the idea once it acquired Tenneco's claims twenty years later. The solicitor of the interior advised that "protective leasing" was necessary to protect the federal government's interest in the potentially significant royalties from oil production around the national park. The slant wells were built in 1975, making TRNP the only national park to be so encumbered.

The park's water quality is generally good, though wastewater discharges, grazing, and oil and gas activities have affected the Little Missouri River and other surface waters. Groundwater is threatened by the increased use of fertilizers and pesticides outside the park in recent decades, perhaps most notably at the Bully Pulpit golf course that opened three miles south of Medora in 2004. Scattered springs and seeps provide the most important source of water in the backcountry of TRNP. Likewise, the park's air is remarkably clear to anyone who is more familiar with the ordinary pollution surrounding large metropolitan areas. In 2005, Billings County, home to the park's South Unit, ranked second in the nation for the least number of fine particulates in the air. That is precisely what the Clean Air Act is trying to preserve.[40]

The 1977 amendments to the Clean Air Act mandate the "prevention of significant deterioration," or PSD, of air that was already clean at the time the provisions took effect. The PSD provisions allow the least amount of new air pollution in national parks and many wilderness areas that are collectively denominated Class I areas. Each Class I area may tolerate a limited decline in air quality, and that permissible decline depends on the initial measurement of air quality (known as the *base level*) and the amount of additional pollution that the area is allowed (known as the *increment*). The PSD regulations limit the amount of sulfur dioxide and particulates that may be emitted by facilities that have been built since 1975. The PSD program has complicated the state's efforts to develop several new energy-related plants in western North Dakota. A coal gasification facility proposed for South Heart, just fifteen miles east of TRNP, is seeking the necessary state permits despite complaints about the facility's possible effect on the national park. An even larger coal-fired power plant is being developed near the tiny town of Gascoyne, fifty-six miles south of the park. The NPS informed North Dakota's Division of Air Quality, which administers the PSD program, that the Gascoyne

plant would adversely affect visibility in the park. The National Parks
Conservation Association was more blunt, warning that "this enormous
new plant would emit in the park area air shed more than 3 million tons
of carbon dioxide, 1,524 tons of sulfur dioxide, 2,286 tons of nitrogen
oxides, and 660 pounds of toxic mercury," all of which would "have a
dramatic and noticeable impact on park visibility." The association thus
lists TRNP as one of the ten national parks that is most threatened by
new coal-fired power plants.[41]

None of this would be possible according to a strict understanding
of the PSD rules. The legality of new sources of pollution depends on
contested understandings of the baseline air quality against which any
additional pollution is measured. Initially, the EPA opposed the state's
plan because the agency contended that North Dakota already exceeded
the permissible increments for sulfur dioxide at TRNP. The North Dakota Department of Health employed estimates of the baseline that were
about 13 percent higher than those used by the EPA, and its estimates of
current emissions were about 19 percent lower than those used by the
EPA. Together, the state's numbers would show that more of the PSD
increment was available to be consumed by new sources of sulfur dioxide and particulates. The EPA accepted most of the state's calculations in
an agreement in December 2003, much to the chagrin of a group of
EPA air-quality modelers who objected that the agreement adopted procedures that "can artificially inflate the baseline, and so artificially expand the available increment." Mark Trechock of the Dakota Resource
Council accused the state of engaging in a process of "backward science"
that began with the desired conclusion and then sought to develop the
model to support it. Much of the discrepancy was due to the conflicting
results of air-quality modeling (preferred by the EPA staff and most environmental groups) and air-quality monitoring (preferred by the state).
The Dakota Resource Council challenged the agreement between the
EPA and the state in federal court, but the case was dismissed after the
agency announced that the agreement was not final and enforceable.
Since then, the EPA has issued a proposed rule that would adopt the approach used in North Dakota as the agency's official position throughout
the country. "To address the uncertainty in how to determine actual emissions for increment consumption purposes," the EPA explained, "we propose to codify a policy that gives the reviewing authority discretion to

select the data and emissions calculation methodologies that are reliable, consistent, and representative of actual emissions." The agency's proposal has provoked congressional opposition and threats of new litigation.[42]

The air-quality dispute is just one example of how TRNP faces more threats from outside the park than from within. Challenges such as elk management, eradicating leafy spurge, and managing visitor activities are much easier to address than the activities that occur outside the park's boundaries. In part, that is because the NPS has scant legal authority over what happens outside the park. "Aesthetics is an important component that contributes to visual or scenic quality and the sense of solitude prized by many park visitors," according to the park, but aesthetic impairments abound. A power line obstructs the view near the park's headquarters in Medora, oil and gas activity can be seen and heard from nearly anywhere in the park, and it was only the persuasive powers of park officials that prevented a cell phone tower from being built in Medora high on a bluff overlooking the park. National park advocates frequently beseech Congress to regulate activities occurring adjacent to national parks, but Congress has shown little inclination to create buffer zones or otherwise expand the NPS's authorities to include nearby activities. Instead, the draft 2006 NPS Management Policies endorses "cooperative conservation" that promises to use "all available authorities to conserve park resources and values" while directing park superintendents to "fully apply the principles of civic engagement" that create an effective dialogue with local interests.[43]

Another solution would be to change the park's boundaries. Indeed, TRNP's boundaries have not been static. Each national park's periodic general management planning exercise includes an evaluation of whether neighboring lands should be added to the park. The TRNP's boundary changed in 1956 (for the park headquarters in Medora), 1963 (for the construction of I-94), and 1978. Most recently, the NPS proposed acquiring 6,581 acres that were once part of T.R.'s Elkhorn Ranch. In 2000, the Eberts family indicated their desire to sell their 5,150-acre ranch to the NPS "to honor Theodore Roosevelt and to ensure that land he once owned and used would not be developed or subdivided by future landowners." National park boundary expansions are subject to the Farmland Protection Policy Act, a 1981 law that seeks to minimize the conversion of farmland to nonagricultural uses, but the NPS concluded that the act would not apply because grazing would still be allowed on the land even if it became part of the national park. The issue became moot, though, when the Forest Service—not the NPS—acquired the Ebert Ranch in 2006 and added it to the Little Missouri National Grassland that surrounds the national park. Even then, Congress enacted a law authorizing the sale of an equivalent amount of national forest lands in Billings County "to offset the acreage acquired by the Federal Government upon the acquisition of the Elkhorn Ranch." The ranch is now part of the national grassland rather than the national park, and I now turn to how the land immediately outside the national park is managed.[44]

THE NATIONAL GRASSLANDS

The TRNP comprises only seventy thousand acres of the hundreds of thousands of acres in the badlands. Befitting a national park, those seventy thousand acres get most of the national attention, and they attracted my initial interest in the area. But the remaining lands actually present legal and policy issues that are unique among the public lands disputes in the United States.

The park is surrounded by the Little Missouri National Grassland, whose 1,028,045 acres make it the largest of twenty national grasslands managed by the U.S. Forest Service. The most contentious issue involving the Little Missouri National Grassland is to whom the land belongs. This is a common issue for all federal public lands, as evidenced by frequent disputes between local constituencies who believe that they hold a privileged position regarding the use of the land and national constituencies who insist that public lands belong to the nation as a whole and should be managed accordingly. But the Little Missouri National Grassland presents a twist on that familiar dynamic.

The legal issues arise because of the odd history of the ownership of the badlands of North Dakota. The United States acquired them as part of the Louisiana Purchase in 1803, and they were treated as part of the public domain thereafter. The 1868 Treaty of Fort Laramie promised land and hunting rights to the Lakota, Sioux, and Arapahoe, but those rights were quickly ignored. When he arrived in the 1880s, T.R. insisted that the badlands were a commons void of private ownership. He never actually owned any land in the area; he was a squatter. Of course, so was nearly everyone else back then. T.R. wrote that the local custom entitled ranchers to a swath of land four miles upriver and four miles downriver from their headquarters, and indefinitely in a perpendicular direction.[45]

That custom began to change as incoming settlers made claims to the land. The first land claims were viewed with hostility by those who had simply used the lands that they needed. Marquis de Mores, for example, was ostracized for buying land claims. But land ownership was inevitable. The Homestead Act, signed by President Lincoln in 1862, promised 160 acres of land to any settler. That inducement was inadequate in the northern Great Plains, so in the Enlarged Homestead Act of 1909 Congress upped the amount to 320 acres for settlers west of the 100th meridian. Most of the badlands passed into private ownership thanks to the population boom that North Dakota experienced during the early years of the twentieth century.[46]

Then the dreaded "Three D's"—depression, drought, and dust—rendered many ranchers destitute. North Dakota experienced the highest level of foreclosures of any state during the Depression, affecting one of every three ranchers in the area. Landowners who wanted to sell their property couldn't find any buyers. The Homestead Act probably made the problem worse by encouraging settlers to try to live on land in the northern Great Plains that could not support agriculture. In 1936, a special committee reported to President Roosevelt: "Mistaken public policies have been largely responsible for the situation. . . . The basic cause of the present Great Plains situation is an attempt to impose upon the region a system of agriculture to which the Plains are not adapted."[47]

So the federal government tried again. Its remedy was to buy back so-called submarginal land—land that could not profitably support farming. All of the sales were from voluntary sellers, with condemnation proceedings employed only if necessary for establishing title or satisfying other legal requirements. The "Resettlement Administrator" within the U.S. Department of Agriculture (USDA) reported in 1935 that the land acquisition program was "allowing many thousands of families to escape from locations where it is impossible to maintain a decent standard of living, and is bringing relief to many thousands of other families by providing employment in the development of the lands being acquired." In North Dakota's badlands, the initial plan was to help the families who sold their farms to resettle in the Pacific Northwest, but many ended up simply moving to northern McKenzie County instead.

The purchased lands were designated Land Utilization Projects that were designed to demonstrate what could be done on such lands. Typically, that meant grazing, not growing crops, on the land that was acquired in western North Dakota.[48]

Congress codified the land reacquisition program in the Bankhead-Jones Tenant Act of 1936 (BJTA). John Hollis Bankhead II (a Democratic senator from Alabama and the uncle of actress Tallulah Bankhead) and Marvin Jones (a Democratic representative from Texas who would soon leave Congress for a long and distinguished career as a federal court of claims judge) were eager to adopt more New Deal legislation to assist the millions of farmers who were suffering during the depths of the Great Depression. The preamble to their law states a desire "to promote more secure occupancy of farms and farm homes." Section I comprised the heart of the law's efforts to promote farm ownership, empowering the federal government to develop farmland for lease and ultimate resale to struggling farm tenants who would otherwise be unable to afford their own land. Unimpressed, North Dakota's Representative Lemke derided this effort as "a joke and a camouflage" that would do little to help farm tenants become farm owners. Section III, which authorized the land acquisition program, was somewhat of an afterthought. Indeed, Senator Bankhead had worried that a single bill that both operated "to buy worthless land and also to sell to tenant farmers good agricultural land" could give the impression "that it was desired to place the tenant farmers upon acquired submarginal land." The scant legislative discussion of Section III described it as "a continuation of the present program" of land acquisition designed "to retire this submarginal land from unprofitable crop production and to turn it back to grass and into grazing and forest areas."[49]

The plan worked. By 1946, the federal government had acquired 11.3 million acres for a cost of nearly $50 million—or about $4.40 per acre. The land in North Dakota's badlands sold for even less, according to U.S. Representative Don Short, who recalled that "there was a lot of it that was sold for $.50 an acre." Once purchased, most of the lands were first managed by the Soil Conservation Service (later known as the Natural Resources Conservation Service), which succeeded in restoring the grasslands to health. The Forest Service assumed control of nearly four million acres in 1954, while a similar amount of lands were assigned to agencies with distinct management duties (including some lands that became part of TRNP).[50]

In other words, one federal law gave the land to private individuals, and another federal law took it back, and the residents of the land today still begrudge the fact that they lost "their" land. That resentment animates two types of legal arguments. The first contention insists that the BJTA obligates the Forest Service to give priority to grazing on national grasslands that had been purchased pursuant to that act. There are three parts to this argument, each of which is unpersuasive. One claim is that grazing was identified as the public use for which the lands were acquired and therefore the Forest Service remains under an obligation to continue to manage them for that use. It is true that grazing was identified as "a proper public use" that justified government condemnation of the lands. For example, the judgment in the 1941 proceedings in *United States v. 17,463.13 Acres of Land, More or Less, in McKenzie County* recited the "establishment of a demonstrational area for the proper grazing of livestock" as one of the public uses. The same proceeding, though, listed several other public uses, including water conservation, prevention of soil erosion, relief of unemployment, and "control of destructive animal life." More importantly, black-letter eminent domain law confirms that the government is not required to maintain the same public use once it acquires property for that use. The Supreme Court so held in *Reichelderfer v. Quinn,* which ruled that land originally acquired for Rock Creek Park in Washington, D.C., could be used for a fire engine house. A second claim, advanced in a law review article written by attorney Elizabeth Howard, emphasizes "that federal agencies cannot act to modify the purposes for which lands were acquired without express congressional authorization to do so." This claim admits that Congress could change the purposes for which the national grasslands are managed but objects that Congress has not done so. The Forest Service responds that the Forest and Rangelands Renewable Resources Planning Act of 1974, which mandates land and resource management plans for all units of the national forest system, defines that system to include "the National Grasslands and land utilization projects administered under Title III of the Bankhead-Jones Farm Tenant Act." Howard returns that volley by insisting that the fact that the grasslands are part of the national forest system doesn't necessarily mean that they must be managed according to the laws governing national forests. The third claim reads the BJTA to favor grazing over other uses of acquired lands. In fact, Section III of the BJTA (as amended on several occasions) lists "controlling soil erosion, reforestation, preserving natural resources, protecting fish and wildlife, developing and protecting recreational facilities, mitigating floods, preventing impairment of dams and reservoirs, developing energy resources, conserving surface and subsurface moisture, protecting the watersheds of navigable streams, and welfare" as the goals of the act's "land conservation and land utilization" program. The Forest Service now relies on those many purposes in justifying its new grasslands management rules. Moreover, as the general counsel's office of the USDA has explained, "it is not at all apparent from the BJTA whether livestock grazing on national grasslands is even one (let alone the only) way that secure occupancy of farms and farm homes may be protected." The legal challenge to the Forest Service's treatment of the national grasslands has never been adjudicated in court, though two cases seem to have presumed that the Forest Service has complied with the BJTA.[51]

The weaker form of the argument suggests that as a policy matter the Forest Service should continue to honor past grazing practices because the Little Missouri National Grassland is federal property only because the federal government exploited the dire straits of the locals during the 1930s. Representative Lemke accused the federal government of driving "some pretty hard bargains, as governments always do. They took advantage of the impoverished conditions of families, and they made promises, as you know, by their local representatives to those people that they did not keep." Grazing proponents often voice this claim. But it is not an argument of legal obligation, but rather one of equitable persuasion.[52]

The Forest Service has not been persuaded. The agency paid little attention to the national grasslands for several decades, effectively allowing the grazing that the BJTA seems to have anticipated. "From the very beginning," writes a historian of the national grasslands, "the national grasslands' concept has been a stepchild within the USDA." That began to change by 1995, when the Forest Service began a series of discussions about the management plans for the national grasslands that are required by the USDA regulations implementing the Forest and Rangeland Renewable Resources Planning Act and the National Forest Management Act. It decided to prepare a plan for all of the Dakota Prairie Grasslands, including the Little Missouri National Grassland. Over the next five years, the Forest Service solicited public involvement on several occasions as it prepared a management plan and associated environmental impact statement (EIS). A draft plan and EIS were released in July 2001, and following another round of comments, Regional Forester Bradley Powell signed the Record of Decision approving the plan in July 2002. Powell described the plan as "a balance," and he sought to both "explain the 'why'" of the decision and apologize for "those places where legality makes for hard reading." The chief of the Forest Service upheld that decision against numerous administrative appeals, and no one sought judicial review of the plan in the courts, so the plan is now in effect. All future decisions regarding permit applications or particular requests for access to the Little Missouri National Grassland must be consistent with that plan.[53]

"The previous management plan for the grasslands," observed Powell, "reflected the desires that the public had nearly 15 years ago, when the primary focus was on what the land could produce. Those desires are changing, and they will continue to change. Today's focus is centered more on the condition of the land, as a basis for providing multiple goods and services." Specifically, the plan is based on five "key themes" or "decision criteria": (1) "ensuring the long-term health of the grasslands," (2) "helping native plants and animals recover and thrive," (3) "contributing to the economic diversity of local economies by using grassland resources in a sustainable way," (4) "protecting special areas and unique resources," and (5) "diversifying recreation opportunities." These goals are employed to satisfy the Forest Service's national grasslands regulations, which require multiple-use management, identification of suitable grazing lands, evaluation of potential wilderness areas, and ongoing monitoring.[54]

What this means is that the management plan adopts a host of specific "goals," "objectives," "standards," and "guidelines" regarding the multiple users who have sometimes conflicting expectations for the grasslands. To highlight just a few, the plan monitors three indicator species that live on the Little Missouri National Grassland—the Plains sharp-tailed grouse, the sage grouse, and the black-tailed prairie dog—to judge the overall health of the grasslands ecosystem. It establishes "special management areas" for bighorn sheep and for ecological restoration. The plan anticipates the reintroduction of black-footed ferrets on the grasslands at an unspecified future date. It emphasizes increased recreational opportunities ranging from hunting to mountain biking to experiencing solitude. The plan supports further improvement of the Maah Daah Hey Trail, which was completed in 1999 and travels ninety-seven miles along the Little Missouri River through the national grasslands while connecting the three units of TRNP. The *New York Times* has acclaimed the trail "as one of the top cross-country mountain biking routes in the United States." The plan also reflects three ways in which the regional forester tweaked it. The area's counties receive 6.25 percent royalty payments for oil production on the national grasslands within their borders, so they want to maximize such production. The final plan allows more oil and gas development than earlier versions, though it still seeks to protect bighorn sheep. The regional forester also emphasized the need to be a "good neighbor" with respect to the divergent views of the prairie dogs on the national grasslands. He thus authorized the poisoning of prairie dogs that threaten public health, damage residences or other facilities, or colonize on adjacent private lands. And the regional forester deferred making a final decision regarding the plan's provisions for grazing.[55]

Grazing generates more passion than any other activity on the Little Missouri National Grassland. T.R. once wrote that "there are very few businesses so absolutely legitimate as stockraising and so beneficial to the nation at large." Of course, he also wrote that "overstocking is the great danger threatening the stock-raising industry on the plains." Overgrazing is not a significant problem on the national grasslands. Indeed, the Forest Service's grasslands management primer advises that "grazing permitees should be recognized for their devotion [to] and care of rangelands." But now, many other interests would like to use the grasslands for different purposes. And so, according to the 2001 summary of the EIS for the management of the Dakota Prairie Grasslands: "Livestock grazing on National Forest System lands is a permitted and traditional use on public lands and plays a part in maintaining and improving ecosystem health, when managed appropriately. However, this use must be balanced with multiple-use objectives, such as flora and fauna diversity, soil and water protection, wildlife food and habitat, outdoor recreation, and other resource values dependent on rangeland vegetation."[56]

The right to graze on the national grasslands is regulated both by the Forest Service and by four grazing associations authorized by North Dakota state law. These grazing associations were established soon after the federal government reacquired the lands in the 1930s, and they produce a unique legal regime. In most parts of the country, grazing permits for federal lands are issued to individual ranchers by the federal agency managing the land (usually the Bureau of Land Management, but sometimes the Forest Service). In the national grasslands of North Dakota, by contrast, the Forest Service enters into agreements with each grazing association with respect to the permissible number of cattle and other requirements, and then each grazing association allots those grazing rights to the ranchers who comprise the association's membership. The grazing associations exercised nearly complete de facto control over grazing on the federal grasslands for decades, so it is not surprising that they chafed as the new management plan threatened both to subject them to greater oversight by the Forest Service and to force them to compete with individuals and organizations who want to use the grasslands for other purposes. Nor is it surprising to see sharply different perspectives on the role of the grazing associations. Keith Winters, the head of the McKenzie County Grazing Association, insists that "the grazing associations practice 'true ecosystem management.'" Two historians even argued that self-government by local ranchers acting through their grazing associations illustrates Robert Putman's theory of social capital.[57]

The issue came to a head when the Forest Service estimated that its plan would result in a 9 percent reduction in permissible grazing levels, while grazing supporters claimed that the actual reduction could be as high as 69 percent. Rather than resolving the dispute by decree, the regional forester decided to "phase in" the new grazing rules by having an independent scientific study team review sixty-four sample allotment management plans (AMPs). "Completion of these sample allotments," explained the regional forester, "will be like taking the new plan out for a test drive." The resulting scientific review team reported in 2005 that it would be possible to implement the new management plans but noted that "the outcome is uncertain." Faced with such continuing uncertainty, Abigail Kimbell—the new regional forester—authorized a "demonstration

project" designed to "(1) develop and implement integrated AMPs col-
laboratively with the respective grazing associations that share in the
management of grazing on the National Grasslands; (2) to determine if
[the management plan's] Goals and Objectives are achievable or in need
of modification; and (3) monitor progress towards meeting resource objectives." Kimbell cited the efforts of the Society for Range Management
to develop a landowner-initiated, consensus decision-making process
involving all of the stakeholders affected by grazing. She also quoted Gif-
ford Pinchot, the first chief of the Forest Service, who said that grazing "is primarily a local issue and should always be dealt with on local
grounds."[58]

The controversy surrounding grazing on the national grasslands
may soon be eclipsed by the debate about increased energy development. The American Petroleum Institute identifies the Bakken Shale
Formation of western North Dakota as a "strategic energy resource"
that may contain more than four billion barrels of oil that are only now
recoverable thanks to new technology. The institute also boasts that the
industry "has explored and drilled in the state's grasslands for 52 years
and has a proven record of producing oil without disruption to the environment or to wildlife." Not so, respond environmentalists and some
local ranchers. One oil producer paid the state a $120,000 penalty after
spilling nine hundred thousand gallons of salt water from a waste pipe-
line into a creek in McKenzie County. The Wilderness Society portrays
the Little Missouri National Grassland as "too wild to drill." "With each
new lease sale, and each new subsequent well and road," worries the
group, "the grassland is further broken apart by industry development,
making it increasingly difficult to ever recover the game corridors, grazing grounds, and sweeping pristine landscapes that provided the character that shaped the American West and the conservation ethic of
Theodore Roosevelt and [naturalist and biologist] Olaus Murie." Such
arguments resonate with Deborah Reichman, a local rancher who
recently moved to the area from Montana. She told me that "it's fright-
ening to see how deeply the oil industry has reached into the local
economy," dividing the community into the haves (who own mineral
rights) and the have-nots (whose "split estates" give them only surface
rights). So Reichman formally objected to a federal Bureau of Land
Management decision to lease nearly two thousand acres of the na-

tional grasslands for oil production. Reichman protested that the agency underestimated the likely extent of oil production given higher gas prices and new estimates of the reserves within the Bakken Formation, failed to protect cultural artifacts left by nineteenth-century settlers, and neglected the data provided by personal observations of wildlife in the area. The Interior Board of Land Appeals rejected each claim.[59]

The grasslands management plan also identifies four areas totaling 41,520 acres that are "suitable for wilderness" designations by Congress pursuant to the Wilderness Act. The plan doesn't actually recommend such a designation because of, in the regional forester's words, a "lack of consensus for support of wilderness in North Dakota at this time." But the commodities interests feared that the Forest Service de facto achieved the same result pursuant to the "roadless rule," or Roadless Area Conservation Rule, that the agency adopted during the last days of the Clinton administration in January 2001 and that made about one-third of national forest lands off-limits to road construction. The roadless rule has been buffered by litigation ever since then. Besides the national debate concerning the legality of the roadless rule, the situation is further complicated in North Dakota thanks to the state's "section line" law. That statute, dating from statehood, burdens the land on either side of a section line with an easement in favor of public highway use. The chief justice of the North Dakota Supreme Court explained in 1921 that the public right to use "the land for two rods on each side of a section line . . . is so well settled there is no occasion for discussing it." And where there are roads—or the right to roads—there won't be wilderness, as demonstrated by an analogous dispute in Utah regarding a nineteenth-century federal law, known as R.S. 2477, that preserves all existing "roads." In North Dakota, the state and several counties in the badlands challenged the application of the Forest Service's roadless rule to lands encumbered by the section line easement. The Forest Service settled the litigation on terms that appear to be more acceptable to the state and counties than to the advocates of wilderness management. And while the challenges to the roadless rule are resolved, the Little Missouri National Grassland is already implementing a January 2001 Forest Service decision banning off-highway vehicles from areas where there are no existing roads or trails.[60]

Finally, consider some of the proposed alternatives that were rejected in the new grasslands management plan. The draft EIS offered five alternatives, and the losing suggestions would have placed greater emphasis on commodity production, ecosystem restoration, or recreation, respectively, or simply maintained the management status quo. Various constituencies offered unsuccessful proposals to establish a conservation reserve and to prohibit all livestock grazing. Several tribes and individual Native Americans sought to restore free-roaming bison to the national grasslands and raised environmental justice issues on appeal when the plan declined to do so. The chief of the Forest Service denied the appeal because the failure to authorize free-roaming bison "does nothing to alter a situation that has existed for over 100 years, and cannot be said to create disproportionately high and adverse human health or environmental effects on minority and/or low-income populations or Native tribes."[61]

The national grasslands are intermingled with privately owned lands throughout the badlands. Generally, this means that state law governs how the land is used, and North Dakota's laws place relatively few restrictions on private property owners. McKenzie County does not have any zoning laws. The North Dakota legislature has rebuffed several recent attempts to enact a conservation easement law, thus making it more difficult for conservation groups to work with private owners to preserve their lands—instead of selling them to outsiders for ranchettes, or rural vacation homes. The state does have a noxious weeds law, which requires people "to eradicate or control the spread of noxious weeds" on state lands that they own or control. The modest legal tools available to direct the use of privately owned lands show why the arguments about the neighboring federal lands have been so contested.[62]

WHAT'S NEXT?

The future of North Dakota's badlands may be the same as their past, which would suit Clay Jenkinson just fine. He extols the badlands as "a magic landscape," "an exotic and self-contained region of 'otherness,' a wild, stark magnificent landscape with a unique aura and a distinctive history." The landscape and its human imprint have remained relatively stable since the last major upheaval during the Dust Bowl and Great Depression of the 1930s. There are mixed suggestions of the potential effect of climate change on western North Dakota, with perhaps the greatest effect on the birds that now live in the grasslands, but it is unlikely that the area will suffer serious climate changes any time soon. It also seems unlikely that it will experience a population boom, especially given its long, slow slide in population and its remoteness from other population centers. The absence of significant transportation facilities limits the willingness of businesses to relocate there, as well as making it more difficult for tourists or early retirees to change the character of the area. The absence of dramatic management problems within the national park—and no, in the broader scheme, too many elk does not qualify—suggests that the park's management will remain much the same as well.[63]

This means that the area's economy will continue to rely on a mix of ranching, oil production, and tourism. Each of these activities is governed by the variety of federal and state laws described above. But those laws offer the greatest opportunity for—or threat to—a change in the natural environment. The TRNP is governed by federal laws prescribing the parameters for management and permissible activities, and few of the locals seriously question what happens within the park. But the story is quite different on the national grasslands. Most local interests favor the existing balance that privileges grazing, encourages some oil production, and accepts certain new recreational and tourist opportunities on the grasslands. But some national organizations would alter that balance to emphasize recreation and the preservation of biodiversity at the expense of unlimited grazing. And environmental law gives them the tools to make that happen. The laws governing those grasslands mandate their management for multiple uses. Management of the national grasslands, like other federal lands, responds to a national constituency with values that are different from those that have traditionally held sway in North Dakota. As Dave Pieper, the supervisor of the Dakota Prairie Grasslands, explained to me: "The livestock community is holding on to something that they've had. It's been a pretty good deal for a lot of people. But the public is demanding something else." More specifically, said Pieper, "This is what the American public wants. It's not necessarily what North Dakota wants. . . . These are national grasslands. They're not North Dakota grasslands." And the balance could tip even more if, for example, the black-tailed prairie dog or another local species were listed under the

ESA, thereby further constraining federal land managers, state agency officials, and private interests.

The laws governing North Dakota's badlands may also change who lives there, and not necessarily for the good of the land. Jenkinson worries that "the Badlands can be drilled, graded, bridged, ranchetted, paved, 'improved,' and even recreationed to death." His solution "is to 'conserve' the existing for-profit family ranching system that has been in place since T.R. and the Marquis arrived in 1883. The working ranches in the Little Missouri River Valley are widely diffused and tucked into the contours of the land. Their environmental impact is low. Their infrastructural 'footprint' is lighter than that of any other economic activity." But the price of the private land in the area has risen sharply in recent years as outsiders build ranchettes as vacation homes or to obtain a hunting tag, and speculators hoping for more of the same drive prices even higher. Land with an agricultural value of less than $200 per acre now sells for up to $2,000 per acre. Many natives in the area worry that an influx of absentee landowners will threaten both the economy and the landscape of the badlands. "We would prefer to see traditional ranches stay on the land," Jan Swenson of the Badlands Conservation Alliance told me. Likewise, Gerald Reichert of the Alliance (who also serves on the staff of the Nature Conservancy) referred me to Wendell Berry's writings for the idea that "if you don't have people that own the land and take an interest in how it affects their daily lives, then you lose something. And so to have people living sustainably on the landscape is a very important part of this."[64]

Most of these changes are occurring slowly, especially when compared with the boomtowns adjacent to other national parks in the West. The best explanation for why few such changes have occurred so far is the absence of an indigenous environmental community within North Dakota. Proponents of traditional uses, governmental officials, and representatives of the state's few local environmental organizations all made this same point. One of the few local activists explained that everybody is "so danged polite" that conflict, let alone litigation, concerning the lands is frowned upon. To be sure, the Sierra Club has a modest office based in Bismarck, the Dakota Resource Council has had some success recruiting local ranchers, and the Badlands Conservation Alliance emerged from the initial debates over the grasslands management plan. But such groups are the exception and typically are characterized as "fringe groups" or "extremists" by everybody else. Clay Jenkinson worries that people may object to a new wilderness proposal "not on its merits, but merely because they cannot stand the idea that the conservation community would win a little victory in the land use wars of North Dakota and the American West. I hear the phrase 'damned environmentalists' almost every day of my life." A Forest Service employee admitted to me that it was unnecessary to "bullet-proof" grasslands management decisions that are otherwise ripe for litigation because there aren't any environmentalists around who are willing to challenge them. The absence of citizen groups is compounded by an alleged unwillingness of state agencies to enforce existing environmental requirements. "We don't have environmental enforcement," the Dakota Resource Council's Mark Trechock explained to me, "because we have environmental agencies that are permit granting agencies, and that's it."[65]

Yet the other common belief among parties on all sides is that they expect the law to decide. "When all this is said and done, you just have to go to the courts," McKenzie County Commissioner Dale Patten told me. "There's all this mess out there, and you have to have the courts sort it out." The strange thing, of course, is that so far the courts haven't decided much of anything in the badlands. The laws governing the national park are notably capacious for most management choices that the NPS would like to make, and the potentially more stringent laws applicable to the national grasslands are only now being implemented. There has never been any reported litigation concerning the management of the TRNP or the grasslands. The courts have not decided much so far, but now everyone expects that to change. The future of North Dakota's badlands may depend on the future of environmental law after all.

CHAPTER FOUR

River Enigma

THE SUSQUEHANNA RIVER

THE SUSQUEHANNA RIVER is simultaneously famous and forgotten. It is the longest river on the Atlantic seaboard, flowing 444 miles from New York through Pennsylvania and Maryland into the Chesapeake Bay. Its 27,500-square-mile watershed drains sixty-seven counties and comprises 43 percent of the Chesapeake Bay's drainage area. The river is a mile wide at Harrisburg, Pennsylvania, and it is shallow for nearly its whole course. The Susquehanna has captured the imagination of artists such as Frederic Edwin Church, Benjamin West, Jasper Cropsey, Samuel F. B. Morse, and Nathaniel Currier and James Ives. Robert Louis Stevenson rhapsodized that when he learned that the "shining river and desirable valley" was called the Susquehanna, "the beauty of the name seemed to be part and parcel of the beauty of the land."[1]

But where some observers see shining beauty, others don't see much of anything. In 1899, a traveler confessed: "I have always considered the Susquehanna such a useless river. It seems so big and lumbering." Eighty years later, a collection of paintings portraying the Susquehanna admitted that the river "never had the glamour" of rivers such as the Hudson, Ohio, Mississippi, Missouri, Rio Grande, Colorado, or Columbia. One writer commented: "Too shallow to serve for long as a great commercial conduit and too quickly overtaken by railroads as a mode of transport, too mean-

"The Valley of Wyoming," painted by Jasper Francis Cropsey in 1865. The Metropolitan Museum of Art, Gift of Mrs. John C. Newington, 1966 (66.113). Image © The Metropolitan Museum of Art.

dering in its course through these states to serve as a line of geographical or political demarcation, too diverse in its resources and the inhabitants of its borders to have engendered one distinctive image, it fades in the memory of Americans in a culture no longer attuned to natural boundaries and regional idiosyncracies."[2]

Perhaps even the meaning of the river's name has faded. There are at least sixteen different translations of the word *Susquehanna,* but it is agreed that it refers to the native peoples who lived at the river's mouth when John Smith arrived in 1610. Smith's voyage has been recounted in numerous writings, even briefly by the D.C. Circuit Court in 1941, which romantically noted that the Susquehanna River was "discovered by Captain John Smith, whose courage and resourcefulness saved the Jamestown Colony from abandonment and destruction, and thus preserved the North American Continent to Anglo-Saxon colonization." The land along the Susquehanna was peopled by various Indian tribes before and after Smith's arrival. The Iroquois viewed the area as a barrier to the westward expansion of white settlements. The whites arrived anyway. David Brainerd, a Congregationalist missionary, fought through "nothing but a hideous and howling wilderness" before reaching the river in 1744. But a 1796 history of the river boasted of "the prospect of internal commerce, with so extensive, so complete, and convenient communication with the Atlantic."[3]

That prospect never quite materialized. The Susquehanna flows through some of the earliest settled and most populated parts of the country, yet the largest city along its banks hosts fewer than fifty thousand residents. Instead, the Susquehanna is "a river of small towns and small cities," as a 1985 *National Geographic* feature described it. Native Americans comprised the dominant population along the river until the late eighteenth century. Now, nearly four million people live within the river's basin. The river begins in Cooperstown, New York, a small town founded by James Fenimore Cooper's father in 1787 and most famous today as the site of the Baseball Hall of Fame. The river crosses into Pennsylvania and then back into New York before encountering its first sizeable city at Binghamton. It again returns to Pennsylvania and flows southeast to Wilkes-Barre, where coal reigned during the end of the nineteenth century and the beginning of the twentieth. One hundred miles or so later, the Susquehanna reaches Harrisburg, the state capital whose forty-seven thousand people make it the largest city on the river. Flowing southeast, the river ends its journey at Havre de Grace, Maryland, and empties into the Chesapeake Bay.[4]

People have used the river for many different purposes. It served as a remarkable fishery for Native Americans and early settlers. It was a waterway for those same people, as well as the millions of trees that were floated down the river when Pennsylvania and New York's forests were felled during the nineteenth century. Its water powers hydroelectric plants and cools nuclear power plants. It has been treated as a convenient waste receptacle by city sewage plants, coal mines, factories, and farms. There is comparatively little recreation along the river, and few cities rely on it for drinking water. The Susquehanna was imbued with spiritual significance by the Iroquois, for whom the "river valley was a Vatican," and by the members of the Church of Jesus Christ of Latter-day Saints—commonly known as the Mormons—whose founder, Joseph Smith, was baptized in the river in May 1829 near what is now Oakland in far northeastern Pennsylvania. The economic value of the river is reportedly $6.8 billion, ranging from the $1.4 billion generated by 521 food manufacturing establishments to the $4 million produced by ten amusement and theme parks.[5]

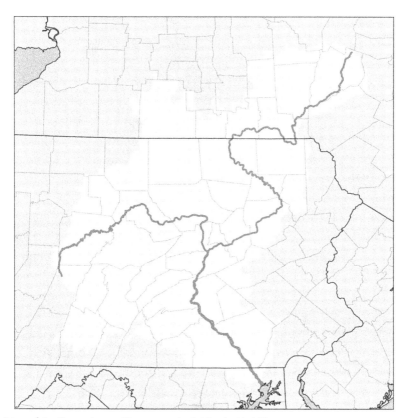

Map of the Susquehanna River watershed. Map by Karl Musser.

Unlike the other places I describe in this book, several excellent books have been written about the Susquehanna River area, including its environmental conditions. *Down the Susquehanna to the Chesapeake* by Jack Brubaker eloquently follows the river from Cooperstown through dozens of communities until it reaches the Chesapeake Bay. Susan Stranahan, a journalist for the *Philadelphia Inquirer* who reported on the nuclear accident at Three Mile Island, wrote *Susquehanna: River of Dreams* in 1993. A few decades earlier, Carl Carmer wrote *The Susquehanna* for the Rivers of America series, and geologist and geographer Richmond E. Myers penned *The Long Crooked River.* Going back to 1899, we find *Down the Historic Susquehanna: A Summer's Jaunt from Otsego to the Chesapeake* by Charles Weather Bump, and in 1796, the quintessentially eighteenth-century-titled *A Description of the River Susquehanna, With Observations on the Present State of Its Trade and Navigation, and Their Practicable and Probable Improvement,* written by Zachariah Poulson Jr.

The story I want to tell here focuses on the management of the river with respect to its environment. The events for which the Susquehanna River is known in environmental law are not happy ones. Pollution from the coal mines of central Pennsylvania got so bad that the state enacted the nation's most stringent water pollution law in the 1930s. The worst nuclear power accident in U.S. history occurred on a small island in the river—Three Mile Island—just south of Harrisburg in 1979. The river's most recent fame occurred in 2005, when the environmental organization American Rivers named the Susquehanna the most endangered river in the United States. That designation prompted a brief flurry of attention to the river and its problems, but soon it faded back to its typical obscurity.

The biggest question is how we should use the river. Daniel J. Flood, a colorful member of Congress from Wilkes-Barre during the 1970s, voiced the traditional view that "we must not forget that the Susquehanna River is to serve man, and, if the people of the Susquehanna River are to prosper, the river must be used to best meet the needs of these people." Today's environmental groups have a much different idea about the purpose of rivers, and the Susquehanna, preferring to restore the river's ecosystem to its natural conditions. The management of the river tries to account for both concerns. One management question is how to use the river, and that question in turn has two subparts. The first issue is how to control where the river goes. The law works to keep the river where we want it. We don't want flooding; we want the river to stay where it belongs. In addition, sometimes we want to take water from the river to use it, and the law facilitates such consumptive uses. The second management question is what to allow in the river. The Susquehanna, like many other American rivers, has a long history of pollution. It is much less polluted at the beginning of the twenty-first century than it was for much of the twentieth century, but it is still threatened by pollution that flows from farms, mines, sewer overflows, and roads. The answers that we offer to these usage questions often depend on who gets to answer them, so let me start there.[6]

WHOSE RIVER IS IT?

No one actually owns the water that flows in the Susquehanna River. Instead, the law specifies who has a right to *use* that water. Historically, the right to use the river's water attached to the countless public and private parties who owned the bordering—or, in legal terminology, *riparian*—land. Generally, riparian owners have a right to make a reasonable use of the water. A 2003 Maryland case involving the proposed expansion of a yacht club on the Susquehanna River at Port Deposit stated that riparian owners enjoy "at least the following rights" of access to the water, construction of a wharf or pier, consumption of the water, use of the water without transforming it, ownership of accretions, and ownership of nonnavigable streams. These common law riparian rights interact with other common law doctrines of contracts, torts, and property to provide the framework for the resolution of conflicts between conflicting users of the river. Some of the conflicts over the Susquehanna River that have been adjudicated by courts applying the common law include an 1837 Maryland case holding that a railroad could build a wharf near the mouth of the river because it would be "a strange doctrine" that would allow exclusive fishing rights to arise from mere use; a 1911 federal case in Pennsylvania in which a paper mill successfully sued an electric power company for breaching its contract by diverting so much water from the river that the mill could not operate; and a 1939 case refusing to enjoin the City of Binghamton from diverting water for its public water supply despite the effect on downstream riparian owners. Notwithstanding the longevity of the application of riparian rights and other common law doctrines, Professor Joseph Dellapenna contends that the riparian system in Pennsylvania suffers from flaws "including the vagueness and unpredictability of the criteria of decision, the instability of the resulting legal decisions, the lack of a process for managing water during shortages or for protecting public values, a systematic bias in favor of large users and the impracticality of markets under such a legal regime." Dellapenna suggests that the root of the problem is the common property aspect of riparian rights.[7]

Even as riparian rights have persisted, the use of the Susquehanna River has always been subject to governmental regulation. The notion that private individuals controlled the Susquehanna River shocked the

Pennsylvania Supreme Court in 1845, which observed that a "surrender of any part of it would have been an act of political suicide." Hundreds of local governments govern land that abuts the river or that lies within the watershed, and those local governments exercise a notorious amount of independent authority in Pennsylvania and New York. The story is different in Maryland, where the state dominates the regulatory scene. Of course, the federal government's actions affect the Susquehanna River, too. Congress enacted the first federal statute addressing the river in July 1789, ensuring that duties would be collected from ships traveling on its waters. Numerous federal agencies, including the EPA, the Army Corps of Engineers, the Federal Energy Regulatory Commission, the FWS, and the Nuclear Regulatory Commission exercise jurisdiction over specified activities involving the river.[8]

But that was not enough. Or maybe it was too much. In any event, during the 1960s, pressure grew to establish a separate entity charged with managing the Susquehanna River. Such an entity would avoid "the duplicating, overlapping, and uncoordinated administration of a large number of governmental agencies which exercise a multiplicity of powers resulting in a splintering of authority and responsibility." The states of New York, Pennsylvania, and Maryland and the U.S. Congress approved the proposed Susquehanna River Basin Compact, and it became law once President Richard Nixon added his approval on Christmas Eve 1970. The parties to the compact recognized "the water resources of the Susquehanna River Basin as regional assets vested with local, state, and national interest for which they have a joint responsibility." The point of the compact was thus to better manage the river. The compact established the Susquehanna River Basin Commission (SRBC) and charged it to "develop and effectuate plans, policies, and projects related to the water resources of the basin." More specifically, the SRBC is empowered to operate its own projects, establish planning standards, allocate waters, conduct research, promulgate regulations, and "exercise all powers necessary or convenient to carry out its express powers and other powers which reasonably may be implied therefrom." The compact contains separate articles addressing water quantity and water quality, as well as articles encouraging watershed management, recreation, hydroelectric power, and "other public values" such as economic, historic, and scenic interests. All of this is to be accomplished by the four commissioners of the SRBC—the governors of New York, Pennsylvania, and Maryland and a commissioner appointed by the U.S. president—who exercise authority over the area drained by the Susquehanna River and its tributaries.[9]

The SRBC has successfully defended its authority in court on several occasions. Two Pennsylvania state court decisions held that the interstate compact preempted the authority of local townships to impose additional conditions on proposed water withdrawal projects that had already been approved by the SRBC. Both cases involved municipalities that were frustrated by the effects of development on water resources, particularly in potentially stressed areas where demand exceeds supply. Initially, the SRBC approved the State College Borough Water Authority's proposal to install wells to provide more groundwater for the community. Several local townships, however, exercised their authority under state law to impose conditions upon the projects. The water authority then challenged those conditions in state court. The Commonwealth Court agreed with the water authority that the interstate compact preempted the power of the townships to impose additional regulations. According to the court, "to permit the imposition of conditions by the board in its desire to protect the Township's residents, would result in a splintering of authority and responsibility, the very mischief that the Susquehanna River Basin Commission was designed to remedy."[10]

In 2006, the SRBC published a rule in the *Federal Register* amending the commission's project review regulations to "include additional due process safeguards, add new standards for projects, improve organizational structure, incorporate recently adopted policies and clarify language." Comments by members of the public betrayed a mistrust of the SRBC. They accused the commission of imposing excessive regulatory burdens, neglecting economic development, failing to be accountable to its constituents, and exceeding its authority under the compact. Not surprisingly, the SRBC defended its record and its authority. It acknowledged "certain short-term administrative and financial obligations" imposed by its regulations, but it quickly emphasized "the long-term benefits of Commission management to a critical resource." Unconvinced, a Pennsylvania concrete company sued the SRBC in federal court seeking a preliminary injunction against the new regulations. The court rejected the suit because the company failed to show that it would suffer an irreparable injury from the enforcement of the regulations, and thus it was not entitled to an injunction. Instead, the court explained, "this is simply an example of a corporation spending money to comply with a government regulation."[11]

The SRBC has displayed more zeal for defending its power than exercising it. Despite its wins in court, it has a modest view of its role. The commission sees itself as coordinating the management of the Susquehanna River basin by the three states, who maintain "primary responsibility" for the river. The SRBC steps in when the states fail to act or when they disagree and thus emphasizes the compact's directive "to promote interstate comity" and "to remove causes of possible controversy." The compact omits any authority to regulate land use within the basin because "local determination is a sacred cow" that the drafters of the compact were unwilling to challenge. The SRBC thus distinguishes its powers from the Tahoe Regional Planning Agency, whose land use authorities have generated enough controversy to reach the Supreme Court. There is also the practical limitation, in the words of Dellapenna, that the commission lacks "sufficient staff to adequately police all water users within the areas they regulate in Pennsylvania," as well as in New York and Maryland. On the other hand, some parties believe that the SRBC has been too aggressive in regulating activities in the Susquehanna River basin. "They have this regulatory pall that they cast over the watershed," according to one New York conservation official. Another planner asserts that the SRBC is "slightly less powerful than God. They own the water, they sell the water, and they pay themselves to do things." "They could be the best thing in the world," James Curatalo of the Upper Susquehanna Coalition told me, but "they live for themselves."[12]

Regardless of who is right, the SRBC has not achieved the lofty goals of its creators. William Voigt wrote a book about his experiences serving as the secretary for the commission that drafted and promoted the compact, which he believed was "destined to influence significantly if not actually to be a chief determinant of the water-related economic and cultural future of the basin and its people." Instead, state politicians and federal administrators still play a central role in the decisions governing the management of the river. Nonprofit environmental organizations play a key role, too, which was probably unforeseen at the time that the compact established the SRBC. For example, American Rivers was not founded until 1973, three years after the SRBC came into existence. It is those private and governmental organizations, along with the SRBC, who battle to determine how the Susquehanna River should be managed.[13]

WHERE THE WATER GOES

There are 2.5 billion gallons of water in the Susquehanna River on an average day. It takes six days for a drop of water to flow from Cooperstown to the Chesapeake Bay. The challenge is to ensure that the water is at the right place at the right time. Much of the law affecting the Susquehanna River is crafted to direct the water's course. The river has a mind of its own, so to speak, and is constantly sending water onto the adjacent land where it is not wanted. In other words, it floods. Not to be outdone, the human communities near the Susquehanna have their own ideas for the water, and they have gone to great expense to try to move the water from the river to places where it can be put to other uses. Dams play a central role in both flood control and water diversions, though other techniques are used as well. The law helps to decide where the water should be amidst the competing challenges of floods, dams, and consumptive uses.

Floods

The Susquehanna has flooded about every twenty years since Europeans began to settle the area and observe the river in the eighteenth century. The first recorded flood occurred in 1744, followed by "The Pumpkin Flood" of 1786 when the river carried ripe pumpkins from central Pennsylvania into the Chesapeake Bay. Other major floods occurred in 1810, 1865, 1889, and 1894. The two largest floods of the twentieth century happened in March 1936, when the waters rose to thirty-three feet in Wilkes-Barre and communities all along the river suffered a total of $67 million in damages; and in June 1972, when Hurricane Agnes stalled over the basin and dumped about fourteen trillion gallons of water there, caused millions of dollars of damage, and claimed the title of "the nation's worst natural disaster" at that time. The most recent serious flood occurred in June 2006, hitting New York especially hard and sending fifteen million tons of sediment into the Chesapeake Bay. Many engineering schemes, dollars, and laws have tried to defend against the river's "sinister side to its personality."[14]

The Susquehanna is sometimes described as the most susceptible to flooding of any river in the United States. The basin's topography "features short, steeply sloping tributary valleys, higher gradient streams in the lower basin, and highly erodible soils related to glaciation." The deforestation resulting from logging during the nineteenth century made matters worse. The Wyoming Valley, the site of Wilkes-Barre in north central Pennsylvania, is particularly susceptible to flooding because the river repeatedly zigzags there before entering a narrow gorge. But flooding is also a historic part of the river's life and essential to the ecology of the basin. What changed is that people wanted the benefits of living near rivers without experiencing the losses caused by floods. In Susan Stranahan's words, "people soon came to regard the riverbanks as their own, their tenancy on them as permanent, and the river as the *intruder*." As early as 1840, a local poet intended to ask Congress to ensure "that the banks of rivers in all towns settled henceforth, shall be government property, to be reserved and planted for public grounds."[15]

Congress did not heed the poet's advice, but neither did it do much to stop flooding. Most legal authorities doubted that Congress had the power to regulate flooding. As Joseph Arnold, a historian of the Army Corps of Engineers, explains, "For reasons that have yet to be investigated adequately, the right of the federal government to improve navigation under the Commerce Clause was extended to flood control in a very slow, halting, and, it must be admitted, occasionally disingenuous manner; sometimes projects were authorized under the guise of navigation improvement when everyone in Congress knew the work was also for flood control." The principal concern was that the construction of levees and other flood control projects provided a much greater benefit to local communities than to the nation as a whole. The Corps limited its work to surveying rivers. Federal public works projects involving rivers did not really begin until after the Civil War, and even then Congress insisted that the local beneficiaries should pay the cost.[16]

The floods of 1849 persuaded Congress to enact the Swamp Land Acts, which began a federal policy of draining wetlands in part to avoid future flooding. The 1889 flood prompted the affected communities to ask Congress for help. That same year Congress enacted its first of what would become nearly twenty laws denominated Flood Control Acts. The Flood Control Act of 1917 represented "the first time that Congress

appropriated funds openly and primarily for the purpose of flood control."
As one congressman said during debate on the bill, the measure "removes
the mask" from years of covert federal flood control spending under the
"pretext" of navigation improvements. The actual provisions of the 1917
law were quite modest, directing the Corps of Engineers to spend $45 mil-
lion on flood control projects for the Mississippi River and $5.6 million on
the Sacramento River—two rivers that had just experienced significant
flooding and where businesses had been engaged in a lengthy effort to
obtain federal assistance to make their products more economically competitive. Ten years later, flooding of the Mississippi River persuaded Congress to pay the entire cost of flood control projects, but a threatened veto
by President Coolidge led to a compromise in which the federal government built the projects and the local governments paid to maintain them.
"The 1928 Flood Control Act," writes historian Karen O'Neill, "marked
the point when the Corps of Engineers embraced flood control as a duty
fully compatible with its navigation improvement work. Presidents and
members of Congress would now likely be expected to respond to all large
flood disasters." O'Neill quotes two supporters who characterize the 1928
law as "the greatest piece of legislation ever enacted by Congress" and "the
greatest piece of internal improvement legislation 'since the world began.'" The Flood Control Act of 1944 has yielded the most litigation, including recent controversies over the management of the Missouri River
that Sandra Zellmer described so well in a 2004 article, but that act and
most of the other Flood Control Acts have had little direct effect on the
Susquehanna.[17]

Pressure mounted in Congress throughout the 1920s and early
1930s for the enactment of more comprehensive flood control legislation. A bill came very close to passing in 1934 until Maryland's Millard
Tydings ridiculed it during a memorable speech on the floor of the Senate. Tydings, whose name now adorns the bridge that carries Interstate
95 across the Susquehanna River, blasted the amount of federal money
that the bill would spend for flood control projects on obscure rivers
throughout the country, especially in the Louisiana home of his enemy
Huey Long. Tydings then observed that the Susquehanna River often
flooded his hometown of Havre de Grace, as well as nearby Port Deposit.
"Did those people ever come to Washington and ask for $385,000? It
would have been the last thing they ever thought of doing. . . . They do

not ask other people to help them. They stay and take it. . . . They do not run to Washington every time they have a little disaster. . . . They never ran to the Government for help for every little thing that happened to them. They have not been pork-barrel raiders." That view was soon overwhelmed by flooding that occurred throughout the country in March 1936, especially in the northeastern states. Perhaps more importantly, members of Congress watched the waters of the Potomac River rise and swamp the National Mall. The *New York Times* editorialized that the flooding "is no credit to a country which prides itself on its technical achievement." Even Senator Tydings acquiesced to the inevitable federal flood control legislation.[18]

The Flood Control Act of 1936 presumed that the federal government should take the lead role in controlling floods. Congress stated "that destructive floods upon the rivers of the United States, upsetting orderly processes and causing loss of life and property, including the erosion of lands and impairing and obstructing navigation, highways, railroads, and other channels of commerce between the States, constitute a menace to national welfare; that it is the sense of Congress that flood control on navigational waters or their tributaries is a proper activity of the Federal Government in cooperation with States, their political sub-divisions and localities thereof." The Corps of Engineers historian concludes that it was "faith in technology and intensity of humanitarian spirit, exhibited especially during the catastrophic floods of 1936, that explains congressional willingness to adopt such sweeping legislation without examining its implications more thoroughly." The law assigned responsibility "for flood control and allied purposes" to the War Department (the Army Corps of Engineers) while charging the Department of Agriculture with investigating watersheds, preventing erosion, and regulating runoff. The act's most immediate effect was to authorize $310 million for dozens of flood control projects throughout the country. About one-tenth of those funds, $27 million, was designated for flood control projects along the Susquehanna River. The act specifically authorized levees in the Susquehanna River basin cities of Bloomsburg, Edwardsville, Forty Fort, Harrisburg, Jersey Shore, Kingston, Lock Haven, Milton, Montgomery, Muncy, Nanticoke, Plymouth, Sunbury, Swoyerville (now Swoyersville), West Pittston, Wilkes-Barre, and Williamsport (all in Pennsylvania), as well as dams, detention reservoirs, or other flood control structures in York, Pennsylvania, and the southern New York cities of Binghamton, Corning, and Hornell. Acting upon this authority, the Corps built thirteen reservoir projects in the Susquehanna watershed. For example, the Whitney Point Dam was constructed between 1938 and 1942 in order to help control flooding in southern New York and eastern Pennsylvania. The resulting Whitney Point Lake eventually became a popular recreational site in Broome County, New York. The Corps also spent the money authorized by the Flood Control Act of 1936 on a system of levees, including a $9.1 million project designed to withstand thirty-seven feet of water in the Wyoming Valley.[19]

Hurricane Agnes topped those levees with three feet to spare. The county civil defense director ordered the evacuation of Wilkes-Barre at 12:15 a.m. on June 23, 1972, and soon the city's downtown was submerged under ten feet of water. Agnes killed about one hundred people and displaced one-quarter million more, resulted in $2 billion in losses, and was repeatedly characterized as the worst natural disaster in U.S. history up to that time. The local congressman, Daniel J. Flood, flew home on a helicopter loaned to him by Secretary of Defense (and Flood's former House colleague) Melvin Laird. Upon landing, the congressman proclaimed, "This is going to be one Flood against another!" True to his word, Flood repeatedly reminded military officers and federal and local agencies that he chaired the defense appropriations subcommittee, and he used that "authority" to direct resources to the area despite the absence of the legal power to do so.[20]

As the waters subsided, the first help to the victims of the flooding came from "thousands of civic, religious, human service, and business organizations." Local banks agreed to defer home payments for three months. Robert Wolensky's history of the response to the flood quotes Alexis de Toqueville's observation that "the health of a democratic society may be measured by the quality of functions performed by private citizens." Judge Max Rosenn, who had been recently appointed to the U.S. Court of Appeals for the Third Circuit by President Nixon and whose own chambers had been flooded, chaired a Flood Recovery Task Force composed of local business leaders that spearheaded the efforts to help the Wilkes-Barre area recover from the flood. Judge Rosenn later recalled that the task force "feared that unless something drastic was done, the community would be abandoned."[21]

The task force immediately sought unprecedented assistance from the federal government. But "the state and federal governments were often slow in reacting." A flood historian adds that "the state at first participated reluctantly, in large part because of a conflict with the federal government over responsibility and philosophy. The federal government, on the other hand, was simply unprepared for a catastrophe of such magnitude." The problem was worsened by the visit of the secretary of Housing and Urban Development (HUD), George Romney, to Wilkes-Barre on August 7. Romney was the former governor of Michigan whom Nixon had defeated in the Republican presidential primary of 1968. Romney was already unhappy with his cabinet position when Nixon ordered him to visit Wilkes-Barre the next day in order "to achieve a more harmonious working relationship" between HUD and local officials. Instead, as the *Washington Post* began its page-one story, "a group of screaming women and their families and Gov. Milton Shapp engaged Housing Secretary George Romney in an hour-long shouting match" at a press conference held, coincidentally, at the Daniel J. Flood Elementary School. When shown a photo of a home ruined by the flood, Romney responded, "At five years of age I was driven out of Mexico, and we didn't even have that left." Romney also observed that "government has a great role to play and they can and must do a great deal. But ultimate action depends on more private effort than government effort." Apparently, that was not the message the White House wanted to send during an election year. Romney announced his resignation upon his return to Washington, and he never served in public office again.[22]

The federal government soon began to respond. President Nixon remarked: "Confronted with so massive a disaster emergency, our response as a Nation must also be massive. Conscience commands it; humanity impels it." The Army Corps of Engineers oversaw the cleanup efforts pursuant to the powers bestowed upon it in the Disaster Relief Act of 1970. That law also provided modest loans administered by the Small Business Administration and the Farmers Home Administration, but those provisions were quickly judged "entirely inadequate to address Agnes' destruction." Congress approved $200 million in emergency relief on July 1, just two weeks after the flood. The Agnes Recovery Act, passed in 1972, added an additional $1.6 billion in low-interest loans, temporary housing, unemployment compensation, food stamps, and

funds for reconstruction and flood control. The act also broke with precedent by authorizing private religious organizations to receive disaster
relief grants. Pennsylvania senator Hugh Scott told his colleagues, "it
is essential . . . to the recovery of the disaster area, in Pennsylvania and
other States, that the private schools rebuild along with the public
schools."[23]

Next, Congress turned to amending federal disaster law in anticipa-
tion of future floods. Pennsylvania's other senator, Richard Schweiker,
testified that "there is no reason why our Federal Government should
not take a responsibility in all kinds of disasters in the future. . . . People
ought to know that the Federal Government cares on these things." That
sentiment shows how much thinking about natural disasters had
changed since Senator Tydings ridiculed federal flood control programs
four decades before. Congress also revised the National Flood Insurance
Act (NFIA). Originally enacted just a few years before in 1968, the NFIA
found that it was "in the public interest for persons already living in
flood-prone areas to have both an opportunity to purchase flood insurance and access to more adequate limits of coverage." When Agnes
struck, only two Wyoming Valley residents had enrolled in the plan.
Congress amended the law to make such insurance mandatory for property within Special Flood Hazard Areas. But it declined to enact the National Catastrophic Disaster Insurance Act that had been proposed by
Representative Flood. That bill would have required all property owners
throughout the nation to participate in a national disaster insurance
plan that would be funded by a tax on fire and property insurance premi-
ums, a tax on the repayment of disaster loans, and congressional appropriations. The residents of Wyoming Valley supported the idea, but
Congress did not. Nonetheless, Judge Rosenn observed that "there has
never been such generous remedial legislation on the part of the federal
government, and I doubt that there ever will be." Susan Stranahan offered a less enthusiastic verdict, observing in her book that "a number of
residents received the equivalent of a full-year's wages from taxpayers"
only to live in "a community driven deeply into long-term debt for property on the banks of a river that will once again deliver a devastating
flood."[24]

Agnes represented the high-water mark of the river. The Susquehanna still floods, but no flood since Agnes has been as devastating, and

Wilkes-Barre above the Susquehanna River today.

no flood has triggered congressional action. Instead, flood control has become the province of the SRBC with assistance from the Corps of Engineers and the state governments. The nature of flood control projects has changed as well. Before Agnes, most flood control projects—and most flood control laws—relied on the construction of levees, dams, and other structures. The Corps dammed fourteen of the Susquehanna's tributaries after Congress passed the Flood Control Act of 1936. Since Agnes, the Corps has worked to raise the levees at certain stretches along the river, including a $147 million project to raise the levees in Wilkes-Barre—again—that Congress authorized in 1986. But reliance on levees and other structural attempts to control floods has waned. "If Congress had given the green light," Jack Brubaker wrote, "the Corps might have regulated the entire Susquehanna by damming each tributary and placing strategically located tourniquets on the river itself." Brubaker added, just four years before Hurricane Katrina, that if the Corps "can force the lower Mississippi not to leave its present channel by employing enormous control structures, they surely could dam the Susquehanna into impotent sections." As a Corps official explained, "If my only interest was flood control and I was a god, there would be dams all over the place—but there are other concerns besides flood control, so we certainly don't want to do that." Those other concerns are often aesthetic. The nineteenth-century mansions that used to look out over the Susquehanna along Wilkes-Barre's Coal Coast now look out over the concrete levees that are across the street. A similar phenomenon prompted one observer to complain that the city of Sunbury had "the feel of an empty swimming pool." Harrisburg declined to install levees through its downtown precisely because of concerns about such visual effects, and today the city is the only one along the Susquehanna that does not have a levee and features recreational paths that run close to the river's banks.[25]

The town of Lock Haven, Pennsylvania, voiced some of those concerns when it filed a lawsuit designed to stop the Corps from building seven miles of levees and dikes along the river. Residents of the town had debated the wisdom of the project for several years, with the mayor and city council supporting the Corps until they were defeated by levee opponents in a municipal election. The new mayor sued the Corps in federal district court in Washington, D.C., preferring that venue to the local federal court in Pennsylvania. The lawsuit alleged that the Corps failed to update its environmental impact statement (as required by the National Environmental Policy Act) to consider how the levees could spread hazardous chemicals and that the Corps did not comply with the National Historic Preservation Act. The court rejected both arguments because it found that the Corps had already addressed the town's concerns in its extensive studies of the environmental consequences of the levees, possible alternatives to levees, and the affected archeological resources.[26]

Floodplain management has become the preferred alternative to new structural efforts to prevent future flooding. "If there are no homes in the floodplain," asks James Curatalo, "is it really a flood?" The Susquehanna River Basin Compact commits its parties "to control flood plain use along and encroachment upon the Susquehanna River and its tributaries and to cooperate faithfully in these respects." Sara Dueling of American Rivers explained to me that it would be more river-friendly and cost-efficient to move things out of the floodplain and to rely on wetlands "to start to mimic the hydrological system that predates" human engineering. Toward that end, the SRBC advocates municipal land use regulations that restrict building in floodplains, as well as compliance with the floodplain development criteria imposed as a condition for participation in the national flood insurance program. Pennsylvania has enacted such laws, including its Flood Plain Management Act of 1978. Section 404 of the federal Clean Water Act requires a permit for development in floodplains that satisfy that law's ambiguous jurisdictional standards. Curatalo suggests another way to remove structures from floodplains: have a municipality acquire properties on higher ground when they are available at tax sales and then trade them to people who suffer from floods.[27]

But there is resistance to floodplain management, too. Environmentalists often accuse the Corps of Engineers of solving any problem by building something, but during the 1920s the Corps complained about "a great indifference on the part of the individual and the public to the necessity of a waterway sufficient to care for floods. For either profit or convenience, there have been established residential subdivisions on areas subject to overflow." Eighty years later, a local resident agreed: "Storm water management is the answer to flooding. You'll never see it. The lobbying groups are too strong. It's the Realtors and the developers. They don't give a damn where they build." Indeed, sometimes the law works against floodplain management. One report blames "a lack of zoning in many towns" that "results in buildings being placed too close to streams, which, in this basin, have a great tendency to migrate. The resulting problems of stream encroachment on roads, driveways, septic systems, and buildings often result in drastic emergency measures, which often compound the unstable stream conditions." Similarly, after Hurricane Agnes, "never once did [the federal government] question the determination of local and state officials to rebuild on the floodplain," complained Susan Stranahan. "In fact, that was a criterion to qualify for some federal money." Even at the time of Agnes, the NFIA directed "State or local communities, as a condition of future Federal financial assistance, to participate in the flood insurance program and to adopt adequate flood plain ordinances with effective enforcement provisions." The affected communities, however, insisted that they should be allowed to rebuild in the areas destroyed by the flood because of the huge existing investment there and because it was not practical to move everyone to higher ground. The Corps bowed to the intense public opinion and finessed the NFIA's mandate by simply defining the floodplain "as the area within the banks of the river itself."[28]

The effort to prevent floods has been accompanied by a recognition that they will still occur despite our best efforts. Accordingly, in 1986 the SRBC joined the National Weather Service, the U.S. Geological Survey, and several other federal and state agencies to establish the Susquehanna River Basin Flood Forecast and Warning System. The system employs radar and gauges of rainfall and stream levels to collect information that is then disseminated to affected communities. The new system performed well in its first real test during the flood of January 1996, save for its initial underestimate of the amount of rainfall and snowmelt. The system worked again during the flood of 2006, providing between seven and seventeen hours of advance warning of imminent flooding. The SRBC has identified several areas for improvement, but mostly what it wants is money. In 2005, it issued a press release lobbying Congress to restore a $2 million appropriation for the system that had been deleted two years before. Maryland's senator Barbara Mikulski followed up with a meeting with SRBC and local officials and then issued her own press release describing the flood warning system as "not elective, it's essential" and noting that "as a senior Democrat on a Senate Appropriations Committee, I get to put money in the federal checkbook for the nation's priorities." She and her Maryland congressional colleague Dutch Ruppersberger made good on that promise by including $2 million for flood forecasting and $67,000 for a Susquehanna River basin low flow management and environmental restoration study in the 2009 omnibus appropriations bill.[29]

Dams

There are countless dams along the Susquehanna River and its tributaries—literally, as no one has been able to count them all. Whatever the number, each dam is designed to alter the flow of the river's water. The dams on the Susquehanna do this for different reasons, including flood control, hydroelectric power, navigation, and recreation. Some dams have unintended benefits, such as creating habitats favored by aquatic birds and anglers alike. One of the first dams was built by Revolutionary War general James Clinton to create a sufficiently large pool of water to enable his supply boats to travel down the Susquehanna from the area that would be Cooperstown to attack the British in the summer of 1779. Shortly thereafter, more dams were constructed across the river in Maryland and Pennsylvania in order to facilitate two canal systems.

Dams offer many benefits, but they also interfere with other uses of the river. Most obviously, they usually obstruct navigation. The earliest laws sought to encourage navigation along the Susquehanna River. A 1771 law enacted by the Pennsylvania legislature, and approved by King George III, asserted that "improving the navigation" on the river and its tributaries "will greatly conduce to the benefit of the inhabitants residing on and near the [river] and the province in general by increasing the trade of the said province." Toward that end, the law declared the rivers "to be public streams and highways for the purposes of navigation up and down the same, and that all obstructions and impediments to the passage of His Majesty's liege subjects up and down the same erected or hereafter to be erected shall be deemed, held and adjudged common nuisances." In 1797, the Maryland legislature enacted a similar law declaring that the Susquehanna River "shall be considered a public highway, free for any person or persons whatsoever to work thereon in clearing the obstructions to its navigation."[30]

But the law could not overcome hydrology. John Smith's exploratory voyage of 1610 stopped just a few miles up the river because the rocks and shallow water blocked further passage. Subsequent efforts to make the Susquehanna navigable in conjunction with a system of canals failed once the railroads spread throughout the region beginning in the 1830s. Even so, legislation was introduced in Congress in 1866 "to ascertain the practicability of having a steamboat navigate from the Chesapeake bay, at the mouth of the Susquehanna river, to Lake Ontario." The legislation failed, as did efforts to allow steamboats to ply more than short stretches of the river. Instead, the Susquehanna's heyday as a navigable river occurred in the second half of the nineteenth century when the timber industry floated logs down the river when the water was high in the spring. Efforts to ship things north against the river's flow failed and, as Susan Stranahan describes it, "the Susquehanna remained what it would always be: a one-way river, and not an especially hospitable one at that."[31]

The law persisted, however. The Rivers and Harbors Act of 1899, best known for prohibiting any interferences with navigable rivers without a permit, designated the Susquehanna River as navigable. But in 1904, Secretary of War—and future President and Chief Justice—

William Howard Taft "re-examined the question as to whether the Susquehanna River can be said to be a navigable river within the provisions of the act of Congress requiring that navigable rivers in two States shall not be crossed by bridges, except by authority of Congress, or should be considered as a navigable river within one state, consent to cross which may be given by the Legislature of the State, with the approval of the Secretary of War." Congress had authorized the construction of bridges across the Susquehanna River in numerous statutes enacted during the nineteenth century. It had not, however, approved the bridge that the Pennsylvania Railroad wanted to build across the river in Maryland. Taft concluded that congressional approval was unnecessary. "My own judgment," he explained, "is that in the present condition of the Susquehanna River it is navigable only within one State. There is no interstate navigation such as was in the mind of Congress making the distinction." The consent of Secretary of War Taft and of the State of Maryland sufficed.[32]

Congress overrode Taft's decision in 1914—the year after Taft left the presidency—but by then the navigation debate had become moot. Large hydroelectric dams blocked the Susquehanna in southern Pennsylvania at York Haven and Holtwood beginning in 1904 and 1910, respectively. The Conowingo Dam, originally authorized by the Maryland legislature in 1884, became the river's largest dam and the world's largest hydroelectric project when it opened in 1928. The Safe Harbor Dam opened upstream in 1931. Together, Jack Brubaker writes, "the four dams have changed the Lower Susquehanna from a free-flowing, rock-encrusted wild river into a series of four placid ponds."[33]

Those dams survived several legal challenges. In 1916, Maryland's highest state court adjudicated a lawsuit brought by the City of Havre de Grace against the builders of the proposed Conowingo Dam. The city claimed that the dam would constitute a public nuisance because it would destroy both the city's fishing industry and "the navigable nature of the Susquehanna river, and thereby render unprofitable and perhaps valueless certain wharf property owned by the municipality." The court held that the dam did not constitute a public nuisance because the river that it blocked was not navigable anyway. The court rejected the city's reliance upon the 1797 state law stating that the river was navigable, observing that "a mere declaration, though by statutory authority, that a stream is navigable, could not make it so unless it was navigable in fact." And, explained the court, "there is no pretense or claim in this case that the Susquehanna is or ever was in its natural state navigable for up-stream commerce between the head of the tidewater and the Pennsylvania line." Another case reached the federal appeals court for the District of Columbia in 1941, objecting to the failure of the owners of the Holtwood Dam to obtain a license from the new Federal Power Commission. Again, the case turned on whether the Susquehanna River was navigable, and this time the court said that it was, given the broad understanding of navigability recently announced by the New Deal Supreme Court.[34]

By then, the legal question had changed from whether the construction of dams was allowed to the regulation of the dams that had been built. For example, in January 2008 PPL Corporation announced plans to expand the Safe Harbor Dam to double the amount of electricity the dam generates. The expansion project would benefit from the incentives contained in the national energy policy that President Bush announced during a visit to the dam in 2001. At the same time, PPL has to satisfy lots of laws. The corporation has applied to the Federal Energy Regulatory Commission (FERC) to amend its license, which otherwise would expire in 2014, to accommodate the changes to be wrought by the project and to extend the term of the license until 2030. PPL's application states that the project must (1) obtain a water-quality certification required by Section 401 of the federal Clean Water Act as administered by the Pennsylvania Department of Environmental Protection (PADEP); (2) receive a National Pollutant Discharge Elimination System permit required by the Clean Water Act in order to discharge storm water; (3) obtain a permit required by Clean Water Act Section 404 in order to add fill material into the water; (4) demonstrate compliance with state laws administered by PADEP, including the Clean Streams Law, the Dam Safety and Encroachments Act, and the Flood Plain Management Act; and (5) gain the approval of the SRBC. In December 2007, "the parties desiring to avoid litigation and intending to be legally bound," PPL and PADEP entered into a consent order and agreement with respect to the project. Kathleen McGinty, the head of PADEP (who previously served as the chair of the White House Council on Environmental Quality during the Clinton administration), said that she "worked closely with PPL to craft this proposal in a way that helps meet our energy needs, while also addressing the environmental and ecological considerations." So far, the only concerns have been raised by whitewater rafting enthusiasts who worry that the expanded dam will eliminate the whitewater on which they rely. Meanwhile, in November 2008 FERC released an environmental impact statement analyzing PPL's proposal "to construct a new powerhouse, install new turbines, construct a new skimmer wall and larger forebay, and reconfigure the project facilities to enhance upstream fish passage through modification of existing facilities and excavations in the tailrace channel" at the Holtwood Dam. FERC's statement concluded that the proposal, with slight modifications, would actually yield a net benefit to the environment.[35]

The other issue facing all of the dams along the Susquehanna River concerns a different kind of navigation problem. The dams obstruct fish as well as human traffic. Early settlers raved about the fisheries in the Susquehanna River, which was "once regarded by some as the greatest fish highway in the United States." John Smith's diary marveled at the "abundance of fish lying so thicke with their heads above the water." Smith undoubtedly saw the American shad, a large herring that sometimes grows to two feet in length and weighs as much as six pounds. Shad live most of their lives at sea, but in the spring they return to spawn in freshwater rivers all along the Atlantic coast from Newfoundland to Florida. Shad were first caught for subsistence. Native Americans depended on the shad runs in the spring; then the fish lured settlers from Connecticut during the eighteenth century because the shad, "unlike the fields, barns, and granaries, could not be burned by the" existing Pennsylvania settlers who were fighting to keep the Connecticut settlers out of the area. Commercial fishing added to the catch for subsistence purposes, so that shad fishing was the region's most important economic activity by the 1820s. Then fishing began to decline as a result of overfishing, the construction of dams for canals and small mills, and water pollution.[36]

The law was quick to try to arrest the decline. Between 1700 and 1866, the Pennsylvania legislature enacted "more than seventy-five laws related either directly or indirectly to shad-fishing on the Susquehanna and its tributaries." The difficulty in applying those laws is illustrated by an 1810 Pennsylvania Supreme Court case involving the owner of 228 acres of riparian land along the Susquehanna. The landowners created a pool for shad by removing rocks from the two hundred yards of the river closest to their land; they then sued several parties who caught one thousand shad, worth $200, using a seine within twenty yards of the shore. Two judges relied on statutes vesting the public with the right to fish in state waters; the dissenting judge relied on other laws that were "utterly inconsistent and incompatible with the common right of fishing in" the pool next to the plaintiff's land. In 1866, the Pennsylvania legislature established a Commissioner for the Restoration of Inland Fisheries, but the first commissioner reported that the laws governing shad fishing were being violated by illegal fish traps, and weirs were catching millions of juvenile shad en route to the sea. By the end of the nineteenth century, a writer noted that "lamentations over the loss of the shad are common among the old inhabitants of the entire Upper Susquehanna." The problem worsened with the construction of the four dams at the mouth of the river during the first decades of the twentieth century and with the effects of increasingly polluted water. Shad had nearly disappeared from the Susquehanna River by 1980.[37]

The efforts to eliminate water pollution from the Susquehanna were soon accompanied by efforts to reintroduce shad. The dams were the biggest obstacle. The technology for allowing fish to bypass the dams did not exist until the second half of the twentieth century, and once that technology became available, the challenge became persuading the utilities that operated the largest dams to employ it. The dam operators installed fish ladders and stocked the river with shad eggs, but they insisted that federal law dictated that electricity generation be given the highest priority along the river. Shad supporters—including the SRBC, the FWS, the Maryland Department of Natural Resources, and the Pennsylvania Fish and Boat Commission (PFBC)—turned to FERC, which periodically reviews the licenses of the hydroelectric dams, to test that claim. The Federal Power Act charges FERC to consider commerce, hydroelectric power, recreation, irrigation, flood control, water supply, "and enhancement of fish and wildlife (including related spawning grounds and habitat)" when reviewing a license application. Applying that test, in 1980 FERC approved the relicensing of the four dams while also ordering further administrative proceedings on the efficacy of additional efforts to assist the shad. In

December 1984, the three upstream dams settled their dispute with FERC and agreed to spend $3.7 million over the next decade on shad restoration efforts. But Philadelphia Electric, the owner of the Conowingo Dam, continued to pursue the issue before FERC. An administrative judge ruled against Philadelphia Electric in January 1987, observing that "fish passage measures are a cost of doing business on a river containing anadromous fish populations."[38]

FERC affirmed that decision one year later. The agencies supporting the restoration of the shad sought to condition the license upon a requirement that the Conowingo Dam be operated to allow the minimum flow of water necessary for the shad. Philadelphia Electric, by contrast, claimed that "the existing fishery is thriving, that existing interim flows are sufficient to protect it, and that increased flows would not enhance it." The dispute centered on the best way to test those claims. The commission acknowledged "that predicting changes in fishery populations in complex ecologies such as in the Conowingo waters is at this point more of an art than a science." Rather than waiting for the science to develop, the commission concluded that its "responsibilities under the Federal Power Act, which go to fish and wildlife as well as power production, are more appropriately discharged by pursuing a more expeditious resolution of the minimum flow issue." The commission also affirmed the administrative judge's orders to build a second fish lift and to modify and build a new entrance to the existing lift. After a series of FERC decisions, the utilities agreed to spend millions of dollars to restore shad to the Susquehanna.[39]

The FERC decision and the settlement agreement prompted the investment of millions of dollars in efforts to help the shad travel upstream to parts of the river that they had not reached in a century. By 2001, nearly 200,000 shad passed the Conowingo Dam. But that success disappeared by 2008, when only 19,914 shad were lifted over the dam—and only 21 passed the York Haven Dam forty-six miles upstream, down from a high of 16,200 in 2001. The Atlantic States Marine Fisheries Commission, which oversees the shad fishery all along the Atlantic coast pursuant to the Magnuson-Stevens Fishery Conservation and Management Act, reported in 2007 that the American shad stocks were "at all-time lows and do not appear to be recovering," citing the Susquehanna

River as one that continues to experience declines. Biologists suggested that predation by striped bass and offshore commercial fishing operations may explain the disappearance of the shad. At some point, the mounting costs of restoring shad will be questioned if the fish themselves fail to benefit. The PFBC has identified economic benefits from recreational fishing, the role of the shad in the region's heritage, and ecosystem restoration as reasons for persevering, along with the argument that "restoring migratory fish to the Susquehanna is the right thing to do!" Perhaps so, but the large hydroelectric dams are no longer the impenetrable culprits that they once were.[40]

The era of dam construction is mostly over, but one proposal to dam the Susquehanna River persisted into the twenty-first century. In 1991, U.S. Representative Paul Kanjorski—who took Daniel Flood's seat in Congress in 1984, four years after Flood resigned because of a corruption scandal—began to promote the idea of building an inflatable dam across the Susquehanna River at Wilkes-Barre. The inspiration for the idea came from Sunbury, a downstream city that has "the world's largest inflatable dam" whose pond "has become one of central Pennsylvania's prime recreational assets." The proposed dam at Wilkes-Barre would be inflated between Memorial Day and Labor Day in order to create a deeper pool of water for recreational users behind the dam. When fully inflated, the dam would stand 9.5 feet high and impound 4.5 miles of the river, producing a body of water that was no wider than the river but that would be about ten feet deeper. The Lucerne County Flood Protection Authority adopted the project to serve as mitigation for the aesthetic and recreational losses that will occur as a result of the further raising of the city's levees. A study performed by Gannett Fleming, the county's consultant, reported that the inflatable dam would "lessen the existing recreational deficit in the Wyoming Valley" while creating one hundred temporary and eighteen permanent jobs and millions of dollars in sales taxes. According to Representative Kanjorski, the inflatable dam "would provide a strong incentive to invest in cleanup of the river, encourage economic growth throughout the region, and enhance the visibility of planned riverfront improvements. . . . The lake [that would be created by the dam] would allow for boating, fishing, picnicking, hiking, sightseeing, and nature studies during the summer." But not everyone was convinced that the inflatable dam was a good idea. The local Audubon Society, for example, argued that the dam would destroy wildlife habitat, degrade the river's fishery, and trap pollutants flowing downstream—all without measurably improving recreational opportunities. A memorable bumper sticker warned, "If you can flush it down your toilet, you can find it in our lake." Opponents outnumbered supporters twenty-one to six at the public hearing on the project. The only public protest was conducted by a solitary individual who spent a day on a bridge with a "no dam" banner, and none of the groups that opposed the dam threatened litigation if it was approved.[41]

Kanjorski secured congressional funding for 75 percent of the costs of the inflatable dam, so the fate of the project depended on the Army Corps of Engineers. In 1970, Congress supplemented the Corps' flood control and navigation responsibilities by designating the agency as the enforcer of the wetlands provisions of the Clean Water Act. According to Section 404 of the act, no one may place any fill material—think "dirt"—into waters of the United States unless the Corps has issued a permit to do so. The regulations that the Corps promulgated for its enforcement of Section 404 provide that a permit will not be issued if there is a practicable alternative that has a less adverse effect on the aquatic environment or if the project is not in the public interest. The dam required such a permit because it would inundate 13.35 acres of riffle pool complexes and permanently fill 1 acre of forested wetlands. In February 2008, the Baltimore district engineer of the Corps denied the permit. Initially, he observed that the inflatable dam "would have an adverse impact on riffle-pool complexes, wetlands, anadromous finfish, eels, resident fish, native mussels, sediment erosion and accretion, water quality, habitat diversity, benthic ecosystem, riparian vegetation, and safety." The argument for the dam suffered from the "high degree of uncertainty regarding whether an inflatable structure will provide the purported enhanced recreational opportunities." The district engineer thus concluded that the project's purpose could be achieved by alternative measures that were less damaging to the river's environment. Those alternatives included the Wilkes-Barre Riverfront Development Plan and the West Bank Development Plan, which are designed to improve recreational opportunities along the river simply by providing better access to it. Representative Kanjorski responded by accusing "bureaucrats within the Army Corps of Engineers" of "narrowly defin[ing] the regulations which implement the Clean Water Act." He also planned "to examine the underlying laws which enable federal bureaucrats to value 'riffle pool' complexes above the needs of human beings." But Kanjorski acknowledged the criticisms of the inflatable dam when he added, "if that's what the people want, who am I to change their position." The county flood authority soon voted not to appeal the permit denial in federal court.[42]

At one time people wanted to build dams, but more recently they have wanted to remove them. This is especially true of dams that were built as early as the nineteenth century for canals and mills, purposes that have long since been abandoned—as have the dams. The SRBC cites the benefits of dam removal to include improving fish migration, eliminating safety and liability threats, facilitating navigation, and restoring habitat and ecological processes. American Rivers has been especially active in championing the removal of small dams that have long outlived their usefulness. It cites the example of the Good Hope Dam, a 5.5-foot-high, 230-foot-wide dam built in the early twentieth century across Conodoguinet Creek—a tributary of the Susquehanna River in Pennsylvania. The PFBC was unable to identify the dam's owner, so it conducted economic and ecological studies and held public meetings to discuss the consequences of removing the dam. The commission also organized a group of a dozen interested entities, including federal agencies such as the FWS and the National Oceanic and Atmospheric Administration (NOAA), and local watershed associations and soil conservation districts. American Rivers paid for half of the $35,000 removal costs with funds provided by the FishAmerica-NOAA Community-Based Restoration Program Partnership, while PADEP issued the necessary permits. More generally, the EPA's Chesapeake Bay Program has provided funding for the removal of other dams in the Susquehanna River basin. PADEP has approached dam owners to find out whether they want to remove their dams, and the PFBC and PADEP have removed dozens of dams beginning in the 1990s. PADEP has even developed a "restoration waiver" that streamlines and expedites the permitting process necessary for the removal of a dam. In New York, the FWS has taken the lead in evaluating whether the removal of dams in the upper Susquehanna River watershed could improve fish passage, and it has identified eight dams whose removal would be especially valuable.

Taking Water from the River

Flood control notwithstanding, sometimes people want to move water from the Susquehanna to use outside the river. This is much less of an issue for the Susquehanna than for rivers in the West, for example, where diversions of water for irrigation and other purposes may account for nearly all of a river's water. Most of the Susquehanna's water is left in the river, though that is beginning to change. A *withdrawal* takes water—perhaps to cool electric generators—and later returns it to the river. Water taken for *consumptive use,* by contrast, is not returned to the river; instead, it evaporates, is diverted to another watershed, or is incorporated into a product such as cement. The leading consumptive uses include public water supply (30 percent), power generation (30 percent), agriculture (18 percent), and industry (11 percent). Consumptive uses and withdrawals have not been much of a concern for much of the history of the Susquehanna River. Few agricultural uses require irrigation water, unlike western rivers whose every drop (and then some) is diverted for irrigation pursuant to complex legal proceedings. Only a handful of communities rely on the Susquehanna River for a public water supply. Baltimore accesses the Susquehanna only when its regular water supplies are inadequate. Even so, consumptive use of the Susquehanna River's water has grown from an average of 157.2 million gallons per day in 1970 to 278 million gallons per day in 2006, and it is estimated to reach 306 million gallons per day by 2025. More than half of those consumptive uses occur in the lower Susquehanna, home to the largest hydroelectric facilities and to a growing number of people. Irrigation is increasing, too, doubling in Pennsylvania's Lancaster County between 1992 and 1997.

The SRBC oversees the removal of water, for both withdrawals and consumptive uses, from the Susquehanna River. It seeks to harmonize the contrasting water management regimes of Maryland (which regulates all withdrawals and consumption), Pennsylvania (which regulates only public water suppliers taking surface water), and New York (which regulates public water suppliers taking surface water or groundwater). Since the establishment of the commission in 1971, it has reviewed any consumptive use of the Susquehanna's waters that exceeds an average of twenty thousand gallons per day. Regulated operations must compensate for their water during periods of low flow in order "to restore the streamflow to the levels that would occur if the regulated consumptive use projects were not in operation." For withdrawals (as opposed to consumptive uses), commission approval is required for any withdrawal of surface water or groundwater that exceeds one hundred thousand gallons per day. That approval may be conditioned upon withdrawing a lesser amount of water if the proposed withdrawal would adversely affect the river.[43]

Those are the rules. In practice, though, "the regulatory program didn't have a lot of maturity to it for a long time," SRBC Deputy Director Tom Beauduy told me. The SRBC finally decided that it needed to be more consistent and cover everyone, or else it should simply just drop its regulations. It opted for the former. The Susquehanna basin's 256 golf courses offer a particularly telling example of the difficulty in regulating water consumption. A typical golf course uses between five hundred thousand and one million gallons of water per day. A 1999 SRBC study disclosed that 98 percent of the courses in the basin were not in compliance with the commission's regulations. That might have been less of a problem in the 1970s when greens and tees were a lot smaller and before courses sought to make fairways more attractive by irrigating them. So the SRBC began regulating the use of that water, only to discover that "the political backlash was unbelievable," as Beauduy put it, because so many legislative fundraisers are held on golf courses. It took the commission three years to get all of the area's golf courses under its docket, and some of the courses had to be modified because they lacked the required water storage capacity to survive a drought. Beauduy boasts that the courses are operating better now, consistent with his view that the SRBC's "fundamental mission is not to penalize people, but to bring them into compliance."

Still, Beauduy recognizes that the commission "should be regulating a lot more" than the six hundred projects it currently tracks. The SRBC is negotiating with the electric utilities that use the largest amount of water in the Susquehanna River basin. The commission's strategy has been to exempt consumptive uses and withdrawals that began before the compact took effect in 1971, and then to impose the regulations when a facility's ownership transfers or when it increases its water usage by more than one hundred thousand gallons per day. The SRBC has also exempted public water supply systems from consumptive use regulations, though they are regulated for the withdrawals, because studies indicated that about 90 percent of the water that goes into those systems is returned. Agricultural uses escaped the SRBC's attention for a long time as well, until a study completed in 2005 found 785 operations that should be subject to the consumptive use regulations. The SRBC's recommended response is to identify and secure the 15.7 million gallons of water per day that are needed to compensate for agricultural consumptive uses during low flow periods.

Natural gas development presents the most recent challenge to the SRBC's regulation of consumptive use of Susquehanna River water. The Marcellus Shale formation underlies parts of eight states extending from Tennessee to New York, including 72 percent of the Susquehanna River basin. There may be as much as five hundred trillion cubic feet of natural gas trapped in the shale, compared with the twenty-three trillion cubic feet that the United States consumes annually. New technologies make the gas accessible for the first time, but those technologies rely on the injection of large amounts of water to fracture the rock and release the gas. The SRBC became involved as exploitation of the Marcellus Shale increased in 2008. Tom Beauduy told a Pennsylvania legislative hearing that the SRBC's "management objective is to have this industry avail itself of the water resources of the basin in the development of this important mineral resource, but to do it in a way that minimizes impact to the basin's water resources." Toward that end, the SRBC issued two cease-and-desist orders to drilling companies that were using river water without the SRBC's approval, and the commission then negotiated seven additional settlements and began processing nearly one hundred consumptive use applications. The SRBC relied on "a previously unused rule" that it had adopted in 2006 for other purposes, but whose provisions fit the challenges presented by development of the Marcellus Shale. In Congress, Representative Phil English introduced a resolution that would have instructed the SRBC to consider national energy needs before regulating natural gas development in the watershed, but the resolution failed to attract any cosponsors before English lost his congressional seat in the November 2008 election. The SRBC proceeded to establish a new "approval by rule process" applicable to the consumptive use of wastewater acid mine water while retaining the existing process for reviewing groundwater or surface water withdrawals. In doing so, the SRBC rejected both the concerns of environmentalists that the new rules are too lenient and the concerns of industrial users that the rules are too burdensome.[44]

The compact gives the SRBC the "power to acquire, construct, operate, and control projects and facilities for the storage and release of waters." The latest such project involves Whitney Point Lake, which was created when the Corps of Engineers built Whitney Point Dam across the Otselic River in Broome County, New York, in 1942. The original purpose of the ninety-five-foot-high dam was flood control, but the latest project will use some of the resulting lake to store water that can be released during periods of low flow. But the law authorizing federal funding for the project—Section 1135 of the Water Resources Development Act of 1986—focuses on environmental restoration, so the SRBC's information sheet describing the Whitney Point Lake environmental restoration project emphasizes that "the health of the aquatic ecosystem would be maintained and have better recovery from drought events" thanks to releases of the stored water. The balance of the funding comes from a $2 million earmark that a New York state senator secured from the state legislature. In other words, the Whitney Lake project uses environmental funds to compensate for water consumption. That bothers Chip McElwee of the Broome County Soil and Water Conservation District because the SRBC threatened to hold local farmers responsible for consumptive uses unless they were able to store enough water behind the dam, but the commission could not explain how an environmental restoration program remedied consumptive use. McElwee further notes that not much water is consumed in the upper reaches of the Susquehanna River, so compensation should not be necessary. Additionally, he worries that the project would take water from the bottom of the river, where it is less conducive to biotic life, and then move it to other parts of the river where it could do more harm than good. All of this means that the Whitney Lake project might be worthwhile, but not for the reasons that the law requires it to articulate.[45]

WHAT GOES INTO THE RIVER

The discussion so far has considered where the river's water goes. The other question that the law confronts is what is allowed to go into the river's water. Little of what we place in the river—intentionally or not—

helps it, so the law seeks to control what goes into the river. Those efforts must now address a longstanding legacy of pollution.

Like many other rivers, the Susquehanna was long regarded as a convenient place to confirm the prevailing axiom that "the solution to pollution is dilution." Dozens of towns were pouring raw sewage into the river by 1900. By 1964, the Susquehanna River earned the unenviable title of "the Garbage Disposal of New York State." But recognition that the dumping of sewage into the river was a problem prompted efforts to solve it long before then. In 1905, Pennsylvania enacted its Purity of Waters Act, which made it illegal to discharge untreated sewage into the river without a permit issued by the secretary of health, the attorney general, or the governor. Eighteen years later, Pennsylvania's new administrative code authorized the creation of a Sanitary Water Board, the first of its kind in the nation. That board spearheaded the state's efforts to clean the Susquehanna of untreated sewage, conditioning permits upon new types of treatment and providing more than $100 million to help municipalities build the necessary treatment facilities. Governor James Duff pushed recalcitrant communities to have operating sewage-treatment plants by 1952, though Wilkes-Barre did not satisfy that mandate until 1969. Pennsylvania now regulates sewage disposal through its Sewage Facilities Act, also known as Act 537, which requires all of the state's municipalities to develop and implement plans to address existing and future sewage disposal needs. Today, 142 wastewater treatment facilities discharge treated sewage into the Susquehanna. Brubaker proclaims that "no city along the Susquehanna has done more to improve water quality than Binghamton," whose plant treats more than twenty million gallons of effluent each day. Most facilities, though, fail to treat the nitrogen that is blamed for so many problems in the Chesapeake Bay. Nor do they detect the pharmaceutical products that are routinely flushed down the drain, so dam owners "are sweating bullets" about the day that they'll have to clean out the sediment behind their dams because they fear there might be some "super bugs" there.[46]

The days of untreated sewage being dumped into the Susquehanna River have passed, but that has not kept sewage from entering the river. The problem lies in combined sewer overflows (CSOs), the term for sewage that overflows certain outdated collection systems. Those systems were built—often a century or more ago—to collect sewage, industrial waste, and runoff and to carry the combined waters to the treatment plant in a single pipe. They generally work fine during dry weather, but during heavy rains or melting snow, they often overflow and discharge untreated water directly into the river. A disproportionate number of the nation's 746 communities with combined sewer systems exist in the Susquehanna River basin, which hosts many of the older communities that are especially likely to have such systems. American Rivers cited the "sewer pollution" from CSOs as the greatest threat to the Susquehanna when it listed the river as the nation's most endangered in 2005. According to American Rivers, "in March 2002 just two of the 16 outfalls [in Wilkes-Barre] sent 150 million gallons of human feces, industrial wastewater, stormwater, hygiene products, pharmaceuticals, and food scraps into the Susquehanna."[47]

Each CSO outfall is a point source that must obtain a National Pollution Discharge Elimination System (NPDES) permit pursuant to the Clean Water Act. An NPDES permit contains technology-based limits that are calculated on the basis of the best available technology economically achievable (BAT) for toxic and unconventional pollutants and the best conventional pollutant control technology (BCT) for conventional pollutants. Compliance, however, has been slow. The SRBC's Beauduy agrees that CSOs are "a major problem in the basin," but he quickly adds that "it's really a money problem." In "these relic industrial cities, the Wilkes-Barres of the world," the costs of retrofitting a sewage-treatment system are "astronomical." So far, funding to address CSOs has come from such sources as the EPA, the Clean Water State Revolving Fund, congressional earmarks, and state appropriations. Congressman Kanjorski responded to the 2005 designation of the Susquehanna as the nation's most endangered river by noting that he had obtained $4.1 million in federal funds to correct CSO problems on the river. As the federal government has moved away from revolving funds, Beauduy encourages affected parties to be more innovative with respect to new kinds of funding sources. He notes that "there are massive infrastructure problems" in the whole system—besides CSO outfalls and dams and bridges and levees in dire need of repair—and he warns that the day is coming when society needs to pay double, triple, or quadruple the money for water supplies in order to pay for the necessary infrastructure.[48]

The next pollution problem is even more costly. "God has truly given wondrous prosperity to the people of the State," extolled a Pennsylvania writer in 1899, "in these glorious anthracite deposits." The world's largest deposits of anthracite coal occur in northeastern Pennsylvania. Mining began in the nineteenth century, peaked in 1917, and ended abruptly on January 22, 1959, when the Knox Coal Company's mine underneath the Susquehanna blew a hole that drained the river like a bathtub until it was plugged by railroad cars, boulders, hay bales, mining cars, and twelve thousand cubic yards of dirt. The softer bituminous coal surrounds the West Branch of the river, and mining there has persisted to a modest extent. But coal mining proved to be an environmental disaster. Pyrite is found near many coal deposits, and when oxygen and water are mixed with the iron and sulfur of pyrite, the result is sulfuric acid. This so-called acid mine drainage killed all of the fish in certain stretches of the river, especially on the West Branch, by the middle of the nineteenth century, and it colored the river banks bright orange.[49]

The coal industry dominated regional politics, and the law, for a century. An industry official told a congressional committee in 1947, "you can't have both fish in inland streams in coal mining districts and coal—one must give way to the other, and certainly coal, being one of our basic industries, must be protected." The courts agreed. "To encourage the development of the great natural resources of a country, trifling inconvenience to particular persons must sometimes give way to the necessities of a great community," ruled the Pennsylvania Supreme Court in 1886 when Eliza McBriar Sanderson complained that the Pennsylvania Coal Company's nearby operations had ruined the pure water of the brook on her Scranton land. The legislature concurred by excluding coal mine drainage from Pennsylvania's Clean Streams Law when the law was enacted in 1937. Attitudes slowly began to change, transforming the court's assertion that "the law should be adjusted to the exigencies of the great industrial interests" to consider other exigencies instead. *Pennsylvania Coal Co. v. Sanderson* itself was the target of hostile legal scholarship as early as 1913 when a writer noted that the "inconvenience" suffered by Mrs. Sanderson was far from trifling and it was suffered "not to satisfy two or more 'necessities of a great community' but the desire of the stockholders of the Pennsylvania Coal Company to make 25 per cent dividends upon their invested capital." A survey of water pollution law published by the *University of Pennsylvania Law Review* in 1951 referred to "the ghost of *Sanderson*" and suggested that the decision had been limited to cases involving acid mine drainage. In 1989, Joseph Sax described *Sanderson* as "perhaps infamous" and as evidence of a bygone era in environmental law. The legislature adopted this view in 1965 when it found that "mine drainage is the major cause of stream pollution in Pennsylvania and is doing immense damage," and therefore subjected the industry to the Clean Streams Law. The state attorney general quickly formed an Environmental Strike Force that relied on the new law to persuade the state supreme court to force the Barnes and Tucker Coal Company to clean up the acid mine drainage caused by its mine along the West Branch. In the course of the company's two appeals, the court overruled *Sanderson*, acknowledged the public's interest in clean streams as expressed in the state constitution, and rejected the company's argument that the mandated cleanup constituted an unconstitutional taking of its property.[50]

The new law did little to clean up the acid mine drainage that had already polluted the Susquehanna. Even the Barnes and Tucker Coal Company avoided liability when it went bankrupt in 2001. Once again, environmental restoration became a question of money. The SRBC has studied several sites within the basin to determine how the acid mine drainage can be eliminated. It announced a remediation strategy for the West Branch in 2006, but it acknowledged that "it will take decades at current funding levels until many of the problem areas are addressed." The Abandoned Mine Reclamation Fund, established by Congress in the Surface Mining Control and Reclamation Act of 1977, has never received enough money to pay for the thousands of sites clamoring for attention nationwide. Lacking federal funds, PADEP has allowed operators to clean up acid mine drainage instead of paying civil penalties, and it encourages "government financed construction contracts" that allow a company to mine and sell coal from an abandoned site and then reclaim it. Trout Unlimited has contributed significant resources, too, in the hope that the elimination of acid mine drainage will restore sport fishing in affected waters.[51]

Mining was not the only industry whose activities polluted the Susquehanna River. Susan Stranahan describes how the country's first steel mills, tanneries, slaughterhouses, food producers, and factories "discharged pickling liquors, dyes, oils, cyanide, phenols . . . acids," and other wastes into the river. The most notorious toxic spill into the Susquehanna River, and the one that most influenced the law, centers on a small hole in the ground behind a gas station several miles from the river in Pittston, just north of Wilkes-Barre. The hole had been drilled to ventilate the coal mines that operated underneath the gas station during the middle of the twentieth century. Years passed, and in 1977 the owners of the Hi-Way Auto Service Station decided to earn some extra cash by allowing various liquid waste transport companies to dump wastes down the bore hole. What they did not know was that the hole connected to a series of old mining drainage tunnels that honeycombed the area underground, including an outflow from the Butler Mine Tunnel into the Susquehanna River three and a half miles away. When oil appeared in the river in 1979, the state police used a dye test that traced the release to the bore hole at the gas station. The owners of the station were criminally prosecuted and convicted of violating the Clean Streams Law, creating a public nuisance, and risking catastrophe. The Pennsylvania Supreme Court affirmed the convictions, including the application of the rare risking catastrophe charge, because "massive discharge of dangerous wastes into the Susquehanna River which, in spite of immediate detection and vast and expeditious containment measures, within two days, contaminated the water way for some 60 miles downstream is conduct that risks a catastrophe." Meanwhile, the EPA and PADEP installed large booms to clean up 160,000 gallons of oil containing thirteen thousand pounds of volatile organic compounds. State officials monitored the site and believed that the problem had been contained. Then, in 1985, heavy rain from Hurricane Gloria flushed the tunnels again, causing 100,000 gallons of waste oil to travel through the Butler Mine Tunnel, into the Susquehanna, and thirty-five miles downstream.[52]

The EPA then began the process of addressing the site pursuant to CERCLA, identifying twenty-five potentially responsible parties (PRPs) whose operation of the gas station or whose wastes were disposed there rendered them liable for the cleanup costs under CERCLA's liability scheme. Seventeen of those PRPs agreed to fund an investigation of the site. The investigation found several hazardous substances, including cyanide, and estimated that several million gallons of oil had been disposed via the bore hole. CERCLA states a preference for removing and

The filled-in bore hole behind the Hi-Way Auto Service Station in Pittston, Pennsylvania.

treating hazardous wastes, but the EPA concluded that there was no single pool of oil or toxic substances that could be pumped out and removed because the oil had adhered to the rocks and gravel in the collapsed mine workings. Instead, the agency's preferred remedy was to continually monitor how much water flows from the tunnel and to be prepared to immediately deploy a river response system equipped with booms, oil skimmers, and barges to prevent any oil from getting far downstream. That solution did not please area residents, who hoped that all of the contamination would be removed. Nonetheless, the EPA issued its Record of Decision in

1996, and it worked with the PRPs on implementing the selected remedial action. The system was successfully tested in 2007. The EPA plans to monitor the area until around 2017, and if there are no further releases, the agency might be able to delist it.

All of this cost the EPA about $1.3 million, so the agency used CER-CLA's liability provisions to seek to recover those costs from the PRPs. CERCLA eschews traditional tort law standards of liability and instead specifies four categories of statutorily responsible parties: the current owners and operators of the site, past owners and operators at the time that wastes were disposed, those who generated the wastes or arranged to ship them there, and those who transported the wastes to the site. The EPA targeted the companies that generated the hazardous wastes that ended up in the Butler Mine Tunnel. Many of those companies had contracted with waste disposal firms owned by Russell Mahler that "collected the liquid wastes from numerous industrial facilities located in the northeastern United States and, in total, disposed of approximately 2,000,000 gallons of oily wastes containing hazardous substances through the Borehole." Eighteen companies and the Department of Defense (whose wastes reached the site as well) settled with the EPA and agreed to pay $828,500 of the cleanup costs, but Alcan Aluminum held out. It manufactured aluminum products in Oswego, New York, from the 1960s through the 1980s, and its production process yielded fragments of various metals that remained in the cooling emulsion even after it was filtered. Alcan employed Mahler's companies to dispose of two million gallons of used emulsion, and about thirty-five thousand of those gallons were dumped down the bore hole. When the EPA approached Alcan, it insisted that it should not be held liable under CERCLA for two reasons: (1) its wastes fell within CERCLA's petroleum exclusion, which specifies that oil is not a hazardous waste for purposes of the statute, and (2) "the level of hazardous substances in its emulsion was below that which naturally occurs and thus could not have contributed to the environmental injury" to the Susquehanna River. The EPA disagreed with those legal arguments and sought to hold Alcan jointly and severally liable for the balance of the cleanup costs. The district court ruled for the EPA, so Alcan appealed to the U.S. Court of Appeals for the Third Circuit.[53]

The Third Circuit quickly rejected Alcan's argument about the petroleum exclusion clause, noting that the company admittedly added hazardous substances to the oily emulsion. The court's response to Alcan's second argument was more nuanced. It recognized that Alcan satisfied the statutory criteria for a responsible party, that CERCLA does not require a demonstration that the wastes caused any environmental harm, and that the law authorized the imposition of joint and several liability—that is, any defendant could be required to pay for the entire cleanup. The court added, however, that Alcan could avoid joint and several liability if its harm was divisible from the harms attributable to the other defendants. Citing the guidance provided by the *Restatement of Torts* concerning the apportionment of harms, the court remanded the case to the district court "to determine whether there is a reasonable basis for limiting Alcan's liability based on its personal contribution to the harm to the Susquehanna River." The court further held that Alcan could escape all liability if it was able to provide that its "emulsion did not or could not, when mixed with other hazardous wastes, contribute to the release and the resultant response costs." In so ruling, the Third Circuit introduced three new ideas to the existing CERCLA jurisprudence: (1) the fact that hazardous wastes are commingled does not necessarily mean that the harm is indivisible, (2) apportionment may be used to avoid joint and several liability, and (3) no liability attaches to the disposal of wastes that do not contribute to the cleanup costs. But Alcan was unable to take advantage of them. On remand, the district court held that Alcan's used emulsion contributed to the cleanup costs, whether or not the individual constituents of the emulsion did so as well, and thus the court ordered the company to pay the $474,000 balance of the EPA's response costs. The district court later dismissed Alcan's separate effort to obtain "equitable contribution" from the settling defendants, finding that their settlement with the EPA protected them from further liability.[54]

Another event occurred while the Butler Mine saga unfolded that would influence environmental law much more. The largest of the thousands of islands located in the Susquehanna River is three miles long and located just ten miles south of Harrisburg, Pennsylvania. Construction of a nuclear power plant on Three Mile Island (TMI) began in 1967, and its first unit began commercial operation in 1974, with a second unit following in December 1978. The plant's opening "did not incite any large demonstrations, prompt lengthy legal proceedings, or generate a great deal of interest even in central Pennsylvania." TMI is one of seven nuclear power plants located along the Susquehanna River, which provides the 4.1 billion gallons of cooling water those nuclear reactors need every day. That water was central to the accident that occurred in Unit 2 on the morning of March 28, 1979, when the reactor was unknowingly deprived of water and began to melt. The problem was arrested and a disaster avoided, and subsequent studies indicate that neither the Susquehanna River nor those living near it suffered lasting physical harms. But the law soon got involved in cleaning up the contamination and responding to concerns about what could have happened. Plans to vent krypton-85 from the reactor to allow cleanup crews to access the damaged core faced public opposition and a federal lawsuit. The Nuclear Regulatory Commission (NRC) approved the venting, and it occurred during the summer of 1980. Nonetheless, the D.C. Circuit ruled in November 1980 that the NRC should have held a public hearing before allowing the venting, but the Supreme Court stayed that decision until Congress amended the law to authorize what the NRC had done. Likewise, "the simplest solution" for the 2.8 million gallons of water that was involved in the accident but had since been purified "would have been to dilute it and then discharge it into the Susquehanna River, but political and public opposition was so strong to this approach that it was abandoned in favor of gradual evaporation into the atmosphere." A 1980 settlement of the City of Lancaster's lawsuit against the NRC blocked the release of "accident-generated water" into the river. Perhaps the greatest concerns about the accident were psychological, and psychologists "who analyzed the situation felt that there was now an absolute distrust of government at all levels." Opponents of the reopening of TMI's Unit 1—which had not experienced any problems during the accident and had been closed since then—faulted the NRC for failing to consider the fears local residents suffered concerning the plant. Their complaints reached the Supreme Court, which unanimously held that although psychological concerns can be evaluated under the National Environmental Policy Act, worries about the risk of another accident would stretch the environmental impact process too far.[55]

The legal challenges to the cleanup were accompanied by lawsuits seeking compensation for various ailments that were allegedly caused by the accident. That litigation occupied the federal courts for two decades, culminating in a 1999 Third Circuit decision affirming a trial court ruling that the plaintiffs were unable to demonstrate that they had developed abnormal tissue growths because of exposure to radiation from TMI. Earlier, the operator of TMI settled with 280 area residents who claimed that they had been injured by the accident, too. The accident prompted numerous changes to the regulation of the nuclear power industry. Most tellingly, public opposition and economic concerns about nuclear power have prevented any new nuclear facilities from being built in the United States since the TMI accident. Susan Stranahan won a Pulitzer Prize for her reporting on TMI, and she concludes in her book: "The Susquehanna has survived every assault human beings have inflicted to date, but they still hold in their hands the capacity to render a whole region uninhabitable. All that is required are a few careless mistakes, and humans have clearly demonstrated themselves quite capable of that."[56]

FROM THE LAND TO THE RIVER

The Susquehanna River is inevitably affected by the use of the land around it. In New York, "the major environmental stressors in the Susquehanna Basin are related to agriculture, stream corridor manipulation, streambank erosion, roadside ditch maintenance, urban sprawl, and forest fragmentation." All of these stressors involve land use. Sediment, nutrients, and debris run off of the land and into the river, where they harm water quality, wildlife habitat, and scenic views. The greatest concern in recent years has not been with the effect on the Susquehanna River as such, but rather on the Chesapeake Bay into which the river flows.[57]

The Susquehanna provides nearly half of the freshwater of the bay. As the water quality of the bay worsened, the affected jurisdictions looked upstream as part of their efforts to remedy the problem. The governors of Maryland, Pennsylvania, and Virginia, along with the mayor of the District of Columbia and the administrator of the EPA, entered into the first Chesapeake Bay Agreement in 1983. The latest agreement, reached in 2000, commits the parties to "work with local governments, community groups and watershed organizations to develop and implement locally supported watershed management plants in two thirds of the Bay watershed" by 2010. The agreement also calls to "strengthen partnerships" with New York (as well as Delaware and West Virginia, which, like Virginia and the District of Columbia, are within the Chesapeake Bay watershed but not the Susquehanna River basin). The agreements established the Chesapeake Bay Commission, consisting of twenty-one legislators, governors, officials, and private citizens from Maryland, Pennsylvania, and Virginia who are charged with implementing the Chesapeake Bay Program that is designed to accomplish the goals of the agreements.[58]

The Chesapeake Bay Program relies on "tributary strategies" prepared for each of the thirty-six primary tributaries to the bay. The strategies crafted by Pennsylvania and New York focus almost exclusively on the Susquehanna River and its own tributaries. The May 2007 draft of New York's strategy contains ninety-two pages of plans for reducing pollution and protecting the water in the river. Prepared by the New York State Department of Conservation in partnership with the Upper Susquehanna Coalition, the strategy outlines the actions that need to be taken by managers of farms, forests, sewage-treatment plants, septic systems, and urban stormwater runoff to achieve the state's commitments in the agreement. "The overall objective," states the strategy, "is to seek the greatest amount of cost-effective reduction from each source category." Pennsylvania has already set aside the 20 percent of land within the watershed as it promised in the 2000 agreement, and the state is now working to achieve its promised reductions in nutrient and sediment runoff. Maryland is managing stormwater runoff, septic systems, and sprawl as part of its strategy. All of this is being done in service of the Chesapeake Bay, rather than the Susquehanna River itself. Indeed, Jack Brubaker complained that "Pennsylvania's Susquehanna has all but lost its own identity and the river in New York has become an afterthought."[59]

The federal Clean Water Act provides another motivation for reducing runoff into the Susquehanna River. Section 303 of the act requires each state to determine water-quality standards based on the quality of water that is needed to support the uses of the water. Drinking water, for example, demands the highest purity; industrial water use can proceed with somewhat less stringent standards. Once a state sets the water-quality standards, then it must calculate the total maximum daily load (TMDL) of each pollutant that the water body can tolerate while satisfying the standards, and the state must allocate that TMDL among the sources of that pollutant. TMDLs must be developed for bodies of water that will not achieve the water-quality standards solely on the basis of the technology-based requirements of the Clean Water Act's NPDES regulation of point sources. The TMDL process encompasses so-called nonpoint sources of pollution (typically runoff from farms and roads) as well as the point sources (including factories and treatment plants) that are already regulated under the NPDES program. TMDLs have evolved slowly, though, because of both the need to identify which waters are still impaired even after the application of the NPDES requirements and the resistance from farmers, highway managers, and other entities who are not as used to federal environmental regulation of their activities. A 2002 study indicated that 37 percent of the impairment of Pennsylvania's waters was attributable to agriculture, 37 percent to acid mine drainage, and 16 percent to urban runoff. Some environmental organizations sued the EPA for not forcing Pennsylvania to draft its TMDLs, and the settlement of that lawsuit in 1997 established a schedule for the completion of all of the TMDLs by 2009. Pennsylvania is on track to satisfy that schedule, and New York should complete its TMDLs by 2010. The SRBC has developed TMDLs for fifty watersheds within the Susquehanna River basin since 2000, and the SRBC began working with Maryland to help with its TMDLs in 2006.

The targets of the tributary strategies and the TMDLs are often the same. Nutrients produced by agricultural operations are the primary focus. Nitrogen and phosphorus occur naturally, but they result in eutrophication when released in larger quantities. The quantities of nutrients are prodigious in Lancaster County, Pennsylvania, whose western border is the Susquehanna River and which enjoys some of the most productive farmland in the country. A 2006 study conducted by the Chesapeake Bay Foundation (CBF) observed that Pennsylvania "administers a host of agricultural programs to address environmental protection, risk management, research, farmland preservation, farm transition, and other goals." In 1993, for example, the state enacted a Nutrient Management Law that requires large farms to develop and implement a nutrient management plan; the resulting regulations convinced the state's Farm Bureau that the law represented "the right way to clean up ground and surface water." But the CBF study also reported that funding was not sufficient for Pennsylvania's agricultural conservation programs, so many farmers "have become so discouraged with the process and wait time that they no longer apply to the programs." In 2007, the state legislature enacted the Resource Enhancement and Protection Act, which provides up to $10 million annually in transferable tax credits to farmers and businesses who develop and implement conservation projects that reduce erosion, control sediment, or manage nutrients. Also since 2007,

PADEP has authorized the voluntary trading of nutrient and sediment reduction credits within the Susquehanna basin, following an approach that is gaining popularity in responding to pollution problems such as acid rain and climate change.[60]

The three states have also employed "forested buffers" to naturally absorb nutrients that would otherwise run off into the Susquehanna. The CBF reports that the presence of trees serving as a buffer between the river and the rest of the landscape can reduce the amount of nitrogen entering a river by as much as 70 percent. Forested buffers also provide habitat for wildlife, prevent erosion, and keep waters at the cooler temperatures preferred by many native fish. Maryland and Pennsylvania support forested buffers with their Stream ReLeaf programs, which provide economic incentives for the establishment or maintenance of buffers of at least one hundred feet along designated waters. Maryland, Pennsylvania, and New York all rely on funding provided by the Department of Agriculture's Conservation Reserve Enhancement Program, which has paid farmers to plant trees to prevent erosion since the program's establishment in 1985. The Upper Susquehanna Coalition secured more funds from the EPA in 2006 to buffer eleven acres and thus protect fifty-three hundred feet of streams, three ponds, and a wetland.[61]

The runoff of sediment affects the Susquehanna, too. A writer lamented in 1753 that "now the country is clear'd, the rain as fast as it falls is hurried into the rivers and washes away the earth and soil of our naked springs." Each of the three states in the Susquehanna River basin has employed their tributary strategy to confront the addition of sediment to the river. My first experience with Pennsylvania's efforts occurred when, as an attorney in the Justice Department, I represented the U.S. Postal Service in a case involving the construction of a new postal distribution facility near Harrisburg. Pennsylvania's Department of Environmental Resources complained that the Postal Service had failed to comply with terms in its Clean Streams Law permit to ensure that the construction process would not cause sediment to go into a tributary of the Susquehanna. The Postal Service asserted federal sovereign immunity from suit by a state. It won in the district court, but the Third Circuit, in an opinion written by Judge (now Justice) Samuel Alito, held that the Postal Service's statutory willingness to "sue and be sued" rendered it susceptible to the department's demand for civil penalties for violating the state law permit.[62]

State and municipal land use regulation is the leading alternative to environmental law as a means of controlling the runoff of pollutants into the Susquehanna River. There is little population growth along much of the river, so in those areas the regulation of land use within the river basin is simply a matter of prioritizing the activities that have long occurred next to it. Only in the lower part of the basin is the human population expanding. People are commuting from communities along the Susquehanna in Maryland and Pennsylvania to the previously distant cities of Baltimore, Washington, and Philadelphia.

Maryland has been especially aggressive in regulating land use. In 1984, the state enacted a Critical Area Act that regulates land use within one thousand feet of the Susquehanna River (as well as other bodies of water). The act channels development to "intensely developed areas," allows some development in "limited development areas," and imposes strict limits on development within "resource conservation areas." The state commission charged with overseeing the act described it in a recent guide prepared for the many citizens who are affected by the law, either because they own property within an affected area or because they do business with those who do: "Like any law or regulation directed toward 'solving' a complicated problem, the Critical Area Law and Criteria are a comprehensive, complex, and detailed body of legislation and regulations." Another study, though, worries that variances have been granted to 76 percent of the landowners who sought to develop within an area protected by Maryland's act.[63]

The example of Harford County is illustrative. The county borders the western bank of the Susquehanna River from the Pennsylvania border to the Chesapeake Bay. Its history features the namesake Henry Harford (the illegitimate son of the Sixth Baron Baltimore) and the birthplace of John Wilkes Booth. Much of the land has been used for farming, though the army's Aberdeen Proving Ground is the largest employer in the county. The military facility is poised to grow by 50 percent as other military bases around the country are closed, and in recent years the county has experienced suburban sprawl reaching northeast from Baltimore. There are lots of new office parks and a number of big residential complexes between I-95 and downtown Havre de Grace; the county officials I interviewed characterized the northwestern part of the county as "McMansion heaven." The Susquehanna River is ignored in much of this development, save as an obstacle that must be crossed on one of the county's few bridges.

The county's master plan, however, views the river as one of the "valuable assets that contribute to the quality of life of its residents," and the plan commits to protect the quality and quantity of the county's water resources. The state Critical Area Act prevents most development next to the river, and the county requires a seventy-five-foot buffer for development near smaller streams and wetlands. The county also boasts of its agricultural land preservation plan, noting that easements had been placed upon nearly forty thousand acres thanks to the county's "use of innovative funding sources, payment options, and a timely manner of settlement." In response, the county has created a development envelope that looks like an inverted T, with the base running west to east along I-95 and a corridor jutting north to the county seat of Bel Air. In those areas— and only those areas—the county provides water, sewer, and other services. And if the school districts are closed to more students, which many are, then the county cannot approve further development.[64]

Whether these efforts will succeed remains to be seen. Maryland might not be able to meet its load allocations because so many people are moving into the Susquehanna River basin there. James Curatalo opined that the only solution may be to establish a fixed population limit within the watershed, "but that's a philosophical, religious thing" that the public may not accept. Meanwhile, Maryland's restrictive sprawl regulation has driven growth across the border into Pennsylvania, where the conversion of farmland to suburban development has become the biggest issue affecting the river. Pennsylvania ranks forty-eighth in the nation in population growth but fifth in the rate of land development. A CBF report thus warned that "there may be no farms, no woodlands or natural areas—just one contiguous sea of subdivisions and strip malls." It then offered a suite of recommendations to prevent that from happening, including zoning revisions that protect open space and "low impact developments" that manage rainfall and return it gradually to the nearest streams.[65]

THE TWENTY-FIRST-CENTURY SUSQUEHANNA RIVER

People have put the Susquehanna River to innumerable uses during the past few centuries. Some of those uses, such as hydroelectric power and waste disposal, will continue. Other former uses may return, for example, if efforts to restore shad to the river are successful. New uses will undoubtedly arise as well; no one could have anticipated the need for cooling nuclear reactors back in the days when logs were floated down the river. These uses of the river are just that: the ways in which people seek to *use* the river for their own purposes. Another emerging movement challenges the presumption of human dominance of rivers and seeks to return the Susquehanna River to its "natural" state. Laws that allow for human assistance—styled ecosystem management—would be necessary to do this. For example, the Comprehensive Wildlife Conservation Strategy for New York recommends "a variety of protection mechanisms such as easements, cooperative agreements, fee title acquisition, donations, development rights acquisition, and others. The type of protection should be determined by the interested parties based on their means and conservation goals."[66]

For all the historical twists and turns of the Susquehanna River's management, the future of that management is relatively easy to identify. It will depend on three things. First, it will depend on public attitudes toward the river. In its failed effort to designate part of the Susquehanna as a scenic river, PADEP "learned a lesson: If citizens who live along the river do not support protective status, no amount of planning by state government or regional environmental associations will produce more than a paper plan." In Wilkes-Barre, many people have a perverse feeling about the river because it was sterile for so long. Sara Dueling of American Rivers suggests that people dump things in the river because they think "that's all it's for"; others view the river as "a killer" that took the lives of several firefighters at a dam on the river a few years ago. In Maryland's Calvert County, county officials say that "the majority of the people don't even know that it exists." The only time that you hear about it "is as a barrier to commerce and growth." All along the river, buildings face the street, not the river. As Broome County's Chip McElwee told me, "We have turned our backs on the rivers out here." To change those attitudes, Professor Brian Mangan of King's College in Wilkes-Barre has created a course to rebut the perception some people have that the river is a sewer or an "an enemy that rises up periodically to smite them." The course instead tries "to convince them that it's an important natural resource that they need to embrace and protect." A tour of the sewage plant gives people "a renewed appreciation that this stuff doesn't just magically disappear, and that ultimately it ends up in the Susquehanna."[67]

A bill introduced by Pennsylvania's Senator Robert P. Casey offers further evidence of changing attitudes toward the river. The bill finds that "for centuries, the Susquehanna River has been an important corridor of culture and commerce for the United States, playing key roles as a major fishery, transportation artery, power generator, and place for outdoor recreation." It then notes that "numerous sites of significance to the heritage of the United States are located" in the lower Susquehanna River corridor, including the "community where the Continental Congress adopted the Articles of Confederation," "the exceptional beauty and rich cultural resources of the Susquehanna River Gorge," and "many thriving examples of the nationally significant industrial and agricultural heritage of the region." The purpose of these recitals is to justify the establishment of a Susquehanna Gateway National Heritage Area whose managers would be charged with "increasing public awareness of and appreciation for the natural, historic, and cultural resources of the Heritage Area."[68]

The future management of the Susquehanna River will also depend on the many governmental jurisdictions involved. For example, there are sixty local governments in Lancaster County, which is one of forty-three Pennsylvania counties within the Susquehanna River basin. Those local governments exercise substantial authority in Pennsylvania and New York, especially with respect to land use decisions. The expertise of local government officials varies. As Sara Dueling explains, "there are communities that do a fabulous job of caring for their resource, and you hate to lose that ability." On the other hand, an official in one environmental organization recounted walking into a meeting where the one commissioner was knitting. And whatever the competence of the individual officials, Dueling explained to me that "you can't manage a river in three- or four-mile segments for a 450-mile river system and have anything that actually functions."

State officials in Pennsylvania pushed hard for the consolidation of local governments in the aftermath of Hurricane Agnes, but nothing happened. Instead, the SRBC is working within the status quo by assisting the local governments that are managing the Susquehanna River. The SRBC's scientific experts identify the open space that is critical for water, so that local officials "can then make informed decisions" and zone the land accordingly. The SRBC's Tom Beauduy reports that the officials "gobble up that information" because "they're all trying to make the right decisions." For its part, the SRBC completed its most recent comprehensive plan in December 2008 and identified twelve "areas of special interest" for upcoming management decisions: (1) abandoned mine drainage; (2) climate change; (3) consumptive use mitigation; (4) drought coordination; (5) economic development, recreation, and other public values; (6) emerging contaminants; (7) energy production; (8) flood forecast and warning; (9) invasive species; (10) migratory fish restoration; (11) potentially stressed areas and water challenged areas; and (12) water and wastewater infrastructure.[69]

Finally, the management of the Susquehanna River will depend on money. Laws authorizing and appropriating governmental funds are more important to the Susquehanna than laws prescribing or proscribing conduct. The ability to improve the river's flood warning system, to clean up acid mine drainage, to modernize sewage-treatment facilities, to remove old dams, and to restore shad to the river depends more on available sources of funds than the regulation of people's conduct. There is never enough money to satisfy all of those desires, which is hardly surprising given the competing interests that governmental appropriators, businesses, and private organizations must consider as well.

Funding has been complicated, though, by the recent controversy regarding earmarks. "We live on earmarks," says James Curatalo, citing the $500,000 congressional appropriation that Representative Maurice Hinchley obtained for the FWS to build wetlands in New York. After Congress overrode President Bush's 2007 veto of the Water Resources Development Act, New York's two senators championed the $30 million that the law provided for efforts to improve the Susquehanna watershed, while Pennsylvania's two senators boasted of the $2 million appropriation for the Susquehanna River Basin Flood System. Dutch Ruppersberger, who represents part of Maryland's Harford County and serves on the House Appropriations Committee, insists that "so-called earmarks are nothing more than targeted spending on specific projects" whose al-

ternative is leaving "the decisions on how to spend money" "to government bureaucrats instead of elected officials." Or, as Curatalo puts it,
"earmarks are bad to pay for the cheese museum, but not when you're
doing something good." But earmark opponents object that such individual legislative spending provisions both short-circuit public debate
about the worthiness of a project and result in more governmental money
being spent.[70]

The cycle resumed in 2009 as the SRBC boasted about Congress
restoring a $1 million annual appropriation that the commission had
received from its establishment in 1971 until 1998. In 1995, the Heritage Foundation targeted the SRBC as providing regional rather than
national benefits, and thus "the responsibility for funding and management should be turned over to the contiguous states." Congress agreed
until 2009, when Representative Tim Holden (who represents a district
stretching east from Harrisburg) persuaded Congress to resume the ap-
propriation because of the SRBC's efforts "to safeguard the residents of
the Susquehanna River Basin, and protect the river itself." More point-
edly, and surprisingly for a governmental agency, the SRBC blamed its
fundless interlude on "misinformation issued by a partisan, Washington-
based think tank."[71]

The debate about earmarks and funding echoes the longstanding
debates about the management of the Susquehanna River. Earmarks
raise questions of how to spend money and who should decide. The multiple public and private actors involved in making decisions about the
Susquehanna argue about the same things: how should the river be managed, and who should decide. Those argument are likely to continue even
as we celebrate the four hundredth anniversary of the river's "discovery"
by John Smith.

CHAPTER FIVE

Lights Out

ALAMOGORDO, NEW MEXICO

THE CITY SNUCK UP ON ME. I was approaching from the north, driving through the New Mexican desert around twilight on a June evening, but few city lights were visible amidst the barren landscape. Actually, that is the whole point. I was visiting Alamogordo because it is reputed to have the most stringent light pollution law in the United States. Once there, I discovered that the area around Alamogordo has long been an ecotourist destination that presents several novel legal questions, even questions of international law.

Alamogordo is a city of about thirty-five hundred people located in southern New Mexico. Days are hot and bright, with an average temperature in the nineties during the summer and 350 days of sunshine. The city sits in the Tularosa Basin at the northern end of the vast Chihuahuan Desert, most of which is located in Mexico. The Sacramento Mountains and the San Andres Mountains bracket the basin to the east and west, respectively. Alamogordo began as the late-nineteenth-century version of a planned community. Before then, various unplanned human communities wandered through the region for centuries, including a pueblo that was located within today's city limits. The Apaches arrived in the area around 1500. Spain claimed the land in 1598, though it never really attempted to exercise control over it. Sovereignty shifted to Mexico in 1821 and then to the United States thanks to the resolution of the

Mexican War by the Treaty of Guadalupe Hidalgo in 1848. Ranchers, miners, and farmers moved into the land from Texas after the Civil War, and not coincidentally, the natives were forced to the Mescalero Apache Reservation just north of Alamogordo by an executive order signed by President Ulysses S. Grant in 1873. Ranching—and overgrazing—soon replaced shoulder-high grama grass with mesquite trees.

The arrival of the railroad a few decades later resulted in the town's establishment. "Alamogordo was built as a part of a speculation scheme," as one writer put it. The Territory of New Mexico received little of the assistance that Congress had provided to encourage the construction of railroads in many other parts of the West, so a series of private investors, including Jay Gould, considered but ultimately declined to pursue a railroad for southern New Mexico. Then, in 1896, Gould sold his interests in the area to Charles Bishop Eddy, a New York entrepreneur who previously developed the town of Eddy (now known as Carlsbad) in Eddy County in southeastern New Mexico. Eddy arranged to build the El Paso and Northeastern Railroad to connect the Southern Pacific Railroad as it passed through El Paso with the Rock Island Railroad and the mines of northern New Mexico. He did so in part thanks to congressional legislation confirming the railroad's right-of-way and approving logging on federal lands located in territories, not just in states. The railroad reached the site of Alamogordo in June 1898, and the city was born fourteen years before New Mexico became a state. Eddy created the Alamogordo Improvement Company to divide the land into plats to be sold to interested residents and businesses. According to one local historian, "Eddy planned a community which was to feature large, wide thoroughfares and irrigation ditches lined with trees," especially the large cottonwoods that gave the city its Spanish name. The city also boasted of having electric lights within one year of its founding.[1]

Alamogordo first sold itself as a destination for those seeking a healthy climate and took advantage of its surroundings to attract tourists as early as the beginning of the twentieth century. The attack on Pearl Harbor provided the next jolt to the city's improvement (as it did for Adak Island, the subject of Chapter 1). The head of the city's Chamber of Commerce later recalled, "as soon as I got over the shock of the news I went to the Western Union Office and sent a telegram to our U.S. Senator Dennis Chavez and asked him who would be in charge of locating bases in our part of the country." That resourcefulness was rewarded with the construction of Alamogordo Army Air Field in February 1942. The sparsely populated, flat, desert land became attractive for all kinds of advanced or secret military activities. The primary mission of the initial airfield was to train heavy bomber crews. The military's most famous activity occurred on July 16, 1945, when the world's first atomic bomb was exploded at the Trinity Site about fifty miles northwest of Alamogordo. The Trinity Site is now within the White Sands Missile Range and is open to the public once each year. The airfield changed names and responsibilities after the war, and Holloman Air Force Base and the White Sands Missile Range now make the military the largest employer in the area. All of these activities earned the city of Alamogordo several nicknames, including Atomic City and Rocket City, and the city has hosted the International Space Hall of Fame since the 1970s. Presumably, the city is less fond of the nickname suggested by one travel guide writer who "came to call it 'Alamegeddin,' mostly because the town itself is fairly desolate without many amenities."[2]

Alamogordo is the largest city in Otero County. In fact, Tularosa (just north of Alamogordo) and Cloudcroft (in the mountains east of Alamogordo) are the only other incorporated cities in the county. Otero is the twenty-sixth largest county in the United States in area, with more than 80 percent of that land owned by the federal government. The Lincoln National Forest, the White Sands National Monument, the White Sands Missile Range, and the army's Fort Bliss are the most prominent federal landholdings within the county. The Alamogordo Chamber of Commerce boasts that the city's cost of living is low, that it is often rated "as one of America's most healthful cities," and that it has yet to experience any earthquakes, riots, tornadoes, smog, hurricanes, tidal waves, or mudslides. The city's 2007 annual report is adorned with photos showing "nothing but blue skies," though there is no mention of its famous dark skies.[3]

My examination of the law's effect on Alamogordo begins with the area just outside of the city. Lincoln National Forest raises several issues of wildlife protection and fire management that are common among federal forest lands. The White Sands National Monument is unique both geologically (thanks to the stunning white gypsum sand dunes) and legally (as an area that was passed over for a national park at the beginning of the twentieth century suddenly confronts a debate over international recognition at the beginning of the twenty-first century). I then consider the values of dark skies, how they are threatened by light pollution, and Alamogordo's atypical responses to its pollution problem. I conclude by imagining how Alamogordo's future growth could moot its dark skies efforts and affect the protected lands around the city.

EARLY ECOTOURISM

The railroad sustained Alamogordo's economy for the first third of the twentieth century. Eventually, the prominence of the railroad declined with the emergence of the automobile, so the city turned elsewhere for its economic development. It turned first to tourism—indeed, what we would describe today as ecotourism—emphasizing the more notable features of the natural environment that lie on either side of the city.

Alamogordo hosts the headquarters of the Lincoln National Forest, best known as the home of Smokey the Bear. The Sacramento Mountains rise quickly from Alamogordo's 4,350-foot elevation, reaching as high as 12,000 feet just east of the city. The arrival of the railroad in Alamogordo made the timber in the mountains accessible to businesses for the first time. Shortly before that, Congress attached the Forest Reserve Act of 1891 as a rider to an appropriations bill. That act authorized the president to withdraw federal lands from the general public domain and to manage them as forest reserves. Congress expanded that law with the Forest Service Organic Act of 1897, which directed that the purpose of national forests is "to improve and protect the forest within the boundaries, or for the purposes of securing favorable water flows, and to furnish a continuous supply of timber for the use and necessities of citizens of the United States." President Theodore Roosevelt exercised his authority under that law to establish the Lincoln Forest Reserve in July 1902, less than a year after he took office. Between 1902 and 1917, the forest reserve changed dimensions and names several times. The forest survived an effort by local leaders to return the land to the public domain in 1913, and the land remained a national forest after a failed attempt to convert it into a national park. Finally, the Lincoln National Forest emerged in 1917. It is now divided into three sections, with the Sacramento District located just east of Alamogordo. The Forest Service boasts of camping, fishing, hiking, skiing, spelunking, and scenic and wilderness opportunities that abound in the forest, and a recreational website describes the forest as "a recreational mecca."[4]

The forest is managed pursuant to a 1986 plan that is due to be updated in 2010. Frank Martinez, the public affairs officer for the forest, told me that he expects the next plan to focus on the overall desired character of the landscape rather than on the management of the forest sector by sector. When I asked him about the laws governing the forest's management, Martinez handed me a one-thousand-plus-page volume that contained only the most important statutes and regulations related to the use of the forest. The forest confronts a variety of claims concerning grazing and mining, both of which federal law allows in national forests subject to permits containing various conditions. In 2003, for example, the federal district court in New Mexico ruled that the Forest Service had violated the ESA by failing to consult with the FWS concerning the effects of livestock grazing on the threatened Mexican spotted owl. Nobody, though, was pleased with the court's remedy: the environmentalists who brought the suit failed to persuade the court to prohibit all grazing pending compliance with the ESA, while the court denied the ranchers' request to reduce the population of elk that were competing for the limited forage. I will skip many of these management issues here, though, in order to focus on how the law confronts the unintentional destruction of the trees in the forest.[5]

Martinez advises that the most pressing management for the forest is the "wildland-urban interface." In other words, the Forest Service tries to prevent forest fires from burning homes. Fires play a crucial role in the ecosystems of forests and grasslands, yet they are among the most terrifying phenomena that humans confront. Fire was the true terror of the night, as A. Roger Ekirch explains in his wonderful book *At Day's Close* (see more below). So the Forest Service spent much of the twentieth century trying to suppress fires from occurring, spreading, or damaging human habitations. The success of that effort helped to eliminate the rich grasslands of the Tularosa Basin, which had depended on periodic fires to eliminate other competing plants. Fire suppression also resulted in the accumulation of huge amounts of brush, leaves, and dead trees in the forests atop the Sacramento Mountains, all of which could become fuel for a truly awful fire.

The Forest Service began to change its fire policies just a few years ago. In 2000, it announced its National Fire Plan, which outlines a series of steps designed to provide assistance to communities in need of wildfire management. Then, in 2002, the Forest Service launched its Healthy Forests Initiative, which seeks to reduce the amount of fuels that could burn in forest fires. This initiative has been praised for addressing the role of periodic fires in forest ecology and criticized as a surreptitious attempt to permit more logging. It has generated repeated litigation, including a 2007 decision by the federal Ninth Circuit appeals court overturning the categorical exclusion of small fuel reduction projects from the environmental assessment requirements of the National Environmental Policy Act. The third step toward establishing a national fire law is the Healthy Forests Restoration Act of 2003, which Robert Keiter describes as "the first significant federal legislation on the role and management of fire on the public lands." The purpose of the act is "to reduce wildfire risk to communities, municipal water supplies, and other at-risk Federal land through a collaborative process of planning, prioritizing, and implementing hazardous fire reduction projects" and to "protect, restore, and enhance forest ecosystem components," including biodiversity and carbon sequestration. Keiter says that the act shows that "Congress perceives fire primarily as a political rather than ecological matter," and the act has generated its own share of litigation. None of the litigation, though, has involved the Lincoln National Forest. Even so, Forest Guardians (now known as WildEarth Guardians) gave the forest an F grade for its recent fire management planning because it "does not include the best available science, guidelines for cost containment or stipulations for public involvement." The Forest Guardians report added that the Lincoln National Forest spent "$54,000 an acre . . . putting out 36 fires that burned a total of just 25 acres," compared with another forest that spent just $24 per acre putting out its fires. Lincoln was the only national forest in the Southwest not to experience any fires that burned more than one hundred acres in 2005 and 2006.[6]

Both Keiter and Forest Guardians agree that the Forest Service properly concentrates on preventing fires from destroying communities within the wildland-urban interface. In the Lincoln National Forest, that means Cloudcroft. The road east from Alamogordo rises two thousand feet in only sixteen miles until it reaches the little town of Cloudcroft, population 750, which is surrounded on all sides by the national forest. Like Alamogordo, Cloudcroft owes its existence to the railroad, though the train there was extremely difficult to build. A resort capped the "cloud-climbing railroad," and a historian noted that the lodge "was to be lighted by electricity," presumably no mean feat in a remote mountain area at the turn of the twentieth century. The Cloudcroft rail line was abandoned in the 1940s once a highway reached the area, but the resort still flourishes. The Forest Service is working to restore the historic Mexican Canyon Trestle—the largest trestle along the route of the railroad and the only one that is still standing—though the local representative to Congress until 2009, Steven Pearce, cautions that the unlikelihood of securing federal funds requires innovative plans to fund the project.[7]

It stretches the idea of a wildland-*urban* interface to apply it to a town of 750 residents, but that is what is happening. Cloudcroft suffers when the threat of fires causes the Forest Service to close the forest to visitors. Dave Venable, the town's mayor, admitted that a two-month fire closure in the spring of 2008 "did affect tourism, and in the short-term, our economic vitality. However, the closure did ensure the continued long-term economic strength of our mountain community livelihoods and helped maintain our natural resources."[8]

So far, the forests around Cloudcroft have suffered more from insects than fires. Nearly fifteen thousand acres of trees have been killed by four insects: the tussock moth, the spruce budworm, the New Mexico fir looper, and *Nepytia janetae,* a moth that first came to the attention of biologists when it defoliated four thousand acres of spruce and fir trees in Arizona between 1996 and 1999. In response, the Forest Service planned to harvest six thousand acres of dead trees in order to reduce the fuel available for fires. The environmental assessment of the project that the Forest Service prepared pursuant to the National Environmental Policy Act in 2008 observed that "the prospect of a high percentage of dead trees covering thousands of acres of forest would be viewed in the short term as being unnatural and a visual eyesore to the majority of National Forest visitors and users." That perception, in turn, could dramatically affect Cloudcroft's economic reliance on tourism. "Dissatisfaction of current visitors," the assessment continues, "translates into reduced likelihood of future visits and, because recommendations from friends and 'reputation' are the most important factors affecting future visitors' destination choices, this could start a downward spiral that can continue for decades." The assessment further noted that the town's economy was already vulnerable to limited tourism on weekdays, reduced winter visits due to reduced snowfall, and fire closures.[9]

But the elimination of four harmful insects could threaten a more desirable one. The only known home of the Sacramento Mountains checkerspot butterfly is within a six-mile radius of Cloudcroft. In 1999, the Center for Biological Diversity petitioned the FWS for an emergency listing of the butterfly as endangered under the ESA. The agency determined that an emergency listing was not warranted, but it initiated a status review to decide whether a regular listing was warranted. The petitioner went to court to force the FWS to complete its status review, and in September 2001 the agency proposed to list the butterfly as endangered. Cloudcroft's expansion, the Forest Service's improvement of three nearby campgrounds, ORV use, livestock grazing, invasive plant species, insecticide spraying, and the absence of fires to create needed openings in the forest were all cited as threatening the survival of the butterfly. Faced with the likely regulatory consequences that would accompany an ESA listing, local government leaders in Cloudcroft and Otero County joined the Forest Service in preparing a conservation plan that they hoped would stave off the listing of the butterfly. The plan noted that Cloudcroft's expansion plans were more modest than originally suggested, and the town adopted an ordinance to protect the butterfly. Otero County enacted an ordinance restricting subdivisions and development within the butterfly's habitat, as well as committing $100,000 to research and monitoring of the butterfly. And the Forest Service promised to adjust its road construction, grazing, and ORV management in order to preserve the butterfly's habitat. The conservation plan also discussed the effect of climate change on high-altitude insects like the butterfly, but it admitted that "the uncertainty of the short-term and long-term response of the Sacramento Mountains butterfly to predicted climate change creates a situation that local management is incapable of addressing." These steps persuaded the FWS to withdraw its listing proposal because the butterfly was no longer in danger of extinction, thanks to the new regulations. The Forest Service's planned harvesting of dead trees around Cloudcroft avoided meadows and forest openings known to have been occupied by the butterfly. But in 2007, Forest Guardians submitted a new petition to list the butterfly, this time highlighting insecticide spraying as the latest threat. Forest Guardians and the Center for Biological Diversity again filed suit in the federal district court in the District of Columbia (not New Mexico) in January 2008 to force the FWS to act on the latest petition, and the agency complied by deciding in December 2008 that the petition presented sufficient information to justify a full review of the status of the species. Meanwhile, the FWS proceeded to spray 4,419 acres of forest affected by the outbreak of defoliating insects, conducting the operation in November 2007 in order to avoid any effects on the butterfly. And, like Colton's endangered fly described in Chapter 1, the prospect of ESA regulation has elicited scorn for "the annual migration of the environmentalists who infest the Sacramento Mountains and the courts," as well as remarks that the rare butterfly is delicious when "[d]eep fried and dipped in a little honey mustard sauce."[10]

In addition to the insecticide, the Forest Service is spraying an herbicide to manage the vegetation in the forest. The Pinyon/Juniper Opening Maintenance program is designed to create more openings in the forest by removing the juniper and piñon trees and shrubs that have covered the forest, thereby improving forage for mule deer and capacities for water and soil retention. The Lincoln National Forest has treated 10,500 acres of juniper and piñon forests during the past twenty years in an attempt to create more open spaces in the forest. In the words of the project's environmental assessment, it is intended to restore the forest to "a more natural condition" by reversing the "significant anthropogenic and natural changes [that] have occurred to the original Lincoln Forest Reserve presettlement woodland resources" during the past century. This goal of re-creating the "native" forest characterizes much of the management of the Lincoln National Forest today, even as traditional commercial activities such as logging and grazing continue to occur in many parts of the forest.[11]

The area's second ecotourism destination lies just southwest of Alamogordo where there is an amazing assembly of white gypsum sand dunes. The gypsum washed from the nearby mountains into the Tularosa Basin, and the gypsum sediments settled in an ancient lakebed as the water evaporated. Wind piled the gypsum sands into the dunes that now encompass and travel through the area. Twice, *National Geographic* profiled the White Sands: in 1935, when an NPS official extolled "a new national playground" and marveled that "the picture afforded in this expanse of white sand is unlike anything known"; and then again in a 1957 article that reported, "enchantment, disbelief, puzzlement—these are typical reactions among startled visitors to the White Sands."[12]

The White Sands story mimics the story of North Dakota's badlands (see Chapter 3), except that the ending is different. The Apaches and other Native Americans had little use for the desolate area. The end of the nineteenth century began a series of "commercial ventures that never seemed to live up to expectations," as a White Sands historian put it. The alternative idea of creating a national park at the site was first suggested in 1898, the year that Alamogordo was incorporated. The initial park proposal envisioned the Mescalero National Park, which would become "the greatest game preserve" in the nation, betraying a local belief that the same land could serve as a national park and as a hunting ground. The park proposal remained dormant until New Mexico became a state in 1912, and almost immediately its new Senator Albert Fall championed the establishment of a national park next to his ranch. Fall was a native of Kentucky who moved to New Mexico in 1887 in part because the climate promised to prevent a recurrence of his tuberculosis. He was a fixture in state, and then national, politics for the next five decades, beginning as a partisan Democrat and slowly shifting to a partisan Republican just before statehood. Fall served as a state senator, an associate justice on the territory's supreme court, one of the original U.S. senators from the new state of New Mexico, and the secretary of the interior under President Warren Harding. Along with Charles Eddy, Fall pushed to move Alamogordo from Doña Ana County to a new county that they presumably would be better able to control. In 1899, the New Mexico territorial legislature approved a bill to place Alamogordo within a new county that was to have been named Sacramento County, but the need to secure the support of Governor Miguel Otero resulted in the establishment of Otero County instead. Actually, Fall spent little time in Alamogordo, first settling in Las Vegas (New Mexico), and later building an elegant home across the Texas border in El Paso. His prized property was the 750,000-acre Three Rivers Ranch just north of Alamogordo, which he acquired in 1906.[13]

That ranch proved the undoing of both Fall and the proposed national park. The park would have been located next to Fall's ranch, and he could expect to benefit from the influx of tourists. Fall introduced bills to establish a national park including the White Sands during the remainder of his eight years in the Senate, sometimes renaming the proposal Rio Grande National Park, but Congress failed to act. Then Fall became the secretary of the interior upon the election of his former Senate colleague Warren Harding, and Fall began to push for the All-Year National Park—so-called because its southern climate could host visitors year-round, unlike national parks such as Yellowstone and Yosemite. New Mexico's Holm Bursum told his congressional colleagues that the area contained "the finest scenery in the world. There is no place more picturesque, more beautiful, more pleasant." By contrast, Robert Sterling Yard, the head of the National Parks Association, told a House committee that the area lacked "the scenic qualities which the public policy and practice of half a century has established as a requisite to national parkhood." Yard further complained that "a group of small isolated spots, no matter how beautiful, can not make a park in any national park sense." Nonetheless, the Senate approved the park in July 1922, but the House failed to act before Fall resigned in January 1923. It was soon learned that Fall had accepted $200,000 to renovate his ranch from two old friends—Henry Sinclair and Edward Donehy—at about the same time that he approved their applications to drill for oil on the federal government's naval oil reserve at Teapot Dome in Wyoming. Fall was the first presidential cabinet member to be convicted for a crime—bribery—that he committed while serving in office.[14]

Another local entrepreneur assumed the cause once Fall was detained by his prison sentence. Tom Charles moved from Kansas to Alamogordo in 1907 hoping that his wife could recover from tuberculosis. She died one year later, but Charles stayed to become a fixture in the community. He viewed the White Sands as a tourist attraction that could benefit the development of Alamogordo. In 1926, Charles seized upon a suggestion that the White Sands should be designated a national monument. Unlike national parks, national monuments are established by the unilateral action of the president. Congress gave the executive that power when it enacted an Act for the Preservation of American Antiquities—commonly known as the Antiquities Act—in 1906. The primary motivation for the law was the protection of Native American relics in the Southwest, where the new professional anthropologists, independent collectors, and mere looters were competing for the relics. The problem was especially acute in northwestern New Mexico's Chaco Canyon, which was featured in the pleas to Congress to enact the law. On the other hand, many westerners opposed the idea of giving the federal government greater control over the land by removing it from the public domain. The Antiquities Act represented compromise legislation that its sponsor, Representative John Lacey of Iowa, assured would apply only to "Indian remains on the pueblos in the Southwest." He was wrong. The text of the law authorizes the president "in his discretion, to declare by public proclamation historic landmarks, historic and prehistoric structures, and other objects of historic or scientific interest that are situated upon the lands owned or controlled by the Government of the United States to be national monuments, and may reserve as a part thereof parcels of land, the limits of which in all cases shall be confined to the smallest area compatible with proper care and management of the objects to be protected."[15]

Acting upon that authority, presidents ever since then have designated monuments not just for archaeological purposes, but also to protect federal lands that Congress had been unwilling to protect itself. For example, President Clinton designated the Grand Staircase–Escalante National Monument in Utah during the final days of his administration in 2001 in order to preserve lands that Congress had not designated as wilderness under the Wilderness Act. Clinton's actions occurred more than a decade after the influential environmental historian Hal Rothman described the Antiquities Act as "the most important piece of preservation legislation ever enacted by the United States government." Rothman further characterized the act as typical of the progressive legislation championed by Theodore Roosevelt, relying on elite government officials to act in the best interests of the public rather than entrusting decisions to the people themselves. The preference for executive instead of legislative action has haunted many westerners who object to unilateral decisions respecting public lands, such as Clinton's actions in Utah. The courts, however, have uniformly rejected challenges to the establishment of new national monuments as beyond the president's authority.[16]

For many years national monuments were often described as "second-class sites" compared with national parks, though at other times a national monument designation was a way station en route to the creation of a national park. President Herbert Hoover entertained more than one hundred monument proposals during the final year of his administration, including the White Sands. The NPS signed off on the idea in 1932, but the monument was almost derailed by the realization that countless people had asserted mineral claims on the land pursuant to the Mining Act of 1872. That law allows individuals to stake claims upon federal lands, and it bedevils environmentalists to this day. But Charles investigated each claim and found that they had all lapsed, so the monument campaign continued to move forward. Finally, in January 1933, a lame-duck President Hoover exercised his authority under the Antiquities Act to create the White Sands National Monument. He designated four other monuments at the same time (the other four have since graduated to national park status: Black Canyon of the Gunnison, Death Valley, Grand Canyon, and Saguaro). The monument opened for business in 1934 in an opening ceremony that featured a baseball game between two African American teams and a speech by a frail Albert Fall.[17]

Charles became the monument's first superintendent in 1933. By 1935, his new superiors at the NPS had to admonish him not to give away samples of the gypsum to visitors. His management duties were limited to counting the number of visitors and preventing vandalism of the entrance station and picnic tables. The 1957 *National Geographic* story quoted a monument official describing the dunes as "just about indestructible" and asking, "What damage can anyone do?"[18]

More ominous management challenges began to occur once the military started using the adjacent lands for flight practice, bombing practice, and missile testing in the late 1930s. The area's desolation made it attractive to military planners who needed vast amounts of land to conduct dangerous and secret operations (such as testing the first atomic bomb). The area was not entirely desolate, though, and the ranchers who were displaced from the land fought the government for decades to obtain compensation for the loss of their federal grazing rights, unpatented mining claims, and improvements. A federal claims court held in 1988 that any additional payment "would constitute a gratuity." An affected rancher then told Congress that the federal government "cheated us out of our deeded land" and "basically cheated us out of our improvements." New Mexico's congressional delegation supported a proposed White Sands Fair Compensation Act of 1989 that would have established a commission to award $17.5 million to the ranchers on the basis of a finding that "these individuals have not been fully compensated by the United States Government for the loss of their land." The Justice Department objected that the bill would contradict the previous court rulings and establish a bad precedent, while admitting the unpopularity of eminent domain proceedings. Congress declined to pass the bill, and the ranchers did not receive any additional compensation.[19]

The White Sands National Monument struggled with its military neighbors, too. A 1942 executive order issued by President Franklin D. Roosevelt directed the military to consult with the NPS "as to the location of bombing target sites, for the purpose of minimizing the effect of demolition bombing in areas valuable for scientific purposes." Those consultations did little to shield the monument from the rockets, missiles, planes, and bombs that swarmed to the area. Soon, the monument was in the middle of what a local editor called "the world's greatest shooting gallery." By 1946, the secretary of the interior deemed it wise to formalize the relationship by granting the military a special use permit authorizing access to the monument subject to numerous conditions, including notification and compensation requirements. That permit was revised and extended during the following decades, even as the NPS struggled with the military's expansion of its operations. The monument also objected to the overflights of jets from Holloman Air Force Base, typically to no avail. Furthermore, the military's continued presence caused the defeat of proposals during the 1970s to designate wilderness lands within the monument pursuant to the Wilderness Act.[20]

Today, White Sands is one of the largest national monuments, with nearly 150,000 acres. It was also one of the most visited, attracting 437,000 tourists in 2007 (just 20,000 fewer, by the way, than the Theodore Roosevelt National Park). The monument hosts a unique collection of fauna and flora. Evolutionary biologists view the white dunes as a laboratory for studying the response of animals to their unusual white surroundings. For many animals, that response is to turn white themselves. One scientist observed that "animals reported to be lighter-colored in the dunes than in non-dune populations include insects, spiders, scorpions,

Yucca plant at White Sands National Monument.

lizards, mammals, and even toads." The bleached earless lizard is a subspecies that is endemic to the White Sands, as is a subspecies of the plains
pocket mouse that features white fur. None of these species is protected by
federal law, though their rarity makes that a future possibility.[21]

During the 1990s, various federal and state agencies supported the
reintroduction of the endangered Mexican gray wolf into the White
Sands, but officials at the adjacent White Sands Missile Range successfully complained about the attention that an influx of biologists would
bring to their secretive facility. Around 1970, though, the New Mexico
Department of Fish and Game introduced African oryx (also known as
gemsbok) to provide an opportunity for game hunting in the area. The
animals were taken from Africa's Kalahari Desert to the White Sands
Missile Range, where they quickly thrived in the familiar desert conditions. As the NPS observes, mountain lions and coyotes are not nearly as
effective as African lions in controlling the oryx population. The rapidly
expanding herd caused the NPS to have to spend $400,000 in a success-
ful attempt to fence the exotic animals from the monument. Similarly,

the monument is plagued by the tamarisk, or salt cedar, that has outcompeted native plants throughout the Southwest. Tamarisk now occupy five thousand acres of the monument.[22]

The latest controversy has been provoked by a seemingly innocuous proposal to bestow another honor upon the White Sands. In January 2008, Secretary of the Interior Dirk Kempthorne added the monument to the tentative list of places that could be named a World Heritage Site by the United Nations Educational, Scientific, and Cultural Organization (UNESCO). World Heritage Sites are places of outstanding cultural or natural value. There are 890 listed sites as of August 2009, including such iconic natural places as the Great Barrier Reef off the coast of Australia and the karst formations of southern China, and cultural sites such as the Angkor temples in Cambodia, the Great Wall, the Sydney Opera House, and Venice. The United States has twenty World Heritage Sites (including more natural sites than any other nation), and New Mexico's three sites—Carlsbad Caverns National Park, the Taos Pueblo, and Chaco Culture National Historical Park—are more than any other state. The U.S. tentative list is awaiting submission for consideration by the World Heritage Committee in 2010.

The idea of an international agreement to preserve the world's cultural and natural heritage originated in a successful 1959 UNESCO campaign to save ancient Egyptian temples that were threatened by flooding from a proposed dam. Subsequent efforts to preserve the world's most important cultural and natural sites combined to produce the Convention Concerning the Protection of World Cultural and Natural Heritage in 1972. The convention encourages nations to identify and nominate candidates for World Heritage Sites, to act to protect sites once they are listed, and to contribute to the World Heritage Fund for the preservation of sites throughout the world. To be listed, a site must be of "outstanding universal value" and possess at least one of ten specific selection criteria. Sites are placed on the list pursuant to a lengthy process that begins with a nation's identification of its "tentative list" of worthy sites. A nation may then nominate a site from that list for evaluation by the International Council on Monuments and Sites (for cultural sites) or by the International Union for Conservation of Nature (for natural sites). The final decision is made during the annual meetings of the World Heritage Committee.

UNESCO explains that the benefits of listing are "belonging to an international community of appreciation of concern," "joining hands" to "express a shared commitment to preserving our legacy for future generations," and generating "prestige" that "often serves as a catalyst to raising awareness for heritage preservation." Listing may also produce funding for preservation, both from the World Heritage Fund and from donors who concentrate on sites that are placed on the list. Additionally, a listed site may be placed on the List of World Heritage in Danger if its protection demands "major operations" and if "assistance has been requested." Sites on that list receive additional attention and funding. Thirty sites are on the danger list, including the Galapagos Islands and the old city of Jerusalem. Several high-profile sites have been removed from the danger list once they were restored thanks to international assistance (including the Angkor temples and the old Croatian city of Dubrovnik) or national actions (including Yellowstone and Everglades national parks). Some nations view the appellation "in danger" as an opportunity for receiving needed assistance, but other nations perceive it as "a dishonor."[23]

Cliff Spencer, the superintendent of White Sands National Monument, submitted a World Heritage Site application in September 2007. The application indicated that White Sands satisfied four of the ten criteria for listing: number seven, "superlative natural phenomena or areas of exceptional beauty and aesthetic importance," which the application said was easily satisfied by "one of the world's greatest natural wonders, the glistening white sand of New Mexico"; number eight, outstanding geological features; number nine, outstanding examples of ongoing evolutionary processes, for which the application cited the numerous white animals in the dunes; and number ten, "the most important and significant natural habitats for in-situ conservation of biological diversity," as evidenced at White Sands by "a high degree of endemic species" and an unusual steady *increase* in biodiversity. These "outstanding universal values" distinguish World Heritage Sites from sites of only national interest, which yields the odd result that even though the White Sands National Monument did not qualify as a national park, it could become an internationally recognized site before such U.S. national parks as Denali, the Grand Tetons, and Zion. Deserts are among the underrepresented areas that UNESCO hopes to add to the list, which helps the chances of White Sands as well as the Petrified Forest National Park (another of Secretary Kempthorne's 2008 additions to the tentative list). The application also cited support for the nomination by New Mexico's U.S. senators Jeff Bingaman and Pete Dominici, Alamogordo mayor Don Carroll, Las Cruces mayor Bill Mattice, state representative Gloria Vaughn, the U.S. Army, Otero County, and U.S. representative Steven Pearce.

But that wasn't quite right. Representative Pearce quickly clarified that he neither supported nor opposed the proposed listing. He compared the idea to the ESA, which "began as something very innocent . . . But over the years, it ended up being used as a tool that twisted and turned things upside down and ultimately did some things that were not so good." Similarly, explained Pearce, "the people at White Sands National Monument will never envision what such a designation could bring in 10 to 15 years from now. . . . The last thing I want to see is some court declaring that Holloman Air Force Base can't exist anymore, or that missiles will no longer be allowed to fly over or near White Sands National Monument." Nor did the application correctly characterize the county's position on the listing. One month after Superintendent Spencer submitted the application, the Otero County Commission enacted an ordinance providing that "no World Heritage Site or buffer zone will be located on or adjacent to any military land or military research base or other facility, or within or adjacent to the boundaries of Otero County." The county commissioners "believe[d] that approval of this application will curtail economic activity and potentially deny local citizens park access," and they questioned the wisdom of the designation "at a time of heightened Homeland security and international relations challenges." The commissioners were responding to numerous individual complaints and a petition circulated by the local director of the conservative interest group Eagle Forum (founded by Phyllis Schlafly) and signed by fourteen hundred people who opposed the listing. One commissioner worried that the United Nations would decide to close the monument. Various individuals feared that listing would result in international patrols or that the monument could be held as collateral for world debt. Several people worried that outsiders would seek to control the huge aquifer underlying the region. One writer suggested that entrance fees would be increased and would be collected by U.N. employees who would replace current park employees. Another letter to the local newspaper asserted that "the U.N., in addition to being a talking shop for useless diplomats, dictators, and assorted do-gooders, also attracts environmentalists, who tend to be anti-military." The writer then asked, "how difficult would it then be for a group of people to find some albino bug or something that might be disturbed by low-, medium-, or high-flying aircraft or missiles and therefore require both Holloman Air Force Base and the White Sands Missile Range to be closed for any future military use." These complaints elicited howls of protest from listing supporters, who complained about "misinformation" and "the lethal combination of paranoia and fear of conspiracy," who were "embarrassed about the dumb reputation that our Alamogordo has created for itself," and who lamented the "'Conspiracy People' who are so totally convinced that there really are 'black helicopters' that we must be so afraid of."[24]

Nothing in the convention supports these claims of the opponents. The press release announcing Secretary Kempthorne's 2008 additions to the tentative list emphasized that "neither inclusion in the Tentative List nor inscription as a World Heritage Site imposes legal restrictions on owners or neighbors of sites, nor does it give the United Nations any management authority or ownership rights in U.S. World Heritage Sites, which continue to be subject to U.S. law." The only sanction for failing to preserve a site is to remove it from the list. That has happened only once, when the Arabian Oryx Sanctuary was delisted in 2007 because Oman reduced the protected area by 90 percent in order to accommodate hydrocarbon exploration. (Ironically, the oryx to be protected in the sanctuary are the same animals that the White Sands National Monument has tried to extirpate.)[25]

It is easy to dismiss the opponents of the World Heritage Site listing as paranoids reminiscent of the 1950s or akin to those who claim to see UFOs in nearby Roswell. But perhaps it is too easy to dismiss the worries of listing opponents. UNESCO proclaims that "World Heritage Sites belong to all the peoples of the world, irrespective of the territory on which they are located," though it disavows any intent to intrude upon national sovereignty. More tellingly, despite all of the official assurances that listing White Sands as a World Heritage Site would not result in additional environmental regulation, one scholar has recently argued that a listing does precisely that. In a 2008 article, Erica Thorson of the Lewis and Clark Law School argued that the convention imposes a legal duty upon the United States to regulate the emission of greenhouse gases that threaten the glaciers for which Glacier National Park (which was designated a World Heritage Site in 1995) is named. Thorson contends that "the obligations imposed by Articles 4, 5, and 6 of the [convention] require that State Parties engage in an aggressive climate change mitigation strategy because they mandate the protection of World Heritage sites and the 'outstanding values' therein." Article 4 imposes a duty upon each nation to "do all it can . . . to the utmost of its own resources" to protect and conserve its listed sites. Article 5 calls upon each nation to "take the appropriate legal, scientific, technical, administrative and financial measures necessary" to conserve a site. Article 6 prohibits each nation from taking "any deliberate measures which might damage directly or indirectly" sites located in other nations. The scope of these obligations remains untested, but it is not silly to imagine that they could affect activities near the White Sands.[26]

Perhaps the most perceptive objection voiced during the Heritage Site debate noted that the application failed to identify any buffer zones that would be needed to preserve the White Sands. The convention provides that "an adequate 'buffer zone' around a property should be provided and should be afforded the necessary protection" when such a buffer is needed to conserve the site. One legal scholar has warned that "the buffer zone principle can be seen as an encroachment on the private property rights of individual landowners." The Otero County Commission echoed that fear when its ordinance objecting to the listing of White Sands blamed Yellowstone's World Heritage Site status for restrictions of private land use and "a proposal to designate some eighteen . . . million additional acres of public and private land as a buffer zone around the park." Yellowstone was added to the List of World Heritage in Danger in 1995 when a gold mine was proposed within three miles of the park. President Clinton relied on the World Heritage Site listing to issue an order that effectively created a buffer zone around the park, thus blocking the mine but infuriating congressional critics of unilateral executive action based on international law. The House responded by approving the American Land Sovereignty Protection Act, which would require Congress to approve all World Heritage Site designations, acting only after the secretary of the interior certifies that the commercial viability of lands within ten miles of the site would not be adversely affected. One member of Congress supported the bill as necessary to respond to "a much larger pattern of furthering the left wing agenda of accomplishing goals through unelected bureaucrats, liberal judges and international organizations like the United Nations." The act did not become law, but the fears that animated it have been resurrected in the debate over the future of White Sands.[27]

The arguments of the listing opponents suggest that the *perception* of the law may be as important as the law itself. A World Heritage Site designation may not produce the land use regulation that some Alamogordo residents fear, but the simple fact that they believe that the listing may have such a result may be enough to defeat it. The assurances offered by listing supporters are probably based on an accurate understanding of how the law has been employed to date, but environmental law is replete with examples of laws evolving to address problems that their drafters could not imagine. And environmental law can achieve those purposes even if it lacks obvious enforcement mechanisms. Consider Cornell political scientist Jeremy Rabkin's testimony regarding the proposed American Land Sovereignty Protection Act: "Even a toothless international program may do some real practical mischief. If these programs have any value at all, it is in the area of moral suasion. If they cannot exert even this degree of encouragement or influence, then they really are entirely silly. But if it is reasonable to hope that they may have some influence in this area—shaming governments to live up to standards advocated by international experts or by respectable international consensus—then it is reasonable to fear that this influence may be abused." The World Heritage Site dispute may turn on the local judgment concerning the likelihood that international law will be abused.[28]

DARK SKIES

I knew little about White Sands or checkerspot butterflies when I first visited Alamogordo. The environment that attracted me there, and that is valued by many other visitors and residents, is one that much of human history has tried to eliminate. "In the beginning," the Bible tells us, "darkness was over the surface" of the earth. Then "God said, 'Let there be light,' and there was light. God saw that the light was good, and he separated the light from the darkness. God called the light 'day,' and the darkness he called 'night'" (Gen. 1:1–5). The moon and the stars appeared on the fourth day, according to that creation story. The scientific explanation for the darkness of the night has troubled astronomers ever since Heinrich Olbers, a nineteenth-century German amateur astronomer, asked why a universe full of stars is not as bright as the sun itself. Today, the accepted answer to what became known as Olbers' paradox emphasizes both that the light from the most distant stars has yet to reach the earth and that the light from other stars dims as the universe continues to expand.

Whatever the explanation, the setting of the sun introduced a dangerous, scary, and unavoidable period of darkness for people throughout much of human history. A. Roger Ekirch, a history professor at Virginia Tech University, tells that story in *At Day's Close: Night in Times Past,* a fascinating book about the history of nighttime in western societies during the period from 1400 to 1900. "Night was man's first necessary evil," Ekirch writes, "our oldest and most haunting terror." Ekirch further explains that "darkness signified more than the temporary absence of light. According to popular cosmology, night actually fell each evening with the descent of noxious vapors from the sky." The darkness provided by night hosted ominous celestial visions, satanic activity, ghosts, witches, deadly falls and accidents, predatory animals, nocturnal pests, fires, and malevolent thieves and murderers. The night also provided cover for adulterous affairs and other illicit sexual activities. Yet the darkness of night did possess some positive values. Churches "viewed darkness, first and foremost, as a sacred time of solitude, prayer, and rest." Or, as a rabbi wrote in the eighteenth century, "God darkened the world so man could study" and "focus and concentrate his mind and thoughts on God." Darkness was also a time of sleep, or of limited work, mostly for servants who needed to prepare for the next day's activities and slept in two intervals separated by perhaps an hour of quiet activity in the middle of the night.[29]

Darkness works a daily transformation on the natural environment, as well. Indeed, one recent book asserts "that all of the conservation planning of the last thirty years told only half the story—the daytime story." The appearance of an ecosystem is often strikingly different at night than during the day, as a whole set of distinctive mammals, birds, insects, amphibians, and reptiles emerges. These nocturnal animals depend on the darkness to allow them to sneak up on their prey or to hide from their predators. In the White Sands, white animals are more likely to survive even at night because they are more difficult for predators to see in the moonlight or starlight. Other animals depend on the moonlight or the stars for celestial navigation. Baby sea turtles, for example, must immediately crawl into the safety of the ocean as soon as they hatch from eggs buried in the sand along the beach, lest they fall prey to birds, foxes, and other animals who would welcome a tasty snack. Arid environments, such as in southern New Mexico, provide additional motivation for animals to behave nocturnally. Many desert species prefer the cooler, more humid nighttime hours to the blazing heat of the day. Meanwhile, the animals that are active during the daylight rely on the darkness for rest.[30]

Long before the era described by Ekirch, human communities— especially indigenous communities—attached great importance to the stars, the moon, and the other celestial objects that they could see only at night. Stonehenge is a famous example, as scientists are still not certain of the meaning of the demonstrable design of the structure to depend on the sun, moon, and stars. Closer to Alamogordo, many native cultures emphasized the importance of the night skies. They were important to the ancient Puebloans who once lived in what is now the Four Corners region and were the ancestors of the Puebloan peoples who live in northern New Mexico today. Their largest community was in Chaco Canyon, within the San Juan Basin of northwestern New Mexico. Sometimes described as the Stonehenge of America, Chaco Canyon contains the remains of great houses, or kivas, that were built there between the ninth and twelfth centuries. The community in Chaco Canyon thrived until around 1150, when a drought scattered the population throughout the Southwest, including to Mesa Verde. As Kendrick Frazier writes, "The people of Chaco were perceptive observers of the sun's seasonal course" who "set up a variety of observing and recording stations." As with Stonehenge, the buildings were designed so that a sliver of sunlight would illuminate designated chambers on the day of the winter solstice. The goal, as recalled by a Hopi Indian who was born in the area in 1890, "was to keep track of the time or the seasons of the year by watching the points on the horizon where the sun rose and set each day." At least that is what archaeoastronomers say.[31]

Today's astronomers are equally committed to dark skies, albeit for different reasons. During the night, sixty-five hundred American professional astronomers work to learn the mysteries of the universe. They are aided by perhaps five hundred thousand amateur astronomers who contribute to our astronomical knowledge or simply enjoy the sights of the night sky. One of those amateur astronomers, the popular science writer Timothy Ferris, wrote a book about how they are "discovering the wonders of the universe" thanks to new telescopes, powerful light-sensing devices, and the Internet. Actually, they do not even need a telescope of their own, for one can operate distant telescopes from a remote location online or one can sift through the unprocessed data generated by other telescopes. All astronomers see the nighttime sky as a unique environment. One dark skies activist proclaims that "our skies and the observation thereof are unique environmental components: they form perhaps the best example of mankind's relationship with his environment." It is a short jump from that imagery to the language of environmental protection. "Night is a vital part of our environment," write three astronomers, "worthy of preservation just as any other natural resource."[32]

Southern New Mexico is an astronomer's paradise. The air is dry and clear. The altitude is high, but not so high that the human eye begins to lose the oxygen necessary for optimal vision. And, of course, there is no sprawling city there with artificial lights hiding the stars, comets, galaxies, and other objects of an astronomer's desire. Not surprisingly, two major professional observatories are located in the mountains just east of Alamogordo. The Apache Point Observatory hosts a 3.5-meter telescope operated by a consortium of universities, a 2.5-meter telescope and 0.5-meter photometric telescope used by a digital survey of the skies, and New Mexico State University's 1.0-meter telescope. It boasts that "airflow over the observatory site is relatively smooth and turbulence-free, with high atmospheric transparency (very low dust and aerosol content), low scattered light from natural and artificial sources, and very dark and transparent at infrared wavelengths (very lower water vapor content)." The nearby National Solar Observatory at Sacramento Peak depends on light—sunlight—for its very existence. There are also hundreds of amateur astronomers who visit the Alamogordo area or

MOONLIGHT ON THE GREAT WHITE SANDS,   26

WHITE SANDS NATIONAL MONUMENT, NEAR ALAMOGORDO, NEW MEXICO

An early postcard illustrating the moonlit skies of White Sands National Monument.

even move there to take advantage of the city's desirable combination of unpolluted air, high elevation, and dark skies. They gather at the annual Hale-Bopp Star Party (previously known as the White Sands Star Party), where dozens of astronomers come from around the country to observe the skies from the White Sands and in the mountains near Cloudcroft. They may also be involved in the Alamogordo Astronomy Club, which fosters astronomy education and works to preserve the area's dark skies.[33]

Lynn Rice is one of those astronomers. She and her husband Mike moved to the area from Alaska around 1997. They searched the entire United States for the perfect location for their interest in amateur astronomy and ended up buying land in the mountains a few miles east of Cloudcroft. They chose that area because it is dark, far from cities, high enough at seventy-three hundred feet but not too high to deprive the human eye of oxygen, and with "softer" mountains that produce a smoother airflow than in Colorado. There they built and now run New Mexico Skies, a high-end bed-and-breakfast for amateur astronomers. It is an amazing place. The lodge accommodates seventeen guests and is equipped with red lights that don't shine outside. Millions of dollars of

Some of the observatories at the bed-and-breakfast New Mexico Skies.

astronomical equipment is housed in white domes that the Rices had shipped from British Columbia. About three hundred astronomers visit New Mexico Skies each year, half of whom are repeat visitors and many of whom are retirees. They come from Hong Kong, Germany, and places throughout the United States to use their telescopes and to record images with incredible computer equipment. Other users do not even visit the site but instead operate their astronomical equipment there via the Internet from remote locations. New Mexico Skies has been profiled in *Conde Nast, Southern Living,* and a film produced by Timothy Ferris. The Rices own all of the land above the observatory sites, so no one can come in and build something that would interfere with their operations. The only visible artificial lights shine from cars traveling along the two-lane highway below or from the natural gas operations in the town of Artesia seventy miles to the east. Rice notes that the darkness astounds visitors who are not used to seeing so many stars. She also told me that the entire operation costs "an astronomical amount of money."

The Rices' operation is unique, but their passion for astronomy is not. Astronomers contribute to the local economy in several ways. My first indication of this appeared in a real estate advertisement for land just north of Alamogordo which proclaimed that the land "did not have any light pollution." Soon, I found similar ads announcing "zero light pollution" and "great southern sky exposure with no light pollution." Darkness thus enhances property values, though a local realtor told me that light pollution issues had never come up in her experience in selling homes. More tangibly, the professional observatories and the local businesses related to dark skies (such as New Mexico Skies) generate substantial revenue for the Alamogordo area. They emphasize that southern New Mexico looks for any clean business, and as dark sky activist Jackie Diehl reminded me, "astronomy is an extremely clean business." Bruce Gillespie, the site manager of the Apache Point Observatory and another local dark skies activist, calculated that astronomy pumps more money into the county than the cattle industry, which has long been regarded as the key to the area's economy. In this regard, he points to, for instance, the jobs at the observatories, "about three hundred very active amateur astronomers that have bought property and moved here specifically because of the southern New Mexico dark skies," retirement homes and second homes for those amateur astronomers, tourists, and a modest amount of astronomical equipment sales. The intangible benefits of Alamogordo's dark skies were acknowledged by David Gottula, the head of the Alamogordo Chamber of Commerce, who told me that "the dark skies add a lot to living in the area."

RESPONDING TO LIGHT POLLUTION

This dark sky environment has become valued just as it has begun to disappear. For most of human history, astronomical insights were in part an instance of necessity serving as the mother of invention. People were at the mercy of the dark because they were unable to generate sufficient illumination to do much about it. Candles and lamps really didn't accomplish much. Many European cities did not introduce public lighting until the second half of the seventeenth century. The cities employed the law in their campaign to light the urban darkness, enacting ordinances that required each household to hang one lantern at designated times. Ekirch reports, however, that "some officers wisely desisted from enforcing unpopular laws at their neighbors' expense, especially when the infractions [were] minor." The Catholic Church voiced another objection, attacking lighting ordinances "as a sacrilege against the divine order." It was not until the nineteenth, and especially the twentieth, century that we learned how to illuminate the nighttime. The invention of electric lighting was the crucial development. Cleveland became the first U.S. city to install electric streetlights in 1879, and one year later Wabash, Indiana, relied solely on electricity for its street lighting. Thomas Edison's inventions and marketing savvy soon resulted in most American cities having electric street lighting by the dawn of the twentieth century. Even Alamogordo. The Alamogordo Electric Light Plant first generated electricity on June 19, 1899. Soon the Board of County Commissioners said that they did not have the authority to pay for streetlights, so the electric company and local business owners paid for them.[34]

Now we live in a time when light threatens to eliminate the darkness, even during the night. Look at a satellite photo of the earth at night: every large urban area appears as a cluster of light, and the light penetrates far into the countryside as well. The absence of light can also illustrate when something is amiss, such as on the Korean peninsula, where there is a dramatic line between the nighttime lights of South Korea and the darkness of North Korea.

But a growing number of voices complain that our nighttime lights are far too much of a good thing. These are not Luddites who seek a return to the good old days of the fifteenth century when there was no way to avoid the darkness of the night. Instead, the complaints are more focused, questioning whether there is too much light at the wrong time and the wrong place. The darkness that was once viewed with dread is now cherished. Once again, scarcity produces value, just as the wilderness that was feared by the European settlers of America is now cherished and protected by federal law. The appellation "light pollution" is thus entirely appropriate, for like most other pollution claims, time and place transform an otherwise valuable substance into an unwanted pollutant in a valued environment.

The campaign against light pollution began in Tucson, Arizona. In 1988, David L. Crawford founded the International Dark-Sky Association (IDA), which "seeks to preserve dark skies worldwide for the benefit of society by promoting good outdoor-lighting practices and educating the public on the rewards of preserving the stars." More specifically, the

IDA works to "stop the adverse effects of light pollution"; "raise awareness about light pollution, its adverse effects, and its solutions"; "educate
about the values of quality outdoor lighting"; and "promote responsible
legislation, public policy, and standards." The IDA now has more than
ten thousand paid members throughout the world. The organization
encourages networking, develops educational materials, provides expertise to government officials, works with lighting manufacturers and engineers, promotes the application of effective lighting fixtures, promotes
research, increases public awareness, and recognizes and awards positive contributions to dark skies. It has also published dozens of papers
describing light pollution and the ways of responding to it.[35]

Light pollution claims take three distinct forms. *Light trespass* occurs
when lighting shines beyond the boundary of the property where the
light is located. *Glare* refers to lights that "dazzle or discomfort those who
need to see, concealing rather than revealing." *Sky glow* is the dull orange
glow seen in urban areas when light is scattered by dust and water in the
atmosphere. Put together, one study claims that 99 percent of Americans
live in areas that are suffering from light pollution. Light pollution even
presents a dictionary example of the meaning of "pollute": the *American
Heritage Dictionary* offers "the stadium lights polluted the sky around the
observatory."[36]

Numerous harms are attributed to light pollution. One author insists
that "bad outdoor lighting is a psycho-social stressor." It can produce "a
garish landscape." Glare causes traffic accidents, and maybe even airplane
crashes. Contrary to popular wisdom, lights may facilitate crime. Lynn
Rice refers to "insecurity lights" because "they help the criminal element.
If it's dark, then the criminal can't see what they're doing." Rice recalled a
couple who installed a bright light as soon as they moved in near her facility, and about three weeks later they were the first in the area to experience
vandalism on their property.[37]

Light pollution causes more traditional environmental harms, too.
Excessive lighting can affect plant growth. An Alamogordo city commissioner suggested in 1985 that the existing lighting "created an artificial
sunlight which encouraged plant growth to linger on into the colder por-
tions of the season and as a result of that would cause shade trees,
shrubs, etc. to continue to grow past their declination point." Light pollution also harms animals. The first book to explore those harms warned

of the "lethal and sublethal effects on species in many habitats and taxonomic groups. Essentially, artificial night lighting is homogenizing the range of physical conditions present in natural ecosystems." The most famous federal litigation regarding light pollution arose when environmentalists blamed the lights along Daytona Beach in Florida for luring hatched endangered sea turtles toward the resorts instead of the safety of the ocean. Additionally, light pollution opponents frequently cite the energy and money that are wasted by unneeded lights, as well as an estimated thirty-eight million tons of carbon dioxide needed to power those lights.[38]

The most common complaint about light pollution is that it makes it difficult to do something that depends on darkness, such as sleeping or visiting a drive-in movie theater. Most obviously, light pollution threatens astronomy. Nearby bright artificial lights limit the ability of astronomers to see the distant lights of stars, planets, and galaxies. Astronomers say that you need to be at least fifty, and ideally one hundred, miles away from a significant community to get away from the light. That has become increasingly difficult as urban areas have expanded into previously desolate places. Tucson first experienced conflicts between astronomers and outdoor lighting when the city was electrified in the 1920s. Since then, urban sprawl has rendered some prominent astronomical observatories obsolete. Mount Wilson, located just north of Los Angeles, has been "rendered all but useless by the light pollution caused by encroaching metropolitan areas," according to famed astronomer and Alamogordo native Alan Hale (of Hale-Bopp comet fame). Millions of dollars of astronomical equipment have become obsolete in this way.[39]

The dark skies proponents in Alamogordo want to avoid that fate. Beginning in the 1970s, just as many other environmental laws were enacted, a small but growing number of jurisdictions adopted light pollution ordinances. The city of Tucson, and also the county, approved its first light control ordinance in 1972. Closer to Alamogordo, Las Cruces passed an ordinance in 2004, and El Paso approved a detailed light pollution ordinance in 2005. Dozens of other cities have enacted restrictions on lighting. Additionally, Arizona, Arkansas, Connecticut, Hawai'i, Maine, New Mexico, Rhode Island, Texas, and Wyoming have adopted statutes regulating outdoor lighting funded by state entities, and several other state legislatures are considering similar laws. The New Mexico outdoor lighting statute, enacted by the state legislature with little opposition in 1999, was one of the first of its kind in the country. The law requires that outdoor-lighting fixtures of more than 150 watts must be shielded or turned off between 11 p.m. and sunrise. The law also prohibited the sale or installation of mercury-vapor lamps beginning in 2000. The Alamogordo dark skies activists view the state law as "a little watered down" and "nowhere near as strict as the ones that the municipalities pass," but they agreed that "it's a step in the right direction."[40]

Generally, these laws require such steps as the usage of lights that produce less glare, the installation of shields on certain lights, limitations on the amount of light that can escape from someone's property depending on the nature of the area, restrictions on the usage of nonconforming lights during the middle of the night, and prohibitions on the illumination of billboards from below. For example, the IDA recommended a "model lighting ordinance template" that stated its purposes of minimizing light pollution, conserving energy while preserving nighttime safety and activities, and "curtail[ing] the degradation of the nighttime visual environment." The model ordinance then divides a community into four environmental zones depending on the need for lots of light (such as in commercial areas) or for dark skies (such as in national parks or near observatories). The "recommended boundary illumination levels" vary in each zone. The IDA is working on a newer model ordinance that would suggest two alternative lighting design methods: a *prescriptive* method that states minimum requirements for each lighting zone, and a *performance* method that establishes a special review process for complex lighting projects. But it is equally telling what this law—and the municipal light pollution ordinances that have been enacted—do not do. Unlike other pollution laws, light pollution laws do not require someone to get a permit before emitting the relevant pollutant—light—into the environment, nor do they aspire for the day when all light will be eliminated. The light pollution ordinances simply try to regulate how, and how much, light is used during the nighttime.[41]

That is how Alamogordo's light pollution ordinance works. The Otero County Dark Skies Association emerged thanks to the efforts of Jackie Diehl, who is based at the National Solar Observatory but who works on light pollution issues outside of her official responsibilities, and Warren Offit, who conducts minor planet research out of his own observatory in the tiny town of High Rolls south of Cloudcroft. The association was a lobby for dark skies legislation and ordinances in the city and county. The Alamogordo City Council first considered the issue during a work session in 1985 featuring a presentation by Kurt Anderson, a professor at New Mexico State University and the director of the Apache Point Observatory, who explained the light pollution problem and outlined several possible solutions. Five years later, Anderson warned the commission about "flood lights [that] were used in certain businesses and which were directed right into the eyes of oncoming drivers at night." A representative of the Alamogordo Amateur Astronomers recommended that billboards should be lighted from above instead of from below.[42]

The city council enacted its light pollution ordinance in December 1990. The council found that scattered light "can be detrimental to aviation and to astronomical observations such as those being conducted in the vicinity of Alamogordo." The ordinance repeats that concern in its purpose section, which cites the harm that lighting poses "to aviation and to astronomical observations." Additionally, the preamble states that "off-street lighting can also be hazardous to traffic and cause annoyance to adjoining residents." The substance of the ordinance contains several types of provisions. It combats light pollution by mandating that "only shielded outdoor light fixtures may be installed for security purposes or for illumination of commercial establishments." The required shielding must ensure that lighting is "projected below a horizontal plane running through the lowest point on the fixture," thus preventing lights from shining into the sky. Existing light fixtures are grandfathered from the shielding requirement until they are replaced, and outdoor recreational facilities are exempt from shielding altogether. The second general requirement says that outdoor light fixtures must be turned off between 11 p.m. and sunrise. Here, the ordinance exempts businesses that operate after 11 p.m., recreational uses that continue after 11 p.m., and lighting that is "necessary for security purposes." The ordinance also prohibits the use of searchlights for advertising or commercial purposes, and flashing lights except when warning of a danger. Diehl told me that dark sky activists felt very comfortable with the language of the ordinance at the time, lots of which was taken from the IDA model ordinance as adapted to the needs of southern New Mexico.[43]

The Alamogordo skyline at night.

The city council amended the ordinance in 1997 to impose a 2005 deadline for the abandonment or replacement of nonconforming lighting fixtures. Another amendment occurred in 1998 when the city council approved state government construction activities that wanted "to use a type of lighting that will not comply with the current ordinance, but, if allowed, will have a minimal effect on dark skies." A 1999 amendment was motivated by the desire "to make all options available to consumers that will comport with the spirit of the outdoor lighting ordinance."[44]

Cloudcroft followed suit in 1995. It was convinced to act on the basis of aesthetics and the effects of glare on drivers, especially as members of the community age. The town updated and strengthened its ordinance in 2005 in response to a loophole identified by a dispute between two neighbors. The operator of a national astronomy software company based in town objected when his neighbor persuaded the electric co-op to install a light that shined onto the operator's property. The village council considered the dispute in perhaps the town's largest meeting ever, and it concluded that there were holes in the code. All of the offended parties joined to rewrite the ordinance, and the original offense was easily remedied with the installation of a shield over the light.

For many people, the passage of the law would seem to solve the problem. Once enacted, the government enforces the law by identifying and sanctioning any violators. Many environmental laws also include a citizen's suit provision that empowers affected citizens and organizations to sue to enforce the law if the government fails to do so. Later, the law may be amended to close any loopholes, respond to new developments, or remedy any other shortcomings. This combination of creating the optimal law and the ideal enforcement mechanism describes how many expect environmental law—indeed, perhaps all laws—to operate.

But that is not how it works in Alamogordo. The ordinance itself does not even say who is responsible for enforcing it. During the 1990 discussion of the proposed ordinance, one of the city commissioners said that he objected to writing an "ordinance that the City didn't have the ability to enforce." (The same problems occurred with the state law. When Jackie Diehl informed the state's environmental protection office in Alamogordo that it was responsible for enforcing the state's light pollution law, the agency did not know that there was such a law or that it was responsible for it.) Eventually, it was agreed that the city's zoning and building code inspectors were responsible for enforcing the law, but that created its own problems because code inspectors work until 5 p.m. and are not allowed to look for code violations outside of business hours. So the city acts only if a private citizen makes a complaint. Paul Carnes, the past president of the Alamogordo Astronomy Club, "found violations at 135 locations in Alamogordo" during his nighttime drives to monitor compliance with the ordinance. Another dark sky proponent accused a sports bar of violating the ordinance; it denied the claim, but the building that it once occupied stood vacant on a main highway through the city when I visited there. But a city attorney once remarked that "very few" people complain about violations of the ordinance. Bruce Gillespie told me that he was not going to act as the light pollution police because he has to live with these people. It is not surprising, therefore, that the city has rarely actually charged anyone with violating the terms of the light pollution ordinance.[45]

Enforcement is also compromised by the unlikelihood of an effective sanction for violators. The city ordinance fails to detail the penalties for violating the ordinance. Instead, the ordinance cross-references the general penalty provisions of the city code, which authorizes a $500 fine and six months imprisonment. The more likely penalty is a $25 fine, which one local store dismissed as the cost of doing business and which Jackie Diehl derided as "a slap on the wrist." Repeat violators are penalized only by going through the whole process again, but the code enforcement office is short-handed even as it must enforce all of the city's codes.[46]

Alamogordo is not unique in its approach to enforcing its light pollution ordinance. The dozens of such municipal ordinances have yielded only one reported judicial decision. In 1998, the Arizona Court of Appeals upheld Tucson's light pollution law against a challenge brought by a billboard company. The city's ordinance prohibited "bottom-mounted outdoor advertising sign lighting," thereby rendering illegal 170 of the company's billboards. The state court of appeals held that the ordinance fit within the state's police powers, and it deferred to the city's judgment with respect to the appropriate type of lighting. Apart from that decision, municipal lighting ordinances have developed without review by the courts.[47]

"The code is good," concludes Gillespie. "The enforcement clause in each of these ordinances is weak." That does not bother many of the proponents of the ordinance. Gillespie has primarily directed his efforts toward regulation, drafting ordinances, and persuading communities to adopt them. "I've discovered that you can spend 90 percent of your time dealing with municipal governments, but the real action is in community education and appreciation." Good ordinances, says Gillespie, "are those that you co-opted the community into adopting, rather than coercing. . . . You promote the spirit of the ordinance rather than enforcing the details of the statute." Alamogordo's dark skies advocates thus see the ordinance as serving an educational function. Their response to violators is to inform them of their violation and work to persuade them to comply with the law. If the situation is really bad, then a member of the group makes a nice phone call and tries to put a positive spin on the effort to reduce the amount of light projected into the night sky, emphasizing, for instance, energy savings, which is a selling point for local businesses. The Alamogordo activists appear to follow the approaches described in an IDA paper titled "How to Talk to Your Neighbor Who Has a Bad Light," which advises concerned individuals to approach their neighbors "in a friendly way," to "help them solve their problems," and to "show them that you care . . . for them." The author Bob Mizon agrees, remarking in his book on light pollution that a "positive approach and politeness usually get results," while "baldly accusing someone of being a polluter is not wise."[48]

The ordinance also serves to advise new businesses of the city's commitment to controlling light pollution. For example, when Home Depot and Lowe's both opened new stores in the north end of the city—demonstrating either a remarkable jump in the need for hardware materials, or perhaps mimicking the aphorism that no city can have one lawyer—some of the activists in the fight against light pollution met with the developers of each store to explain how the stores could aid in the city's effort to prevent light pollution. Both stores voluntarily said that they would wholeheartedly embrace dark skies legislation and that they were already dealing with it around the country. They now position their lights to minimize any light pollution and shut off most of their lights once they close, producing a result that is noticeably different from the other Home Depot and Lowe's stores that I have seen elsewhere in the country. The lights in the Lowe's parking lot have large skirts to prevent the light from shining into the adjacent neighborhood. Additionally, both stores agreed not to sell mercury-vapor lights and other kinds of light bulbs and fixtures that cause the most light pollution. One astronomer blames retailers for selling "poor-quality, overbright security lighting" that is "imported in large numbers and usually sold very cheaply." Dark skies activists fault the local electric cooperative for installing any lights that a customer requests, even though it is illegal to install certain lights under state law. Home Depot and Lowe's have helped to reduce such lighting simply by not selling it. Gillespie credits both stores for doing a good job, being sensitive to dark skies concerns, and acting in a cooperative way. One of the ordinance's supporters cited Home Depot and Lowe's as future recipients of a possible award that could be given to businesses that are friendly to dark skies, an idea that may be modeled on the good-lighting awards presented by the IDA or the British Astronomical Association.[49]

The city is addressing light pollution through its purchasing decisions, too. Besides more darkness, perhaps the most visible effect of the ordinance is the yellow streetlights. The city is installing such low-pressure sodium lights once each existing light burns out after ten or fifteen years. Some elderly drivers complained that they could no longer distinguish the color of the traffic signals from the streetlights, which is a fair concern given my own first experience driving there in the nighttime. But the complaints soon abated. "We looked at it as lowering the amount of light being projected into the night sky," explained Jackie Diehl. Alamogordo was one of the first communities to change its streetlights.

The Alamogordo light pollution ordinance thus represents a different application of what legal scholars have called *symbolic legislation*— the term for laws containing provisions that no one really believes will be literally enforced. For example, in 1972 Congress provided in the Clean Water Act that *all* water pollution in the United States would end by 1985. In case you have not noticed, that did not happen. Nor did Congress expect it to happen. The academic critique of symbolic environmental legislation argues that such provisions distort the regulatory process and undermine popular respect for the law. My colleague Michael Kirsch has described similar problems in the context of tax law, where Congress legislates simply to demonstrate that it cares about a problem of interest to voters. But Alamogordo's experience suggests that symbolic legislation can perform an educational function that could be obscured by laws containing very specific provisions designed to achieve active enforcement. Amitai Aviram speaks of the law's "placebo effect"— its ability to change subjective perceptions of risk. The legal codification of the city's goal of controlling light pollution serves to notify businesses and residences throughout Alamogordo that light pollution is to be avoided. It also empowers advocates to urge their neighbors to heed the law's commands. That message may be far more effective in actually reducing light pollution than a detailed statute—something like the Resource Conservation and Recovery Act—that tries to prescribe exactly what constitutes pollution, how much may be tolerated, and how it is to be regulated.[50]

But, like any pollution problem, some polluters persist. Bruce Gillespie listed three interests that object to lighting regulation: (1) commercial interests such as gas stations that think they need light for safety, (2) power companies that make money from selling electricity, and (3) billboard owners who think that it is more expensive to install lights on top of billboards shining down than on the bottom shining up.

Several local residents reminded me that Alamogordo shares the western culture of fierce independence and hostility toward government intervention in their lives. John Lattauzio best displays that character. Lattauzio opened a convenience store in Alamogordo in 1962 and retired in 2008 after opening five J&J Minimarkets and serving as chair of the county and state Republican Party for ten years. In 1995, he testified before Congress that his company was "quite simply drowning in federal and state environmental regulations." It is not surprising, then, that Jackie Diehl singled out Lattauzio as the leading opponent of Alamogordo's dark skies legislation. Diehl and other local dark skies activists complained that Lattauzio's stores were lit excessively at night. He responded that he was most concerned about "the safety of my customers." He saw the ordinance as a thorn that he wanted the city commission to remove, but the proponents of the law blocked him at every turn. Lattauzio was never cited for violating the ordinance, nor did he sue to invalidate it. In fact, Diehl counts Lattauzio as a friend, and his service to Alamogordo was celebrated in the local newspaper when he retired in 2008.[51]

There is also the problem of lighting outside of the city. Holloman Air Force Base is outside the city's jurisdiction—as both a geographic and a legal entity—but it has responded to light pollution concerns. The base has scaled down some of its tarmac lighting, and it lowered its lights from 120-foot poles to 60 feet and put shields on them. The base also turned off many of its lights and added security for a Star Party weekend. As I drove north of the base after watching the sunset over the White Sands National Monument, I was struck by two sources of lights on the highway south of Alamogordo. One was the baseball fields, whose lights were supposed to turn off later in the evening, but they sometimes malfunction and stay on later. They were easily the brightest lights in the area. The second most striking lights were on four billboards along the highway. Each was lit from the bottom, not the top, which is one of the leading light pollution no-no's. The fact that one of the billboards advertised the local campus of New Mexico State University was a particular source of embarrassment to some locals. But when I returned to Alamogordo again in 2008, the billboard lights were all turned off by 9 p.m. The bright light on the large sign outside a restaurant was still on, but it, too, was dark when I left the city at 4 a.m. to catch my flight home.

The city ordinance is only the beginning of the legal tools intended to reduce light pollution in the area. The forty acres of land along the ridge opposite Lynn Rice's astronomical bed-and-breakfast demonstrate a particularly innovate approach. Star's End Estates is one of the world's first subdivisions catering to astronomers. To achieve that end, the developer of the property has employed traditional legal tools created by the common law of property nearly two centuries ago. Each of the lots in the subdivision is burdened by covenants prohibiting unwanted lighting. Specifically, the covenants prohibit artificial lights that can be seen from sites used for astronomical observations, as well as driving at night except in an emergency. Those covenants may be enforced by the homeowner's association against any landowners who violate them. Importantly, the covenants "run with the land" so that any future owners of the property must abide by those provisions as well. They may be amended or repealed only upon the vote of at least 75 percent of the landowners at least ten years after the covenants were established. Restrictive covenants are also used to protect dark skies in the San Pedro Creek Estate development east of Albuquerque and in the land that the Nature Conservancy purchased surrounding the McDonald Observatory in west Texas.[52]

Alamogordo had experienced such reliance on restrictive covenants before. The deeds to the original lots conveyed by Charles Eddy's Alamogordo Improvement Company at the turn of the twentieth century provided that the manufacture or sale of alcohol on property within the city would result in the land reverting back to the company. The lots were also burdened by covenants prohibiting commercial uses of the land. (The covenants included a similar stipulation against the use of the land for "immoral purposes" that was never litigated.) The same set of covenants was imposed upon the land in Cloudcroft six years later in 1906. Those anti-alcohol covenants were litigated in the New Mexico courts for decades. In its first decision, the New Mexico Supreme Court held in 1936 that property obtained at a tax auction was not subject to the reverter remedy stated in the original covenant. Four years later, though, the court upheld the covenant itself, observing that there had been only four attempts to violate the covenants in their first forty years, none of which was successful. As recently as 1984, the New Mexico Supreme Court held that a group of neighbors could enforce the covenants against four restaurants that wanted to sell alcoholic beverages. The court agreed that the benefits of the covenants may have been reduced by subsequent changes in the community, but those changes did not defeat the purpose of the covenants. Likewise, the restaurants could not defeat the covenants simply because "restaurants located within the boundaries of the original townsite" are "less competitive than those located elsewhere." A dissenting justice, by contrast, would have extinguished the covenants because of changed conditions. He understood the purpose of the covenants as "to facilitate the development of the original Alamogordo townsite," a purpose that had already been accomplished. That view finally prevailed when a Safeway grocery store challenged the covenant later in 1984. At the trial in the district court, the plaintiffs who were asserting moral objections to liquor admitted that their attorney's fees were being paid by other local liquor stores that would suffer from competition with Safeway. The district court held that the covenant could not be enforced against Safeway because of changed conditions, and the neighbors declined to appeal. Meanwhile, the anti-commercial covenant was less durable than the anti-alcohol covenant. In 1969, the New Mexico Supreme Court held 3–2 that the Cloudcroft covenants against commercial uses were no longer enforceable because of changed conditions. The three justices in the majority emphasized the changes wrought by the noisy highway and existing commercial enterprises already in the vicinity; the two dissenters viewed the restricted property as serving as a needed buffer zone between outside commercial uses and residences.[53]

Covenants—under which landowners must agree, for instance, to adhere to certain architectural norms, not to have too many pets, or not to operate a business from their homes—have become ubiquitous in suburban developments throughout the United States, especially in rapidly growing cities in the West. These covenants have been derided as establishing "private governments" that are insulated from the constitutional and statutory provisions that govern the establishment of similar norms through municipal zoning. Paula Franzese, for example, argues that "the patterns of regimentation that accompany" new developments burdened by restrictive covenants "promote cultures that do more to destroy community than to build it." But Star's End Estates shows how covenants can be employed to create—and equally importantly, to retain—a special community whose features cannot be found elsewhere, and thus attract buyers who depend on the promise that their neighbors will not interfere with their commonly desired use of their properties. The covenants also demonstrate how landownership can solve some pollution problems. If you own the land that is adjacent to your property, or if you have a legally recognized interest in that land, then you get to decide what happens there.[54]

Alamogordo has not employed some of the other legal tools to protect dark skies from light pollution. There are a modest number of cases holding that excessive light may constitute a private nuisance, though none in New Mexico and most are aimed at the light of one objectionable neighbor rather than multiple lights that cast a glow in the entire sky. A more promising approach appears in the dark sky preserves that have been established in Indiana, Michigan, and Pennsylvania. The Michigan preserve was created by a 1993 state statute designating a dark sky preserve at the Lake Hudson State Recreation Area. Additionally, several national parks have included dark skies as part of the environment that they are charged with preserving. For example, "the night sky at Chaco Culture National Historical Park has long been recognized as a precious natural resource," reports the NPS's description of the Endangered Night Sky Darkness Project in Chaco Culture National Historical Park. Indeed, the park's website brags that visitors to the park are "treated to some of the most spectacular views of the dark night sky available anywhere in America." The park's 1993 general management plan designated the night sky as a natural resource. Since then, the park's managers have eliminated unnecessary lights and placed motion sensors and shields on the lights that remain. More than fourteen thousand visitors attend astronomy programs, slideshows, solar observations, and star parties at the park each year. Similar programs exist at national parks throughout the West. The visitor guide that I received on entering Black Canyon of the Gunnison National Park in southwestern Colorado included an article titled "Darkness in Danger," which reported that "our national parks and other protected areas are quickly becoming some of the last places where dark skies are still the norm, where the Milky Way is regularly visible, and where one can look up and become lost in seemingly billions of stars and planets." "Here at the canyon," the guide explained, "there is very little light pollution, which is what often makes it difficult to stargaze in urban areas." More generally, the 2006 version of the NPS's management policies promises that the agency "will preserve, to the greatest extent practicable, the natural lightscapes of parks, which are natural resources and values enjoyed by many visitors."[55]

AS THE CITY GROWS

Alamogordo has experienced cyclical growth throughout its history. The railroad provided an immediate boost to the new city at the beginning of the twentieth century. By 1907, though, the law caused the city's fate to plummet when the federal government obtained an injunction prohibiting the Alamogordo Lumber Company from cutting timber on most of its land because the company began operations before it received title to the lands from the government. The city's population spiked again with the arrival of the military at the onset of World War II, but by 1962, when John Lattauzio arrived, Alamogordo was in the throes of a lengthy recession.[56]

There are conflicting reports about the city's growth today. It appears to be growing, though not as quickly as other cities in the Rocky Mountain region. Ray Backstrom, the county's assistant manager, told me that most of the newcomers to Alamogordo are retirees, many of whom had worked for the military or the government and who are attracted to the good quality of life and the low cost of living. The Forest Service is designing more recreational opportunities for those retirees. Some national chains have moved to Alamogordo, including a Chili's restaurant, a Holiday Inn Express and Hampton Inn, and the Home Depot and Lowe's. Several residents reminded me that Alamogordo is still waiting for its first Starbucks (and they are likely to continue waiting since Starbucks announced plans in 2009 to close six hundred stores nationwide). "Sad to say," says Backstrom, Otero County's growth industry is prisons, with several new prisons and a new Immigration and Customs Enforcement facility located along the highway south of Alamogordo. Farther south, Backstrom expects that Fort Bliss is "looking at a huge influx" of new personnel over the next few years as a result of the base's expansion, thanks to the military's overall realignment.

All cities seem to want economic growth, but too much growth could ruin Alamogordo's dark skies. Light pollution will be impossible to control if the city gets much larger. "At some level you can't win," laments Bruce Gillespie. "You can have very, very good lighting control, but if you get a growth of humanity in the area, you're still going to see an increase in light pollution." Even Tucson, the model city for dark skies, is beginning to experience light pollution despite the laws that it has in place.

That fate may not afflict Alamogordo because of another environmental constraint: the scarcity of water. The authors of a proposal to conduct astronomical research at the Apache Point Observatory were thus pleased to report that "the growth of nearby Alamogordo is expected to be limited by availability of water." Alamogordo has long struggled to secure an adequate water supply. Most of the city's water has come from the Sacramento Mountains, as most recently permitted by the Forest Service in a June 2008 decision that requires the city to protect the endangered Sacramento prickly poppy that grows in the affected area. In recent years the city has embarked upon an aggressive conservation campaign, including a 2002 city ordinance that requires swimming pools to be equipped with recirculation systems, directs restaurants to "provide drinking water to customers only upon request," and limits outdoor watering to three alternate days each week while daylight savings time is in effect. Those efforts reduced the city's water use by 27 percent between 2000 and 2008. But that is not enough to satisfy the area's projected water needs, so the city is developing an extensive desalination project. A vast underground aquifer underlies the Tularosa Basin, but the water is very brackish. Alamogordo secured the rights to drill into the aquifer north of the city, prevailing over the objection of local water rights holders who feared that their own water usage would be adversely affected. The legal issue has been resolved, so now the city is waiting to see whether the project works.[57]

There are social constraints on Alamogordo's growth, too. During the 1990s, the U.S. Air Force invited the German Air Force to conduct a training program at Holloman Air Force Base. The first Germans arrived in 1996, and Holloman proposed the next step in the expansion of its facilities one year later. The proposed expansion would house thirty additional German aircraft and 640 additional German personnel while requiring ninety-six acres of construction and a new target complex. The air force prepared the necessary environmental impact statement analyzing the effects of such a project. But the public hearings on the project in Alamogordo revealed significant latent hostility to the air force's plans, with several speakers recalling the damage that the German air force had done to the United States during World War II. One speaker proclaimed it "an abomination to the Constitution . . . to have to work side-by-side" with the Germans. Another local resident complained that "outsiders view this country as wasteland and nobody lives there, who gives a damn? You want to blow up an atomic bomb, let's do it in New Mexico. . . . You want to fire missiles in White Sands, let's do it in New Mexico." Another speaker insisted that "one reason the logging industry is down is because of some liberal judge and somebody said we've got a spotted owl out there you've got to protect." When the air force decided to pursue the project, several ranchers challenged the adequacy of the environmental impact statement in court. The federal Court of Appeals for the Tenth Circuit held that the statement satisfied the requirements of the National Environmental Policy Act by discussing the noise and other effects of the additional flights and by convincingly explaining why Holloman was the only alternative that would achieve the project's needs.[58]

Alamogordo experiences a tension between the logging and grazing interests that helped to found the city, the extensive presence of the military, the recreational opportunities on the nearby national forest and national monument, and the recent interest in dark skies. None of these interests is likely to disappear, but it is intriguing to imagine what would happen if they did. Whatever the drawbacks of the military's presence, everyone knows the alternative is even scarier. Ray Backstrom told me that Alamogordo would be "devastated" by the closure of Holloman. Another resident once observed that people have known since 1941 "that if the base closed down . . . Alamogordo would be a ghost town." One writer thoughtfully observed that "federalization was attractive" to Alamogordo "because it added an element of security to an otherwise harsh and insecure environment."[59]

The continued popularity of Alamogordo's dark skies is difficult to gauge. Despite the city's efforts to control light pollution, the June 2006 newsletter of the Alamogordo Astronomy Club warned of failing interest, and this issue is the last monthly newsletter uploaded on the club's website, which itself has not been updated since 2007. Backstrom told me in 2008 that he had not heard about light pollution issues in nearly a dozen years. Perhaps, though, dark skies advocates lack the fear of loss that characterizes many environmentalists. Timothy Ferris raved about the opportunities that are available for astronomy even in large urban areas, finding it unnecessary to address light pollution except in one paragraph on page 294 in the first appendix of his book on amateur astronomers. Popular astronomy magazines such as *Sky and Telescope* are far more likely to discuss viewing opportunities and new equipment than the disappearing night sky, a striking contrast to the content of many popular environmental journals that repeatedly warn of threats to the natural environment. There is no similar sense of urgency in Alamogordo. The city's unique environment may remain relatively dry, and thus relatively undeveloped, and thus relatively dark—to the delight of amateur and professional astronomers alike.[60]

Conclusion

I BEGAN THIS BOOK without any preconceived notions of what I would learn as I studied the five places that I had selected. I was surprised by much of what I discovered. The controversy regarding the ownership of the national grasslands in North Dakota's badlands has no parallel in the law. Disputes about public land management are common, and calls for the federal government to divest itself of public lands have been heard from the nineteenth century to the Sagebrush Rebellion of the 1970s to the present day. But it is rare to encounter a serious legal argument that insists that lands that are demonstrably under the control of the federal government instead actually belong to the descendants of the ranchers who left North Dakota during the Dust Bowl. Nor did I expect to learn that Alamogordo is embroiled in a controversy over the possible designation of the White Sands National Monument as a World Heritage Site. There were mundane realizations, too, such as Colton's industrial legacy, which has been forgotten amidst the attention that it receives as the home of the Delhi Sands flower-loving fly; the inability of Adak Island to lure more ecotourists; and the overriding importance of money as the solution to much that ails the Susquehanna River.

My goal, however, was not to write a travelogue of interest only to environmental law junkies. Recall my thesis that existing studies of environmental law overlook how multiple laws operate to affect the

natural environment of specific places. I have not proved the precise relationship between the law and other factors that account for a changed
environment, nor did I expect to do so. But three themes impress me as
I review the stories of the places that I examined.

The first was the elusive nature of values. What kind of natural environment do people want? Laws are based on how society values the natural environment, but the ways in which we value environments evolve
and change over time. Dark skies mattered little to the nineteenth-century
settlers of Alamogordo, or even to the individuals who were brought
there by the military during World War II. Fish played an insignificant
role in the Russian and U.S. development of Adak Island. The natural
flow of the Susquehanna River and its aesthetic virtues were of little
interest to the settlers who used the river for transportation, waste disposal, and electricity generation. The Delhi Sands flower-loving fly was
unknown to the residents of Colton until fewer than two decades ago.
Yet in each instance, the law is now actively engaged in protecting those
newly realized environmental values. On the other hand, rats have lived
on Adak Island for several centuries, yet no one argues that their longstanding presence makes them desirable or entitled to that environment.

It is also important to remember that the environmental values that
animate many twenty-first century constituencies—especially those who
are interested in the working of environmental law—remain foreign to
many individuals. People care about other things. This is most obviously
observed in the difficulty that environmental advocates have encountered in persuading Colton residents of the value of the native dune
ecosystem and the Delhi Sands flower-loving fly, which suffers from the
traditional human disdain for flies, the lack of appreciation of insects
generally, and skepticism about the need to preserve a subspecies. Not
only is the fly unloved in Colton, but few are concerned about the pollution that threatens the community's health. The environmental values of
the Susquehanna River have been met with a similar ambiguity, uninter-
est, or even fear. Many communities along the Susquehanna face away
from the river, or they perceive it as simply irrelevant to their lives. At
the same time, the historic view of the Susquehanna as a threat—a view
born of repeated devastating floods—has been difficult to extirpate. Con-
versely, the badlands of North Dakota tell a story of environmental values
being promoted before their time. Persistent local pressure overcame

broader, but shallower, national attitudes to achieve the establishment of TRNP well before its ecological values were fully appreciated.

The transition from one environmental value to another is often rocky. Ranchers who have seen North Dakota's grasslands as forage for their livestock resent being asked to accommodate recreational users and rare wildlife on the same lands. Colton is struggling to encourage economic development even as it protects its little remaining open space. The advocates of redirecting the flow of the Susquehanna River are unwilling to heed the calls of those who prefer to let the river take its natural course. Representative Kanjorski complained that the rejection of his inflatable dam proposal showed that federal bureaucrats valued riffle pools more than people, but even he acquiesced to the new reality. The Susquehanna River story also reveals changing attitudes toward the federal government's responsibility for flood control and disaster response. One cannot imagine a member of Congress responding to Hurricane Katrina by echoing the ode of Senator Tydings to local responsibility for recovering from floods.

The often conflicting values demonstrate the importance of who gets to decide how the law should affect a place. Institutional battles recur throughout the stories. In Colton, local leaders and the federal FWS have been at odds for more than a decade. Local grazing interests in North Dakota's badlands resent the authority of the federal Forest Service over the national grasslands. Congress established the SRBC to oversee the Susquehanna River watershed, but that agency has ceded power to innumerable and competing local, state, and federal agencies that continue to fight for their preferred vision of the river. And some Alamogordo residents worry, probably erroneously, that the United Nations would rule their lives if the White Sands are designated a World Heritage Site. Much environmental law scholarship analyzes such institutional disputes.

The importance of environmental values in each of these places affirms the ongoing efforts to inculcate those values. Norm entrepreneurs, as scholars describe them, are busily working to teach local, national, and global societies about the importance of biodiversity and the threat of climate change. As Michael Vandenbergh explains, "norms include both social norms—informal obligations that are enforced through social sanctions or rewards; and personal norms—obligations that are enforced through an internalized sense of duty to act and guilt or related emotions for failure to act." Vandenbergh's work contains an excellent description of how environmental norms have developed in the past and how the law can help new norms develop in the future. The process is further illustrated by the professor at King's College who has developed a course to teach teachers about the environmental values of the Susquehanna River. The goal of the course is to change the common perception of the river as a threat to life and to property, and so far the course has had the desired effect upon its students.[1]

The second, and related, theme that characterizes my five stories is the changing nature of the law. Values change faster than the law, but sometimes the law is surprisingly resilient in tracking those changes. The common law that has been developed by U.S. courts for several centuries (and before that in English courts) has proved capable of adapting to modern environmental concerns. Property law's ancient equitable servitudes are being employed both to restrict access to areas still littered by munitions on Adak Island and to keep Alamogordo's skies dark. The traditional riparian doctrine for adjudicating water rights still governs much of the Susquehanna River. And, of course, the common law serves as the baseline against which any statutory or regulatory changes occur.

Sometimes, though, the law fails to respond to pressure to accommodate desired uses of the environment. That has been Colton's experience in trying to get the FWS, Congress, the courts, or anyone to relieve it of the strictures of the ESA. Nor did the Agua Mansa Enterprise District achieve the intended economic redevelopment in Colton—though the ESA complicated that state law effort, too. The new residents of Adak were unable to persuade the navy or the EPA that CERCLA required the elimination of the aesthetic harms resulting from the piles of junk that the military left behind.

In other instances, the law has actually guided the change in environmental values. Federal law decreed in 1913 that Adak Island was a wildlife refuge, then another law confirmed that the island was the site of a military base, followed by a 1971 law that created the Aleut Corporation and another that transferred half of the island's land to that corporation; most recently, Congress inserted a provision into the 2004 appropriations bill that awarded special fishing rights to Adak. That summary includes only the laws that specifically mentioned Adak; it omits the CERCLA hazardous waste cleanup statute, the Wilderness Act, and other statutes that have significantly affected the island. The law, in short, has overseen the evolution of Adak Island from a wildlife refuge to a military base to a native Alaskan community that is attempting to survive by developing a sustainable fishery. The Susquehanna River has experienced a similar transition as numerous eighteenth- and nineteenth-century state and federal laws authorized bridges, canals, and other means of facilitating transportation; then the law began to try to arrest the river's increasing pollution and declining fisheries; and now it focuses on the relationship of the river to the larger Chesapeake Bay ecosystem. The law's effort to respond to changing values has been particularly contentious in North Dakota's badlands, both during the awkward move from a failed farming economy on land provided by the federal government to a ranching economy on lands repossessed by the government, and more recently as recreational and energy interests have begun to assert their legal rights to use grasslands that were once regarded as the exclusive province of the ranchers. Colton's story includes fruit growers struggling with the cement industry during the nineteenth century, and then urban planners opposing the protection of the Delhi Sands flower-loving fly in the twenty-first century, with each interest turning to competing legal tools to defend their positions in the community.

The laws that have the greatest effect on a community's natural environment are often those that are outside the realm of environmental law. Alamogordo, Colton, and North Dakota's badlands experienced their first significant human settlements as a result of federal laws that encouraged the building of railroads to those places. The federal highway law yielded an interstate that split Colton into two parts and brought air pollution from the trucks carrying cargo shipments east from Los Angeles and cars commuting west toward Los Angeles. The laws that designated military bases near Alamogordo and especially on Adak Island brought many more people to those places, and on Adak the law closing the base produced another series of changes whose ultimate effects are yet to be seen. Adak's fate may depend on two federal statutes that are even farther removed from the purview of environmental law. One is Section 1001 of the federal criminal code, the prohibition on false statements that Senator Ted Stevens was convicted of violating, for

Adak benefited immeasurably from the congressional funding and pre-
ferential treatment that Stevens was able to secure for his home state
during his forty-one years in Congress. The second statute is Vision
100—Century of Aviation Reauthorization Act, the latest congressional
authorization of the Essential Air Service program operated by the U.S.
Department of Transportation to subsidize air travel to remote towns
that could not survive without such service. Federal appropriations statutes are also crucial to the future of the Susquehanna River, where everything from mine runoff to sewage-treatment plant renovations to
flood protection depends on a flow of federal funds.[2]

Environmental law works unexpected results as well. The ESA
brought economic development in Colton to a standstill. The combination of the congressional establishment of TRNP and the enactment of
the Clean Air Act has limited energy development in western North
Dakota. The NPS relied on its statutory powers to reintroduce elk to
TRNP, only to confront criticism that the agency's laws blocked the state's
preferred method for reducing today's elk population. The multiple-use
requirements of the national forest laws and their extension to national
grasslands are beginning to change the way in which North Dakota's
grasslands have been used for the past seventy years. On Adak Island,
the fur trade that President Taft cited in his establishment of the wildlife
refuge in 1913 helped to devastate the island's native seabirds, and consequently its native flora, and it took the refuge many years and substantial
resources to eliminate the foxes that we once tried to keep on Adak. The
next task is to employ FIFRA, the federal pesticides law, in a perhaps
vain attempt to eliminate rats from Adak. Only if that effort succeeds
and the seabirds return will the island revert to its "original" conditions.
A similar effort to undo the fruits of earlier laws is occurring along the
Susquehanna River. The Clean Water Act provides funding to update
sewer systems that were early efforts at environmental protection. FERC
is using its legal authorities to aid the shad whose historic route was
blocked by the dams that earlier federal laws authorized. The SRBC is
addressing the new problems posed by natural gas development with a
dormant regulation that was originally promulgated with other water
uses in mind. Federal and state agencies alike are relying on a broad
collection of legal powers to try to clean up the acidic pollution that

endures long after the end of the mining that the law once eagerly encouraged throughout the Susquehanna River basin in Pennsylvania.

The unexpected effects of the law on the natural environment further complicate the difficulty of identifying the role of the law and the role of other ecological, social, and cultural forces in producing environmental changes. Just as anthropologists debate whether law produces culture or culture produces law, any study of the changing conditions of the natural environment of a particular place elicits the question of whether law determines the environment or the environment determines the law. William Cronon's canonical book *Changes in the Land: Indians, Colonists, and the Ecology of New England* acknowledges: "We cannot always know with certainty whether a governmental action anticipated or reacted to a change in the environment. When a law was passed protecting trees on a town commons, for example, did this mean that a timber shortage existed? Or was the town merely responding with prudent foresight to the experience of other localities?" Cronon was writing about the seventeenth century; much more information is available to judge the purpose of more recent laws and the environmental conditions to which they were responding. Law depends on other societal variables, but it operates in ways that are distinct from those variables as well. Law is a tool, but it is a tool that is often wielded by those who seek to achieve results that reach beyond the normative goals that the laws were originally designed to accomplish. It is striking, for example, that Matthew Klingle's environmental history of Seattle begins by praising the salmon as "the fish that might save Seattle" from the fruits of urban development and sprawl. But it is not the *salmon* that might save Seattle; it is the regulatory restrictions of the ESA that were triggered by the salmon's endangered status. Congress did not think much about salmon when it enacted the ESA in 1973, yet that law may play a primary role in shaping Seattle's environmental future. The same law is governing Colton's future, while the Magnuson-Stevens Fishery Conservation and Management Act may determine whether Adak succeeds as a sustainable fishing community.[3]

The difficulty in accounting for environmental changes and the unexpected applications of existing laws confirm the work of environmental law scholars who appreciate the importance of flexible legal instruments. For example, the idea of *adaptive management* has become integral to ecosystem management strategies. J. B. Ruhl describes adaptive management as "a process for continuous monitoring, evaluation, and adjustment" that is built into the framework for regulatory implementation. Ruhl has explained how adaptive management has been incorporated into the application of the ESA, and how it could be employed to preserve species whose survival is threatened by the unpredictable path of climate change. My colleague Alejandro Camacho has also endorsed the need for adaptive management though he has questioned its actual implementation under the ESA. Camacho contends that more resources are needed to make regulatory evolution possible, better legislative directives are needed to make it plausible, and regulated parties need more incentives to make it probable. Most of this work on adaptive management has been limited to the context of preservation issues rather than pollution, and it presumes that agencies will do the adapting rather than legislatures. My five stories indicate that increased flexibility needs to characterize all areas of environmental law, and all makers of environmental law.[4]

The third and most prominent theme of the five stories is that the law operates much differently from what is suggested by the stories told in the judicial decisions that are our most familiar accounts of the operation of environmental law. It is unusual in these five places for courts to resolve legal disputes concerning the environment. Only Colton has experienced repeated environmental litigation in recent years, and the city's pleas to the courts to redirect the course of the law have been notably unsuccessful. Occasionally, the use of the Susquehanna River has been subjected to litigation, especially with respect to the construction and operation of dams, but those cases influenced a tiny proportion of the river management decisions that have been made during the past several centuries. The only litigation affecting Alamogordo's environment dates to the nineteenth century. There have not been any environmental lawsuits amidst the constant changes on Adak Island or in North Dakota's badlands. The most curious case arises in the badlands, where everyone expects the law to adjudicate disputes involving the use of the national park and the national grasslands, but where no one is contemplating a lawsuit to make that happen.

This is not to say that the law has been irrelevant. Rather, legal disputes have been resolved without recourse to the courts. Environmental law is typically thought to be the province of the federal government, with Congress legislating broad environmental commands and federal administrative agencies working to implement them. That pattern is seen in several of this book's stories. The FWS's application of the ESA has hamstrung Colton. The NPS and the Forest Service have prescribed the permissible uses of the national park and national grasslands, respectively, in western North Dakota. The EPA, FERC, the Nuclear Regulatory Commission, and the Army Corps of Engineers are all involved in managing the Susquehanna River. The North Pacific Fishery Management Council has become one of the most important institutions involved in determining the fate of Adak Island, along with the navy, the EPA, and the FWS.

Local governments play an important role in shaping their natural environments, too. The city councils of Alamogordo and Cloudcroft enacted the light pollution ordinances that have served as a catalyst for preserving dark skies in the area. Hundreds of local governments are involved in the management of the Susquehanna River and its watershed, though their activities complicate the plans of those who prefer a more holistic approach to the river. Other local governments have been less successful. McKenzie County leaders have battled the Forest Service over the control of the western North Dakota grasslands that are divided between federal and private ownership. Colton's city leaders have pushed their development vision at the expense of the Delhi Sands flower-loving fly, albeit with little to show for their efforts so far. Only on Adak Island is the local government a minor player in environmental governance. Between federal and local law, of course, lies state law, but it is surprisingly absent from many of the disputes in these five places. State law has been most prominent in the case of the Susquehanna River, where three states have worked to coordinate their potentially competing jurisdictions over the area. The Susquehanna River is also the only place I examined that is governed by an institution specially created for the purpose: the SRBC. The idea of establishing a single institution that is responsible for overseeing the regulation of the environment in a specific place would seem to be a sensible approach to environmental management.

The SRBC, however, has not achieved the success that would cause anyone to want to replicate that model.

Of course, the law applies even without any formal governmental implementation. That is most obvious in Alamogordo, where proponents see the city's light pollution ordinance as a tool for teaching the public about the importance of dark skies. The Alamogordo ordinance is remarkable in the way that it has been employed to respond to the problem of light pollution without resorting to traditional means of legal enforcement. But the ordinance is also unique among the stories in this book. More often the law is not persuasive, or it is simply seen as an obstacle to be overcome. The recovery plan for the Delhi Sands flower-loving fly that the FWS prepared pursuant to the ESA promotes public education regarding the values of the fly and the ecosystem of which it is a part. Those educational efforts have been conspicuously unavailing in Colton, where nobody appreciates the fly. The failure of the teaching model of environmental law has been attributed to the absence of an indigenous environmental movement in western North Dakota, which implies that the law cannot stray too far from the local values of a place.

There are even instances in which people rely on a blatant misunderstanding of the law. The City of Colton neglected to follow the cleanup process dictated by CERCLA's National Contingency Plan, so the city was unable to recover the money that it spent cleaning up perchlorate from its water supply. Daniel Flood of Wilkes-Barre ignored the niceties of federal law when he ordered federal officials to respond to Hurricane Agnes, though with happier results than Colton experienced. Sometimes people cling to beliefs that are demonstrably at odds with what the law actually says, such as the persistent belief that the national grasslands in western North Dakota belong to the ranchers who have lived there since the federal government acquired the property from their ancestors during the Great Depression. Alamogordo offers another example. There is no basis for the contention that the designation of the White Sands National Monument as a World Heritage Site will introduce international law and international organizations into local land use decisions. Yet that belief prompted the county to oppose the designation, notwithstanding the reassurances of Bush administration officials who were generally sympathetic to claims of unwarranted international interference in U.S. law.

Or the law is seen as an obstacle to be circumvented. That occurred in Wilkes-Barre in the aftermath of Hurricane Agnes. The federal flood insurance law refused to subsidize rebuilding in flood zones. Undaunted by that legal command, and pressured by local officials, the federal government deemed the floodplain to be limited to the river itself—thus enabling rebuilding right up to the river's banks. North Dakota's badlands experienced a similar dodge when the Clean Air Act's more rigorous provisions applicable to areas near national parks threatened to block the construction of new coal-fired electric power plants. Again, local officials and the state's congressional delegation pressured the EPA to graft their preferred result into the law, and the EPA obliged by reinterpreting the way in which it calculates the permissible level of air pollution. Such subtle efforts to avoid the law's commands have been more common than more forthright efforts to change an objectionable law. Adak Island offers the exception, having procured a congressional amendment that awarded the community fishing privileges that otherwise would have been denied under the existing provisions of the Magnuson-Stevens Act. Colton, by contrast, failed miserably in its quixotic quest to eliminate the Delhi Sands flower-loving fly from the coverage of the ESA.

This diverse use and understanding of the law is hardly limited to the context of environmental law. It does, however, present significant challenges to the relationships between individuals who are affected by changing environmental conditions; institutions that are responsible for guiding them; and attorneys, regulators, and judges who are called upon to use the law to resolve a dispute. The fact that there were so few occasions for judges to decide what the law means in the course of these five stories highlights the importance of understanding how other actors perceive the law. Perhaps the most important lesson of these stories is that further research into the actual functioning of the law will well serve anyone who is interested in pursuing a vision of the natural environment of specific places.

I relate these three themes as tentative suggestions, for as I finished the study of Alamogordo's light pollution in the book's final story, I discovered Timothy Ferris's aphorism, "storytelling, like the Sun in the sky, obscures as much as it reveals." Zygmunt Plater has voiced a similar warning. Before recounting his role in the case of the Tellico Dam versus the snail darter, which remains the most famous environmental law case thirty years after it was decided, he warned of the "danger that storytellers . . . will believe that what they have experienced deeply is a metaphor for everything else in human society." Duly cautioned, I am not suggesting that these five stories reveal all that one needs to know about environmental law. Rather, I hope that they and their tentative lessons will encourage us to learn more about the actual effects of environmental law and other laws upon the environment. The stories suggest that there is a special need for additional research to recover the importance of places in environmental law. The operation of the law appears quite different from the perspective of how numerous laws affect a particular place than it does from the perspective of how a single law applies in a variety of places. The former approach—the one that I have taken in this book—holds promise for cultivating a more robust understanding of whether our environmental laws actually achieve what we write them to do. Stories about how places are affected by the law may change the ways that we look at environmental law, and in doing so, change the ways that the law works with other tools to govern our natural environments.[5]

NOTES

INTRODUCTION

1. Bill McKibben, ed., *American Earth: Environmental Writing since Thoreau* (New York: Library of America, 2008).

2. Jody Freeman & Daniel A. Farber, "Modular Environmental Regulation," *Duke L.J.* 54 (2005): 795, 837–76; Oliver Houck, "Unfinished Stories," *U. Colo. L. Rev.* 73 (2002): 867, 867–68.

3. Martha Minow, "Stories in Law," in Peter Brooks & Paul Gewirtz, eds., *Law's Stories: Narrative and Rhetoric in the Law* (New Haven, Ct.: Yale University Press, 1996), 26, 36; Daniel A. Farber & Suzanna Sherry, "Telling Stories Out of School: An Essay on Legal Narratives," *Stan. L. Rev.* 45 (1993): 807, 838, 851; Richard Delgado, "Storytelling for Oppositionists and Others: A Plea for Narrative," *Mich. L. Rev.* 87 (1989): 2411, 2413.

4. Ted Steinberg, *Down to Earth: Nature's Role in Environmental History* (New York: Oxford University Press, 2009), x. Steinberg's third ecological turning point was the first to occur: the arrival of Europeans in North America. The recent environmental histories of specific places include Matthew Klingle, *Emerald City: An Environmental History of Seattle* (New Haven, Ct.: Yale University Press, 2009); Gregory Summers, *Consuming Nature: Environmentalism in the Fox River Valley, 1850–1950* (Lawrence: University Press of Kansas, 2006); and William Cronon, *Changes in the Land, Revised Edition: Indians, Colonists, and the Ecology of New England* (New York: Hill & Wang, rev. ed. 2003).

5. Richard Lazarus, *The Making of Environmental Law* (Chicago: University of Chicago Press, 2006), 5; Eric Freyfogle, *Why Conservation Is Failing and How It Can Regain Ground* (New Haven, Ct.: Yale University Press, 2006), 3; David Schoenbrod, *Saving Our Environment from Washington* (New Haven, Ct.: Yale

University Press, 2006), 192; Aaron Sachs, *The Humboldt Current: Nineteenth-Century Exploration and the Roots of American Environmentalism* (New York: Viking Press, 2006), 346.

6. Robert Weisberg, "Proclaiming Trials as Narratives: Premises and Pretenses," in Brooks & Gewirtz, *Law's Stories,* 83.

CHAPTER 1. THE END OF THE EARTH

1. *Swoboda v. United States,* 662 F.2d 326 (5th Cir. 1981); Eliot Asinof, "Adak: 'A Woman behind Every Tree,'" *Saturday Evening Post,* July 17, 1965, 67. Huston's documentary, *Report from the Aleutians,* is available from the Internet Archive at http://www.archive.org/details/ReportFromTheAleutians.

2. Gore Vidal, *Williwaw: A Novel* (New York: E. P. Dutton, 1946), 104.

3. W. H. Dall, *Tribes of the Extreme Northwest* (Washington, D.C.: Government Printing Office, 1877), pt. 1, 44–45.

4. Exec. Order No. 1733 (Mar. 3, 1913).

5. Asinof, "Adak," 69; FWS, Alaska Maritime National Wildlife Refuge, http://alaska.fws.gov/nwr/akmar/wildlife.htm.

6. North Pacific Research Board and North Pacific Fishery Management Council, Comprehensive Baseline Commercial Fishing Community Profiles: Sand Point, Adak, St. Paul and St. George, Alaska, Final Report, June 2008, 3-1, http://www.fakr.noaa.gov/npfmc/current_issues/crab/CommunityProfiles/AK%20Community%20Profiles%20Vol%202.pdf.

7. City of Adak, Alaska, Emergency Ordinance E05-2005-06, § 1 (amending § 9.02.25(B)(1) of the city code).

8. Jeffrey C. Williams and Vincent Tutiakoff Jr., "Aerial Survey of Barren-Ground Caribou at Adak Island, Alaska in 2005" (Sept. 2005), http://alaskamaritime.fws.gov/visitors-educators/caribhunting/2005%20Caribou%20census.pdf.

9. Federal Insecticide, Fungicide, and Rodenticide Act, 7 U.S.C. §§ 136–136y; Katie Rooney, *Time* online, "The Top 10 Everything of 2008: Top 10 Outrageous Earmarks: 10. $150,000 for 'Rat Island,'" http://www.time.com/time/specials/2008/top10/article/0,30583,1855948_1863903_1863888,00.html; FWS, AMNWR, Restoring Wildlife Habitat on Rat Island: Alaska Maritime National Wildlife Refuge, Aleutian Islands Unit, Environmental Assessment (Dec. 2007), http://alaskamaritime.fws.gov/pdf/rat_assessment_508.pdf; FWS, Restoring Alaska's Islands: Alaska Maritime National Wildlife Refuge's Invasive Species Program (Apr. 2008), http://alaskamaritime.fws.gov/pdf/fact_sheet_restoring_408.pdf.

10. Brian Garfield, *The Thousand-Mile War* (Anchorage: University of Alaska Press, 1969), 195.

11. D. A. Croll et al., "Introduced Predators Transform Subarctic Islands from Grasslands to Tundra," *Science,* Mar. 25, 2005, 1959, 1961.

12. Endangered and Threatened Wildlife and Plants, Determination of Threatened Status for the Southwest Alaska Distinct Population Segment of the Northern Sea Otter, Part VI, 70 Fed. Reg. 46366 (2005); Martin Renner &

Kevin Bell, "A White Killer Whale in the Central Aleutians," *Arctic*, Mar. 2008, 102.

13. Joel K. Bourne Jr., "Alaska's Wild Archipelago," *National Geographic*, Aug. 2003, 78; Beth Bryant, "Adapting to Uncertainty: Law, Science, and Management in the Steller Sea Lion Controversy," *Stan. Envtl. L.J.* 28 (2009): 171, 175 (noting "there are at least nine plausible hypotheses proposed to explain the decline and lack of recovery of the Alaskan Steller sea lion population"); Asinof, "Adak" 69.

14. Garfield, *The Thousand-Mile War*, 140–41, 146, 149.

15. Cpl. Dashiell Hammett & Cpl. Robert Colony, "The Battle of the Aleutians 1942–1943," in Terrence Cole, *The Capture of Attu: Tales of World War II in Alaska* (Anchorage: Alaska Northwest Publishing, 1984); Garfield, *The Thousand-Mile War*, 196 ("pathological boredom"); Asinof, "Adak" 68–71.

16. Pub. L. No. 101-510, 104 Stat. 1808 (1990); Defense Base Closure and Realignment Commission, 1995 Report to the President (1995), 1–39, http://www.defenselink.mil/brac/docs/1995com.pdf; Department of Defense, Base Closure and Realignment Report, Mar. 1995, 5–45, http://www.defenselink.mil/brac/docs/1995dod.pdf.

17. Comprehensive Environmental Response, Compensation, and Liability Act of 1980, 42 U.S.C. §§ 9601–9675.

18. Community Environmental Response Facilitation Act, Pub. L. No. 102-425, 106 Stat. 2174 (1992); Superfund Amendments and Reauthorization Act, Pub. L. No. 99-499, 100 Stat. 1613 (1986).

19. EPA Superfund Record of Decision: Adak Naval Air Station, OU1 (Mar. 31, 1995).

20. EPA Superfund Record of Decision: Adak Naval Air Station, OU3 (Dec. 10, 2001), iii, 5–9.

21. Agency for Toxic Substances and Disease Registry, Public Health Assessment: Naval Air Facility, Adak (Sept. 2002), http://www.atsdr.cdc.gov/hac/PHA/adak/ada_toc.html; EPA Superfund Record of Decision: Adak Naval Air Station, OU2 (Mar. 31, 2000), App. B, 7 (clearance technology).

22. EPA Superfund Record of Decision: Adak Naval Air Station, OU2, 10-5.

23. *Id.* at App. B, 18. A recent study concluded that the extent to which Adak was occupied before World War II remains uncertain. There were probably some seasonal trapping camps, and at least some individuals were displaced when the U.S. military arrived in August 1942. *See* North Pacific Research Board/North Pacific Fishery Management Council Fishing Community Profiles, 3-2 and n.8.

24. Alaska Native Claims Settlement Act, 43 U.S.C. §§ 1601–28; The Aleut Corporation: 2008 Annual Report (2008), http://www.aleutcorp.com/images/annualreports/annualreport2008.pdf.

25. Act of Oct. 11, 2002, Pub. L. No. 107-239, 116 Stat. 1438.

26. *Future of Missile Defense Testing Programs: Hearing before the Subcomm. on Strategic Forces of the House Armed Services Comm.*, 111th Cong., 1st Sess. 19

(Feb. 25, 2009) (testimony of Philip E. Coyle, former director of Operational Test and Evaluation), http://armedservices.house.gov/pdfs/STRAT022509/Coyle_Testimony022509.pdf; Southwest Alaska Municipal Conference, The Aleut Corporation: 2008 Annual Report, 16–17; "Adak," http://www.swamc .org/index.php?option=com_content&task=view&id=105&Itemid=64; Aleut Real Estate, "Available Adak Residential Properties for General Public Bid Sale," http://www.aleutrealestate.com/images/stories/documents/15jun09-list%20of%20available%20housing%20for%20adak%20residential%20housing%20sales%20to%20the%20general%20public.pdf (housing prices).

27. Scott McMurren, "Cruise the West Coast, Cash in Miles for an Alaska Trek," *Anchorage Daily News*, Mar. 4, 2007, K4 (Anchorage travel writer).

28. Robert S. Broff, "Bonuses to Nowhere," *San Antonio Express-News*, Mar. 19, 2009, 6B (AIG).

29. 16 U.S.C. § 668dd(a)(3) (management of national wildlife refuges).

30. Wilderness Act, Pub. L. No. 88-577, 78 Stat. 890 (codified in scattered sections of 16 U.S.C.).

31. *Washington Toxics Coalition v. EPA*, 413 F.3d 1024 (9th Cir. 2004), *cert. denied*, 126 S. Ct. 1024 (2006) (relationship between FIFRA and the ESA).

32. American Fisheries Act, Pub. L. No. 105-277, 112 Stat. 2681-616 (1998); Sustainable Fisheries Act, Pub. L. No. 104-297, §§ 108–110, 110 Stat. 3559, 3574–92 (1996); Magnuson-Stevens Fisheries Management Act, Pub. L. No. 94-265, 90 Stat. 331 (1976) (codified as amended in scattered sections of 16 U.S.C.).

33. Josh Eagle, Sarah Newkirk, & Barton H. Thompson Jr., *Taking Stock of the Regional Fishery Management Councils* (Washington, D.C.: Island Press, 2003), 3.

34. 16 U.S.C. § 1853(a)(4).

35. Eagle, Newkirk, & Thompson, *Taking Stock*, 3.

36. H.R. Rep. 401, 108th Cong., 1st Sess. § 803 (2003) (pollack rider); 150 Cong. Rec. S153 (daily ed. Jan. 22, 2004) (statement of Sen. Stevens); National Oceanic and Atmospheric Administration, National Marine Fisheries Service, Environmental Assessment/Regulatory Impact Review for Amendment 82 to the BSAI FMP and Regulatory Amendments to Allow the Allocation of Future Aleutian Islands Pollock Harvest to the Aleut Corporation as Required by Public Law 109–199, Jan. 2005, xlviii (economic development), http://www .fakr.noaa.gov/analyses/amd82/bsai82finaleao205.pdf.

37. Fisheries of the Exclusive Economic Zone Off Alaska; Proposed Information Collection; Comment Request; Aleutian Islands Subarea Directed Pollock Fishery, 70 Fed. Reg. 9856, 9858 (2005); Walter R. Borneman, *Alaska: Saga of a Bold Land* (Harper Perennial, 2004), 276 (salmon canneries).

38. "Draining Adak for Cod," *Highliner*, Mar. 31, 2008 (quoting Adak Mayor Rod Whitehead); Jim Paulin, "A Fish Battle Is Brewing between Adak, Dutch Harbor," *Alaska Journal*, Dec. 9, 2007. The crab rationalization program is summarized in Scott C. Matulich et al., "Policy Formulation versus Policy

Implementation under the Magnuson-Stevens Act: Insight from the North Pacific Crab Rationalization," *Envtl. Aff.* 34 (2007): 1.

39. NOAA Fisheries, Office of Law Enforcement, "NOAA Issues $3.44 Million Penalty for Violations of the American Fisheries Act" (Nov. 29, 2004), http://www.nmfs.noaa.gov/ole/news/news_AKD_112904.htm; Neil A. Lewis, "Prosecutors in Stevens Case Are Ruled in Contempt," *N.Y. Times*, Feb. 14, 2009, A16; Richard Mauer, "Ben Stevens' Secret Fish Deal," *Anchorage Daily News*, Sept. 18, 2005, A1.

40. Department of Transportation Order 2003-1-8 (Jan. 3, 2003); Senator Ted Stevens, press release, "Sen. Stevens Urges Senate to Reauthorize the Indian Health Care Improvement Act," Jan. 22, 2008; James Halpin, "Tangled Web Leads to Adak Power Shutdown; Emergency: Fuel Is There, But City Can't Afford It; Citizens Advised to Leave," *Anchorage Daily News*, Sept. 15, 2008, A3. For one of the blogs commenting on Governor Palin, see http://alaskareal.blogspot.com/2008/09/exodus-from-alaskan-village.html.

CHAPTER 2. THE MAYOR'S OVERSIZED FLYSWATTER

1. A photo of Mayor Bennett wielding her flyswatter and a report about her press conference appeared in Ellen Braunstein, "Cities Hope to Swat Flies: Endangered: Colton and Fontana Mayors Push to Clean Up Areas Designated as Delhi Sands Habitat," *Press-Enterprise* (Riverside, Cal.), Sept. 26, 2002, B1.

2. *Colton v. Rialto,* 230 Cal. App. 2d 174 (Cal. Ct. App. 1964); Duane W. Gang, "Colton Calls Off Its Annexation Plans; Proposal: The City's Mayor Apologizes after Three Hours of Negative Public Comment," *Press-Enterprise* (Riverside, Cal.), Sept. 20, 2006, B7; City of Colton, California, Economic Development: Colton History, http://www.ci.colton.ca.us/Colton_History_070505.html.

3. *United States v. Colton Marble & Lime Co.,* 146 U.S. 615 (1892); California Department of Parks and Recreation, Office of Historic Preservation, *Five Views: An Ethnic Historic Site Survey for California* (December 1988), http://www.nps.gov/history/history/online_books/5views/5views.htm; Harry S. Truman Library and Museum, Colton, California (Rear platform, 1:56 p.m.), http://www.trumanlibrary.org/whistlestop/50yr_archive/colton.htm (President Truman's remarks).

4. *Hulbert v. California Portland Cement Co.,* 118 P.928, 929–30 (Cal. 1911); "Cement Company Buys Dust-Blighted Zone," *L.A. Times*, July 9, 1914, p. II-1.

5. Jose Pitti, Antonia Castaneda, & Carlos Cortes, "Mexican Americans in California," in *Five Views*.

6. Nonprofit Management Solutions and Tax Technology Research, LLC, Report to the California Department of Housing and Community Development on Enterprise Zones, Aug. 18, 2006, 23, 73 (available from the authors at http://www.taxtechresearch.com/index.html).

7. Roger Vincent, "Inland Empire: Where the L.A. Dream Landed," *L.A. Times*, Apr. 16, 2006; Matt Woolsey, "In Depth: How Low Will Real Estate Go?,"

Forbes, Apr. 28, 2008; National Public Radio, "All Things Considered," Mar. 24, 2004.

8. *United States v. Gaytan,* 342 F.3d 1010, 1011 (9th Cir. 2003) (quoting *United States v. Miss. Valley Generating Co.,* 364 U.S. 520, 562 (1961)); Cindy Martinez Rhodes, "Ex-Chamber Figure to File Claim against Colton, Mayor; $1 Million: The Action Alleges Defamation of Character Tied to Budget Shortfalls," *Press-Enterprise* (Riverside, Cal.), May 28, 2008, B4; Cassie MacDuff, "Colton in Therapy," *Press-Enterprise* (Riverside, Cal.), Feb. 22, 2008, B1; Massiel Ladrón De Guevara, "Mayor: Colton on the Mend; State of the City: Ethics Among Leaders, Growth and Open Communication Top the Agenda, She Says," *Press-Enterprise* (Riverside, Cal.), June 1, 2007, B3 (quoting Mayor Chastain's concern about "the cancer of corruption that plagued our elected leadership").

9. EPA, "Brownfields Assessment Demonstration Pilot: Colton, CA," May 1998, 1, http://www.epa.gov/brownfields/html-doc/colton.htm.

10. Department of Toxic Substances Control, "Investigation and Results at Colton Iron & Metal, Colton, CA," Jan. 2008, 2, http://www.dtsc.ca.gov/Hazardous Waste/Projects/upload/Colton-Iron-and-Metal-Fact-Sheet-Investigation-and -Results.pdf; In re Portion of Lot 2, Covenant to Restrict Use of Property: Environmental Restriction, Apr. 18, 2005, 4.

11. *City of Colton v. American Promotional Events, Inc.,* No. CV-05-1479-JFW(SSx), *2 (C.D. Cal. Oct. 31, 2006) (National Contingency Plan case); H.R. Rep. No. 359, 109th Cong., 1st Sess. (2005) ($1.25 million earmark); City of Colton, California, "Finance: Utilities," http://www.ci.colton.ca.us/Utilities_Electric .html; Letter from Anjali I. Jaiswal et al. to Tom Doduc, State Water Resources Control Bd., May 31, 2007, 3.

12. Federal-Aid Highway Act of 1944, Pub. L. No. 521, 58 Stat. 838, 842, § 7.

13. Larry Sheffield, *Images of America: Colton* (Charleston, S.C.: Arcadia, 2004), 8.

14. Joe D. Corless, "Air Pollution Challenges for California's Inland Empire: Testimony Submitted to the Sen. Env't & Pub. Works Comm.," Oct. 10, 2007, 1, http://epw.senate.gov/public/index.cfm?FuseAction=Files.View&FileStore_id =5e77b113-3e45-4810-b844-e635d6ca0495; Penny J. Newman, "Field Briefing for the Sen. Env't & Pub. Works Comm. on Air Pollution Challenges for California's Inland Empire," Oct. 10, 2007, 6, http://epw.senate.gov/public/ index.cfm?FuseAction=Files.View&FileStore_id=cd0af6e5–544a-48eb-8c8d -c44b54a5ac6e (institutional racism); "Statement of Chairman Barbara Boxer, Field Briefing on 'Air Pollution Challenges for California's Inland Empire,'" Oct. 10, 2007, 5, http://epw.senate.gov/public/index.cfm?FuseAction=Files .View&FileStore_id=086be7f4-8811-42bb-a221-745d32345bb9.

15. Clean Air Act, 42 U.S.C. §§ 7651–7651o.

16. In re Alliance Colton LLC, R9-2001-10 (EPA Region IX, Apr. 25, 2001) (Administrative Order on Consent); *People ex rel. Brown v. County of San Bernardino,* No. CIVSS-0700329, *2 (Cal. Super. Ct. Aug. 28, 2007) (Order

Regarding Settlement Agreement); Draft Environmental Impact Report (SCH No. 2007071010) for the Agua Mansa Commerce Center, Feb. 2008, 4.1-45; California Environmental Protection Agency, Air Resources Bd., Staff Report, Proposed 2007 State Implementation Plan for the South Coast Air Basin—PM2.5 Annual Average and 8-Hour Ozone National Ambient Air Quality Standards, Sept. 21, 2007; Bob Dutton, "Listen Up: Delay AB 32 to Save Jobs," *Inland Valley Daily Bulletin* (Ontario, Cal.), Mar. 4, 2009; Joe Nelson, "Air Near Colton Cement Plant Deemed Relatively Safe: Emissions 20 Times Higher in Rubidoux," *Inland Valley Daily Bulletin*, http://www.DailyBulletin.com, May 30, 2008.

17. EPA, "Brownfields Assessment Demonstration Pilot," 1.

18. *Tennessee Valley Authority v. Hill*, 437 U.S. 153 (1978). Recent litigated ESA controversies include *California Trout v. FERC*, 2009 U.S. App. LEXIS 15930 (9th Cir. 2009) (dam vs. toad); *Oregon Natural Res. Council v. Allen*, 476 F.3d 1031 (9th Cir. 2007) (logging vs. owl); *Alabama v. United States Army Corps of Eng'rs*, 424 F.3d 1117 (11th Cir. 2005) (mussels vs. water withdrawal), *cert. denied*, 547 U.S. 1192 (2004); *Rancho Viejo, LLC v. Norton*, 334 F.3d 1158, 1161 (D.C. Cir. 2003) (Roberts, J., dissenting from denial of reh'g en banc) ("hapless toad" vs. suburban development), *cert. denied*, 540 U.S. 1218 (2004).

19. 16 U.S.C. § 1532(6) (ESA exclusion of pests); Ezquiel Lugo, "Insect Conservation under the Endangered Species Act," *UCLA J. Envtl. L. & Pol'y* 25 (2007): 1, 12; FWS, "Summary of Listed Species," http://ecos.fws.gov/tess_public/TESSBoxscore (number of endangered insects.).

20. Agua Mansa Enterprise Zone, Draft Environmental Impact Report, No. 397, Nov. 1985, 6–49; Wilson C. Hanna, "The White-Throated Swifts on Slover Mountain," *The Condor: A Magazine of Western Ornithology* 11 (May–June 1909): 77.

21. FWS, Carlsbad Fish and Wildlife Office, "Delhi Sands Flower-loving Fly (*Rhaphiomidas terminatus abdominalis*): 5-Year Review: Summary and Evaluation," Mar. 2008, http://ecos.fws.gov/docs/five_year_review/doc1898.pdf [hereinafter FWS 5-Year Rev.]; J. N. George & R. A. Mattoni, "Rhaphiomidas terminatus terminatus Cazier, 1985 (Diptera: Mydidae): Notes on the Rediscovery and Conservation Biology of a Presumed Extinct Species," *Pan-Pacific Entomologist* 82 (2006): 30–35 (El Segundo flower-loving fly). The FWS has suggested that the Delhi Sands flower-loving fly should really be called the Delhi Sands *giant* flower-loving fly because it belongs to the Mydidae family instead of the Apioceridae family as previously thought.

22. M. A. Cazier, "A Revision of the North American Flies Belonging to the Genus *Rhaphiomidas* (Diptera, Apioceridae)," Bulletin *of the American Museum of Natural History* 182 (1985), 181-263; M. A. Cazier, "A Generic Review of the Family Apioceratidae with a Revision of the North American Species (Diptera-Brachycera), *Am. Midl. Nat.* 25 (1941), 589-631.

23. Letter from Greg Ballmer to Chris Nagano re Petition for Emergency Listing of *Rhaphiomidas terminatus abdominalis* as an Endangered Species, Mar.

25, 1992, 1; Greg Ballmer, "Petition to the United States Fish and Wildlife Service for Action to List an Endangered Species Pursuant to the Conditions and Regulations of the Federal Endangered Species Act," Oct. 18, 1989.

24. 16 U.S.C. § 1532(16) (defining "species"); Endangered and Threatened Wildlife and Plants, Determination of Status for 12 Species of Picture-Wing Flies from the Hawaiian Islands, 71 Fed. Reg. 26835 (2006); *Endangered Species Act—Vancouver, Washington: Hearing before the Task Force on Endangered Species of the House Resources Comm.*, 104th Cong., 1st Sess. 65 (1995) (testimony of Barbara Tilly, chairman, Chelan County Public Utility District Board of Commissioners); *Endangered Species Act: Washington, DC—Part III: Hearing before the Task Force on Endangered Species of the House Resources Comm.*, 104th Cong., 1st Sess. 261B62 (1995); Endangered and Threatened Wildlife and Plants, Determination of Status for 12 Species of Picture-Wing Flies from the Hawaiian Islands, 71 Fed. Reg. 26835, 26839 (2006).

25. Endangered and Threatened Wildlife and Plants, Proposed Determination of Endangered Status for the Delhi Sands Flower-Loving Fly, 57 Fed. Reg. 54547 (1992); Endangered and Threatened Wildlife and Plants, Notice of 90-Day Findings on Petitions to List the Delta Smelt and Delhi Sands Flower-Loving Fly as Endangered, 55 Fed. Reg. 52852 (1990).

26. 16 U.S.C. § 1532(6) (definition of "endangered"); 16 U.S.C. § 1532(20) (definition of "threatened"); 16 U.S.C. § 1533(a)(1) (factors for determining whether a species is endangered or threatened); Endangered and Threatened Wildlife and Plants, Determination of Endangered Status for the Delhi Sands Flower-Loving Fly, 58 Fed. Reg. 49881, 49883–85 (1993).

27. *Natural Resources Defense Council v. U.S. Dep't of the Interior,* 113 F.3d 1121 (9th Cir. 1997) (gnatcatcher case); Determination of Endangered Status for the Delhi Sands Flower-Loving Fly, 58 Fed. Reg. at 49886 (vandalism).

28. FWS, Pacific Region, "Final Recovery Plan for the Delhi Sands Flower-Loving Fly" (1997), 11, 15–16, 26.

29. 16 U.S.C. § 1538(a)(1) (ESA take prohibition); 16 U.S.C. § 1532(19) (ESA definition of "take" to include "harm"); 50 CFR § 17.3 (defining "harm"); *Babbitt v. Sweet Home Chapter of Communities for a Great Oregon,* 515 U.S. 687 (1995); In re *Cooperative Conservation Listening Session #24,* Colton/San Bernardino (U.S. Dep't of the Interior, Sept. 28, 2006), 38 (Mayor Bennett).

30. Roger A. Smith, *Portraits in History: The San Bernardino County Medical Center, 1855–1998* (San Bernardino: Act I Publishing, 1999), 160.

31. U.S. Const., art. I, § 8, cl. 3 (interstate commerce clause); *Rancho Viejo, LLC v. Norton,* 323 F.3d 1062 (D.C. Cir. 2003) (frog); *Rancho Viejo, LLC v. Norton,* 334 F.3d 1158, 1160 (D.C. Cir. 2003) (Roberts, J., dissenting from denial of rehearing en banc); *National Ass'n of Home Builders v. Babbitt,* 949 F. Supp. 1 (D.D.C. 1996), *aff'd,* 130 F.3d 1041 (D.C. Cir. 1997), *cert. denied,* 524 U.S. 937 (1998); John Copeland Nagle, "The Commerce Clause Meets the Delhi Sands Flower-Loving Fly," *Mich. L. Rev.* 97 (1998): 174.

32. Chris H. Sieroty, "IVDA Ratifies Staters Accord; Brown: 'First Big Step' to Airport Move," *San Bernardino Sun*, Apr. 15, 2004.

33. Jonathan Abrams, "Pact May Be Ointment for Colton's Fly Problems," *L.A. Times*, Jan. 22, 2007, B3 ($175 million).

34. In re *Cooperative Conservation Listening Session #24*, 97–98; Paul Larocco, "Colton Tries to Pry Land from Fly Habitat; Development Rights: Officials Make Their Annual Pitch That Involves an Endangered Species," *Press-Enterprise* (Riverside, Cal.), Apr. 17, 2005, B5 (quoting Pierson's daughter).

35. In re *Cooperative Conservation Listening Session #24*, 37 (Bennett); Cook Barela, "Saving the Fly," *Press-Enterprise* (Riverside, Cal.), Sept. 26, 2002, A12 (tequila bottle); Joanne Glenn, "Saving the Fly," *Press-Enterprise* (Riverside, Cal.), Sept. 26, 2002, A12 (no help); William Booth, "Developers Wish Rare Fly Would Buzz Off; Flower-Loving Insect Becomes Symbol for Opponents of Endangered Species Act," *Wash. Post*, Apr. 4, 1997, A1 (Biggs); Congressman Joe Baca, press release, "Assembly Votes to Remove Protection for the Delhi-Sands Flower-Loving Fly," May 29, 1997 (Baca).

36. Malcolm Tait, *Going, Going, Gone? Animals and Plants on the Brink of Extinction and How You Can Help* (London: Think Publishing, 2006), 68–69 (Xerces Society); "Soaring Species?," *Press-Enterprise* (Riverside, Cal.), July 6, 2007, B8; Lindsey T. Groves, "Letters; More on the Colton 'Fly' Fiasco," *L.A. Times*, Mar. 16, 2003, § 9, 4; Booth, "Developers Wish," A1 (Mattoni).

37. David W. Almasi et al., *Shattered Dreams: 100 Stories of Government Abuse* (Washington, D.C.: National Center for Public Policy Research, 5th ed. 2007), 63; CBS Evening News (CBS Television, Aug. 27, 1999); "Lords of the Flies," *Wash. Times*, Aug. 28, 1999, A11; David G. Savage, "Buzz Over a Fly Presents Challenge to Species Act; Environment: Protections Could Be Drastically Limited by Insect Dispute Born in San Bernardino County," *L.A. Times*, June 15, 1998, A1; Booth, "Developers Wish," A1; "Small California Town Fighting Environmentalists and Federal Government over Delhi Sands Fly Habitat Regulations," NBC Nightly News (NBC Television, Feb. 14, 1997).

38. FWS 5-Year Review, 4 (Ontario recovery unit); Paul Larocco, "Delhi Sands Flower-Loving Fly: Relief in Sight for Developers; Fly-Habitat Deal Holds Out Hope; Colton Landowners See End of Nightmare," *Press-Enterprise* (Riverside, Cal.), June 26, 2005, A1 (Ballmer).

39. *Examining Impacts of the Endangered Species Act on Southern California's Inland Empire: Hearing before the House Resources Comm.*, 108th Cong., 2d Sess. (2004) [hereinafter Inland Empire Hearing], 9; In re *Cooperative Conservation Listening Session #24*, 38 (Mayor Bennett).

40. In re *Cooperative Conservation Listening Session #24*, 38 (Mayor Bennett), 42 (Parrish), 91 (wildlife biologist Greg Miller); Stephen Wall, "Colton Seeks Fly Accord," *San Bernardino County Sun*, May 6, 2006 (Nuaimi).

41. *Tennessee Valley Authority v. Hill*, 438 U.S. 141 (1978); Endangered and Threatened Wildlife and Plants, Final Rule Reclassifying the Snail Darter (*Percina*

Tanasi) from an Endangered Species to a Threatened Species and Rescinding Critical Habitat Designation, 49 Fed. Reg. 27510 (1984); *5-Year Review of the Delhi Sands Flower-Loving Fly*, 1–10 (submitted by Mayor Bennett to the FWS on Jan. 3, 2006).

42. FWS 5-Year Review, 6–8, 14–15.

43. Inland Empire Hearing, 1–2 (Pombo), 4 (Baca), 8–11 (Bennett), 14–15, 23 (Nuaimi), 48 (Silver).

44. In re *Cooperative Conservation Listening Session #24*, 38.

45. Riverside County, "Riverside County Integrated Project," http://www.rcip.org/conservation.htm; Alejandro E. Camacho, "Can Regulation Evolve? Lessons from a Study in Maladaptive Management," *UCLA L. Rev.* 55 (2007): 293.

46. Inland Empire Hearing, 17–18 (testimony of Rialto mayor Grace Vargas), 49 (Silver); Letter from Regional Director to Mayor Karl E. Gaytan, June 13, 1997.

47. Michael J. Bean & Melanie J. Rowland, *The Evolution of National Wildlife Law* (Westport, Ct.: Praeger, 3d ed. 1997), 234.

48. Inland Empire Hearing, 49.

49. FWS, "Conservation Banking: Incentives for Stewardship," July 2005, http://www.fws.gov/endangered/landowner/banking.7.05.pdf; Letter from Gail Koetich, Field Supervisor, FWS Carlsbad Field Office to Mr. Gary Thornberry, California Portland Cement Company, Aug. 14, 1996.

50. Jennifer Bowles, "Site Gets Fly Out of Inland Ointment; Habitat: A Company Sets Aside 150 Acres for an Imperiled Insect That Has Blocked Many Projects," *Press-Enterprise* (Riverside, Cal.), June 23, 2005, A1 (Linton); Governor Arnold Schwarzenegger, "2006 Governor's Environmental and Economic Leadership Awards," Dec. 5, 2006, 11, http://www.calepa.ca.gov/awards/geela/2006/AwardProgram.pdf.

51. *Calmat Co. v. City of Colton*, No. SCVSS 135476, *2 (Cal. Super. Ct. Jan. 9, 2007).

52. FWS 5-Year Review, 10.

53. Stephen Wall, "City Plan for Fly Questioned," *San Bernardino County Sun*, Feb. 15, 2007 (quoting Mayor Chastain); Stephen Wall, "Colton Nears Fly Trade-Off," *San Bernardino County Sun*, Dec. 13, 2006 (quoting Nuaimi); Paul Larocco, "Federal Officials Visit Colton to Tour Fly Habitat," *Press-Enterprise* (Riverside, Cal.), Apr. 21, 2005, 1; "Letters," *Press-Enterprise* (Riverside, Cal.), July 1, 2005 (letter from Paul Brode).

54. Michael J. Sorba, "Colton City Council to Select City Manager Recruiter at Tuesday's Meeting," *San Bernardino County Sun*, June 15, 2009 (cemetery dispute); Michael J. Sorba, "Exit of Colton City Manager Won't Hold Back Projects," *San Bernardino County Sun*, May 18, 2009 (Target); Cindy Martinez Rhodes, "Vision Still Clouded for Colton's Superblock," *Press-Enterprise* (Riverside, Cal.), May 4, 2008 (opponents).

55. *Draft Environmental Impact Report (SCH No. 2007071010) for the Agua Mansa Commerce Center*, 4.2-6–4.2-13; Agua Mansa Enterprise Zone, Draft Environmental Impact Report, No. 397, Nov. 1985, 6–49.

56. *Vasquez v. National Metal & Steel Corp., Inc.*, 2008 Cal. App. Unpub. LEXIS 7588, *3 (Cal. Ct. App. Sept. 15, 2008).

CHAPTER 3. HEAVEN OR HELL?

 1. Landgon Sully, *No Tears for the General: The Life of Alfred Sully, 1821–1879* (Palo Alto, Cal.: American West, 1974), 189.
 2. Clay S. Jenkinson, *Theodore Roosevelt in the Dakota Badlands: An Historical Guide* (Dickinson, N.D.: Dickinson State University, 2006), 20.
 3. *Id.* at 45.
 4. Bruce M. Kaye & Henry A. Schoch, *Theodore Roosevelt National Park: The Story behind the Scenery* (Las Vegas, Nev.: K. C. Publications, rev. ed. 1999), 3.
 5. Jennifer C. Urquhart, "Theodore Roosevelt: Dakota Adventure," in *America's Hidden Treasures: Exploring Our Little-Known National Parks* (Washington, D.C.: National Geographic Society, 1992), 71; National Park Service, "1989 Statement for Management," 16; "2003 Mall Shopping Patterns: Consumers Spent More Time in the Mall," *ICSC Research Quarterly* 11 (Summer 2004): 1; National Park Service, Ranking Report for Recreation Visits in: 2007, http://www.nature.nps.gov/stats/viewReport.cfm.
 6. National Park Service, *Management Policies 2006* (Washington, D.C.: Government Printing Office, 2006), 8–10, http://www.nps.gov/policy/MP2006.pdf [hereinafter *2006 NPS Management Policies*]; National Park Service, "Secretary Lane's Letter on National Park Management, 1918," May 13, 1918, http://www.nps.gov/history/history/online_books/anps/anps_1j.htm.
 7. 70 Cong. Rec. 4629–35 (1927); Jane Jaree Lynn, "The Ouachita National Park: A Failed Proposal from the 1920s," *Arkansas Historical Quarterly* 55 (1996): 410.
 8. 74 Cong. Rec. 2164 (1931) (statement of Rep. Cramton); John Ise, *Our National Park Policy: A Critical History* (Baltimore: Johns Hopkins University Press, 1961), 139; David Harmon, "Sully's Hill and the Development of National Park Standards," *North Dakota History* 53 (1986): 2.
 9. 15 U.S.C. §§ 1125(c)(1), 1127 (Trademark Dilution Act); *Starbucks Corp. v. Wolfe's Borough Coffee, Inc.*, 2007 U.S. App. LEXIS 3372 (2d. Cir. 2007); Robert Sterling Yard, "Gift-Parks the Coming National Park Danger," *National Parks Bulletin* 4 (Oct. 9, 1923): 4.
10. David Harmon, *At the Open Margin: The NPS's Administration of Theodore Roosevelt National Park* (Medora, N.D.: Theodore Roosevelt Nature and History Ass'n, 1986), 2, 4.
11. Edward C. Blackorby, *Prairie Rebel: The Public Life of William Lemke* (Lincoln: University of Nebraska Press, 1963), 195.
12. *Theodore Roosevelt National Park: Hearings before the House Comm. on Public Lands,* 79th Cong., 2d Sess. 3–4, 14, 17, 20 (1946); Letter from Oscar L. Chapman to J. Hardin Peterson, Feb. 14, 1946, *reprinted in* S. Rep. No. 1897, 79th Cong., 2d Sess. 2 (1946).

13. Harry S. Truman, "Memorandum of Disapproval of Bill to Create a Theodore Roosevelt National Park in Medora, North Dakota," Aug. 10, 1946, http://www.presidency.ucsb.edu/ws/print.php?pid=12491.

14. H.R. Rep. No. 49, 80th Cong., 1st Sess. 2 (1947); *Theodore Roosevelt National Memorial Park: Hearings before the Subcomm. on Public Lands of the House Public Lands Comm.*, 80th Cong., 2d Sess. 3, 17 (1948); Harmon, *At the Open Margin*, 21, 23.

15. Harmon, *At the Open Margin*, 40 ("only historical resource"); *National Parks and Recreation Act of 1978: Hearings before the Subcomm. on Parks and Recreation of the Senate Energy & Natural Resources Comm.*, 95th Cong., 2d Sess. 339 (1979). The official name change occurred in the National Parks and Recreation Act of 1978, Pub. L. No. 95-625, 92 Stat. 3467, 3521, § 610.

16. Harmon, *At the Open Margin*, 5 (quoting Burroughs); Theodore Roosevelt, *Ranch Life and the Hunting Trail* (New York: Century, 1888), 47, 82; D. Jerome Tweton, *The Marquis de Mores: Dakota Capitalist, French Naturalist* (Fargo: North Dakota Institute for Regional Studies, 1972), 13 (quoting the *New York Times*); Olaf T. Hagen & Ray T. Mattison, "Pyramid Park—Where Roosevelt Came to Hunt," *North Dakota History* 215, 215–16 (quoting Sherman and Sully); *Bismarck Weekly Tribune*, June 28, 1879 (quoted in Hagen & Mattison, "Pyramid Park," 221); City of Medora: Community, http://www.medorand.com/community.htm.

17. Twelve reasons are listed in the park's recent study of elk management. *See* National Park Service, Theodore Roosevelt National Park Elk Management Plan and Draft Environmental Impact Statement, p. ii (Dec. 2008), http://parkplanning.nps.gov/document.cfm?parkId=167&projectId=10833&documentID=25353 [hereinafter TRNP Elk Management Plan].

18. U.S. Department of the Interior/National Park Service, General Management Plan, Development Concept Plans: Theodore Roosevelt National Park, North Dakota, p. 1 (1987) [hereinafter TRNP General Management Plan].

19. Clay Jenkinson, "A New Year in a Petrified Forest," *Bismarck Tribune*, Jan. 6, 2008, 1C.

20. Dan Kaercher, *Parklands of the Midwest: Celebrating the Natural Wonders of America's Heartlands* (Guilford, Ct.: Globe Pequot Press, 2007), 117.

21. Joseph L. Sax, "America's National Parks: Their Principles, Purposes, and Prospects," *Natural History* (1976): 56; National Park Service, "Secretary Lane's Letter."

22. Eric Bailey, "Federal Judge Halts 9 Renovation Projects in Yosemite Valley," *L.A. Times*, Nov. 7, 2006.

23. *National Park Service's Draft Management Policies: Hearing before the Subcomm. on National Parks of the Senate Energy & Natural Resources Comm.*, 109th Cong., 2d Sess. 5, 32, 36 (2005); *The National Park Service Organic Act and Its Implementation through Daily Park Management: Hearing before the Subcomm. on National Parks of the House Resources Comm.*, 109th Cong., 2d Sess. (2005) (statement of Rep. Pearce and testimony of Chuck Cushman,

executive director of the American Land Rights Ass'n); *2006 NPS Management Policies*, 10–11.

24. NPS, History: Famous Quotes Concerning the National Parks, http://www .nps.gov/history/history/hisnps/NPSThinking/famousquotes.htm (Mather).

25. Act of April 25, 1947, 61 Stat. 54, ch. 41, § 5 (codified at 16 U.S.C. § 245); "Statement of Management: Theodore Roosevelt National Park," Nov. 1994, 5.

26. TRNP General Management Plan, 9, 23; Kaye & Schoch, *Theodore Roosevelt National Park*, 20, 23.

27. Jenkinson, *Theodore Roosevelt in the Dakota Badlands*, 33 (quoting Roosevelt).

28. Theodore Roosevelt, "Hunting Trips of a Ranchman," in Theodore Roosevelt, *Hunting Trips of a Ranchman & the Wilderness Hunter* (New York: Modern Library, 2004), 266–67.

29. S. 684, 110th Cong., 1st Sess. (2007); 153 Cong. Rec. S2232–33 (daily ed. Feb. 26, 2007) (statement of Sen. Dorgan); *Fiscal Year 2010 Budget Request for the Department of the Interior: Hearing of the Interior, Environment, and Related Agencies Subcomm. of the Senate Appropriations Comm.*, 111th Cong., 1st Sess. (June 3, 2009) (testimony of Secretary of the Interior Salazar).

30. Act of Sept. 24, 1950, Pub. L. No. 81-787, 64 Stat. 849, 851–52, § 6 (hunting in Grand Teton National Park); Clay Jenkinson, "So, When Does It Cease to Be a National Park?," *Bismarck Tribune*, Mar. 11, 2007.

31. N.D. H. Con. Res. No. 3007 (2009); TRNP Elk Management Plan, 9 (quoting *New Mexico State Game Comm'n v. Udall*, 410 F.2d 1197, 1201 (10th Cir. 1969)) ("need not wait"), 10 (quoting *2006 NPS Management Policies*), 51–94 (explaining the plan's alternatives), 95–98 (discussing rejected alternatives); Brian Duggan, "Volunteers Get OK to Reduce Elk," *Bismarck Tribune*, Aug. 11, 2009, 1A (TRNP official); Byron Dorgan, "A Regulated Elk Hunt: Senator Dorgan's View," *N.Y. Times*, July 15, 2009, A24; "Elk Hunting in the Badlands," Editorial, *N.Y. Times*, July 8, 2009, A24.

32. *State v. Miller*, 129 N.W.2d 356, 364 (N.D. 1964) (quoting Theodore Roosevelt, "Pronghorn," in Hedley Peek & F. G. Aflalo, *The Encyclopaedia of Sport* 2 (London: Lawrence & Bullen, 1898): 137).

33. Dave Foreman, *Rewilding North America: A Vision for Conservation in the 21st Century* (Washington, D.C.: Island Press, 2004).

34. 153 Cong. Rec. S2233 (daily ed. Feb. 26, 2007) (statement of Sen. Dorgan); TRNP General Management Plan, 29; Theodore Roosevelt, "The Home Ranch," in *Ranch Life in the Far West* (Dillon, Colo.: Vistabooks, 1991), 27; Gary A. Warner, "50 States, 50 Memories: Favorite Recollections from Each of the United States," *Buffalo News*, Oct. 1, 2006, H1; North Dakota Game and Fish Dep't, North Dakota Prairie Dog Hunters Guide Book (Bismarck: N.D. Game and Fish Dep't, n.d.).

35. Endangered and Threatened Wildlife and Plants; Finding for the Resubmitted Petition to List the Black-Tailed Prairie Dog as Threatened; 69 Fed. Reg. 51217 (2004); John G. Sidle et al., "Role of Federal Lands in the Conservation

of Prairie Dogs," in John L. Hoogland, ed., *Conservation of the Black-Tailed Prairie Dog: Saving North America's Western Grasslands* (Washington, D.C.: Island Press, 2006), 223, 228–29 (citing the number of prairie dogs in the TRNP and the NPS's policy).

36. 153 Cong. Rec. S2233 (daily ed. Feb. 26, 2007) (statement of Sen. Dorgan); Roosevelt, "The Home Ranch," 27.

37. In re Saylor, 121 P.3d 532, 536 (Mont. 2005); Urquhart, "Theodore Roosevelt: Dakota Adventure," 74–75 (quoting Myron Freeman, Dickinson State naturalist).

38. TRNP General Management Plan, 91; Harmon, *At the Open Margin*, ch. 12.

39. TRNP General Management Plan, 91; "1989 Statement of Management," 16–17.

40. Lyle Witham, "Monitored Air Quality in North Dakota," Aug. 18, 2005, http://www.ndhealth.gov/AQ/Dockets/ModelingProtocolfinal/Tab%20F%20Air%20Quality%20in%20ND-cor.pdf, 2 (citing the American Lung Association's data for Billings County).

41. Letter from David M. Verhey, acting assistant secretary for Fish, Wildlife, and Parks to Terry O'Clair, director, Division of Air Quality, North Dakota Dep't of Health, July 26, 2007; National Parks Conservation Ass'n, "Dark Horizons: 10 National Parks Most Threatened by New Coal-Fired Power Plants," May 2008, http://www.npca.org/darkhorizons/pdf/Dark_Horizons_Report.pdf.

42. Prevention of Significant Deterioration New Source Review: Refinement of Increment Modeling Procedures, Part II, 72 Fed. Reg. 31372, 31386 (2007) (proposed modeling rule). The North Dakota modeling dispute is described in "EPA Air Quality Modelers on North Dakota Modeling Protocol," *Env't Rep.* (BNA) 35 (2004): 968; "Regional Staff Warn against EPA Agreement with North Dakota on Measuring Pollution," *Daily Env't Rep.* (Apr. 27, 2004): A-1. The Clean Air Act's Prevention of Significant Deterioration provision is codified at 42 U.S.C. § 7473; it is well summarized in Craig N. Oren, "Prevention of Significant Deterioration: Control-Compelling Versus Site-Shifting," *Iowa L. Rev.* 74 (1988): 1. The story of North Dakota's air-quality disputes is told in Lauren Donovan, "Air Pollution Dispute in Final Hours," *Bismarck Tribune*, Dec. 29, 2003, 1B; "A Change in the Air: Two Views on What a Change in North Dakota's Emission Standards Could Mean," *Bismarck Tribune*, Mar. 3, 1997, 1C.

43. NPS, Theodore Roosevelt National Park, Environmental Assessment: Boundary Expansion Study, Public Review Draft, Nov. 2002, 37, http://home.nps.gov/applications/parks/thro/ppdocuments/FINAL%20PUBL%20EA-NOVEMBER.pdf; *2006 NPS Management Policies*, 21.

44. Department of the Interior, Environment, and Related Agencies Appropriations Act, 2008, Pub. L. No. 110-161, 121 Stat. 1844, 2150–51, § 424(a) (2007) (Elkhorn Ranch offset); NPS, Boundary Expansion Study, 3.

45. Treaty with the Sioux—Brule, Miniconjou, Yanktonai, Hunkpapa, Blackfeet, Cuthead, Two Kettle, Sans Arcs, and Santee—and Arapahoe, 1868, 15 Stat.

635 (1868); Jenkinson, *Theodore Roosevelt in the Dakota Badlands,* 35 (citing *Hunting Trips of a Ranchman*). In 1980, the Supreme Court upheld an award of $117.5 million in damages and interest for the violation of the treaty. *See United States v. Sioux Nation,* 448 U.S. 371 (1980).

46. Enlarged Homestead Act of 1909, ch. 160, 35 Stat. 639 (repealed by 43 U.S.C. § 218 (2000)).

47. Timothy Egan, *The Worst Hard Time: The Untold Story of Those Who Survived the Great American Dust Bowl* (New York: Mariner Books, 2006), 267 (quoting the report of the Great Plains Drought Area Committee).

48. Resettlement Administration, First Annual Report of the Resettlement Administration, June 1936 (quoted in H. H. Wooten, "The Land Utilization Program, 1934 to 1964: Origin, Development, and Present Status," *USDA Econ. Res. Serv. Agric. Econ. Rep. No. 85* (1965): 10).

49. Bankhead-Jones Farm Tenant Act, 50 Stat. 522 (1937); 81 Cong. Rec. 8351 (1937) (statement of Rep. Lemke); *id.* at 8380 (statement of Rep. Coffee); *id.* at 8618 (statement of Sen. Bankhead).

50. Congressman Don Short, interview, *North Dakota History* 43 (Spring 1976): 65.

51. 16 U.S.C. § 1609(a) (range act); *Reichelderfer v. Quinn,* 287 U.S. 315 (1932); *United States v. 17,463.13 Acres of Land, More or Less, in McKenzie County,* No. 1002 (D.N.D. Feb. 6, 1941); Elizabeth Howard, "Management of the National Grasslands, *N. Dak. L. Rev.* 78 (2002): 409, 431; Eric Olson, "National Grasslands Management: A Primer," Nov. 1997, 16 (report prepared by the USDA's Office of the General Counsel's Natural Resource Division). *See Duncan Energy Co. v. USFS,* 50 F.3d 584, 589 (8th Cir. 1985) (describing the application of the BJTA to national grasslands); *Sharps v. USFS,* 28 F.3d 851, 852 (8th Cir. 1994) (same).

52. *Theodore Roosevelt National Park: Hearings before the House Comm. on Public Lands,* 79th Cong., 2d Sess. 18 (1946).

53. U.S. Forest Service, "Record of Decision for Dakota Prairie Grasslands: Final Environmental Impact Statement and Land and Resource Management Plan" (July 2002), http://www.fs.fed.us/ngp/plan/Dakota_Prairie_ROD.pdf [hereinafter Grasslands ROD], 1; Francis Moul, *The National Grasslands: A Guide to America's Undiscovered Treasures* (Lincoln: University of Nebraska Press, 2006), 6.

54. 36 C.F.R. § 219.11 (U.S. Forest Service grasslands regulations); Grasslands ROD, 10–15.

55. Grasslands ROD, 7 (good neighbor); Stephen Regenold, "Good Ride in the Badlands," *N.Y. Times,* Aug. 18, 2006, F1.

56. USDA, Forest Service, Northern and Rocky Mountain Regions, Summary of the Final Environmental Impact Statement: Dakota Prairie Grasslands, Nebraska National Forest Units, Thunder Basin National Grassland (Chadron, Neb.: USDA Forest Service, 2001), 10; Theodore Roosevelt, "In the Cattle Country," in *Ranch Life in the Far West,* 7, 14; Report of the National Grasslands Management Review Team, 5.

57. Myron P. Gutmann & Sara M. Pullum, "From Local to National Political Cultures: Social Capital and Civic Organization in the Great Plains," *Journal of Interdisciplinary History* 29 (Spring 1999): 725, 759; Michael Milstein, "Change on the Plains," *High Country News,* June 5, 2000, 32 (quoting Keith Winters).

58. Grasslands ROD, 5; Report of the Scientific Review Team: Dakota Prairie Grasslands, May 2005, 32; USDA, Forest Service, Northern Region, "The Livestock Grazing Record of Decision for Dakota Prairie Grasslands: Final Environmental Impact Statement and Land Resource Management Plan," Sept. 2006, http://www.fs.fed.us/r1/dakotaprairie/projects/livestock_grazing/final_record_of_decision_sig.pdf, 7–8.

59. In re Reichman, 173 I.B.L.A. 149 (2007); American Petroleum Institute, "Strategic Energy Resources: Bakken Shale, North Dakota," Winter 2008, http://www.api.org/policy/exploration/upload/StrategicEnergyResources-BakkenShale.pdf; The Wilderness Society, "Too Wild to Drill: Little Missouri National Grassland, North Dakota," http://www.wilderness.org/Where WeWork/NorthDakota/TWTD-LMNG.cfm; Mark Wolski, "Oil Company to Pay More Than $120,000 to North Dakota for Spill from Waste Pipe," *State Env't Daily,* Oct. 1, 2007.

60. *California ex rel. Lockyer v. U.S. Department of Agriculture,* 2009 U.S. App. LEXIS 17440 (9th Cir. 2009) (describing and reinstating the Forest Service's Roadless Rule); N.D. Cent. Code § 24-07-03; *Huffman v. Board of Supervisors,* 182 N.W. 459, 461 (N.D. 1921) (Robinson, C. J., concurring); Grasslands ROD, 21 (lack of consensus).

61. *Decision for Appeal of the Dakota Prairie Grasslands Land and Resource Management Plan Revision,* http://www.fs.fed.us/ngp/plan/appeals/appeals.html (Dakota Prairie), Feb. 2004, 15.

62. TRNP General Management Plan, 24.

63. Clay Jenkinson, "Best Future for the Badlands: Working Ranches," *Bismarck Tribune,* Mar. 1, 2009, 1C.

64. *Id.* at 1C.

65. Clay Jenkinson, "A Modest and Extremely Important Wilderness Proposal for North Dakota," *Bismarck Tribune,* Aug. 24, 2008, 1C.

CHAPTER 4. RIVER ENIGMA

1. Robert Louis Stevenson, *Across the Plains* (London: Chattus & Windus, 1892), 7.

2. Charles Weather Bump, *Down the Historic Susquehanna: A Summer's Jaunt from Otsego to the Chesapeake* (Baltimore: Press of the Sun Printing Office, 1899), 1; Roger B. Stein, *Susquehanna: Images of the Settled Landscape* (Binghamton, N.Y.: Roberson Center for the Arts and Sciences, 1981), 11–12.

3. *Pennsylvania Water & Power Co. v. Federal Power Comm'n,* 123 F.2d 155, 160 (D.C. Cir. 1941); Stein, *Susquehanna,* 17 (quoting Brainerd); Zachariah Poulson Jr., *A Description of the River Susquehanna, with Observations on the Present*

State of Its Trade and Navigation, and Their Practicable and Probable Improvement (Philadelphia, 1796), 7.

4. Peter Miller, "Susquehanna: America's Small-Town River," *National Geographic*, Jan. 1985, 352, 354.

5. Jack Brubaker, *Down the Susquehanna to the Chesapeake* (State College: Penn State University Press, 2003), 50 (quoting an Iroquois descendant); SRBC Information Sheet, "Economic Value of Water Resources: Direct Water-Dependent Businesses in the Susquehanna Basin" (rev. Nov. 2006), http:// www.srbc.net/pubinfo/docs/FactSheetEconValue1106.pdf.

6. Brubaker, *Down the Susquehanna*, 48 (quoting Flood), 143 (quoting Babbitt).

7. *York Haven Paper Co. v. York Haven Water & Power Co.*, 194 F. 255 (M.D. Pa. 1911); *Conrad/Dommel, LLC v. West Development Co.*, 815 A.2d 828, 845 (Md. Ct. Spec. App. 2003); *Delaware & Md. R.R. Co. v. Stump*, 8 G. & J. 479 (Md. 1837); *Lyon v. Binghamton*, 22 N.E.2d 354 (N.Y. 1939); Joseph W. Dellapenna, "Developing a Suitable Water Allocation Law for Pennsylvania," *Villanova Envtl. L.J.* 42 (2006): 1, 15–16.

8. *Susquehanna Canal Co. v. Wright*, 9 Watts & Serg. 9, 12 (Pa. 1845); Act of July 31, 1789, 1 Stat. 29, 32.

9. Susquehanna River Basin Compact, May 1972, 8, 13–14, 16, 24, http://www .srbc.net/about/srbc_compact.pdf.

10. *Levin v. Board of Supervisors*, 669 A.2d 1063, 1078 (Pa. Comm. Ct. 1995), *aff'd*, 689 A.2d 224 (Pa. 1997) (citing *State College Borough Water Authority v. Board of Supervisors*, 659 A.2d 640 (Pa. Comm. Ct. 1995)).

11. *Pennsy Supply, Inc. v. SRBC*, 2007 WL 551573, at *3 (M.D. Pa. Feb. 20, 2007); Review and Approval of Projects, Special Regulations and Standards, Hearings and Enforcement Actions, 71 Fed. Reg. 78570, 78570–71 (2006).

12. Susquehanna River Basin Compact, § 1.3(5), Pub. L. No. 91-175, 84 Stat. 1509, 1512 (1970); Dellapenna, "Developing," 74. On the Tahoe Regional Planning Agency, see *Tahoe-Sierra Preservation Council v. Tahoe Regional Planning Agency*, 535 U.S. 302 (2002) (rejecting a takings challenge); GAO, "Interstate Compacts: An Overview of the Structure and Governance of Environment and Natural Resource Compacts," http://www.gao.gov/new.items/d07519.pdf (Apr. 2007) (comparing the SRBC and the Tahoe agency). "The Upper Susquehanna Coalition is a network of county natural resource professionals who develop strategies, partnerships, programs, and projects to protect the headwaters of the Susquehanna River and Chesapeake Bay watersheds." Upper Susquehanna Coalition, http://www.u-s-c.org/.

13. William Voigt Jr., *The Susquehanna Compact: Guardian of the River's Future* (New Brunswick, N.J.: Rutgers University Press, 1972), ix.

14. Susan Q. Stranahan, *Susquehanna, River of Dreams* (Baltimore: Johns Hopkins University Press, 1993), 117 ("sinister side"); Robert P. Wolensky, *Better Than Ever! The Flood Recovery Task Force and the 1972 Agnes Disaster* (Stevens Point, Wis.: Foundation Press, 1993), 3.

15. New York State Dep't of Environmental Conservation, "Comprehensive Wildlife Conservation Strategy (CWCS) Plan," 473, http://www.dec.ny.gov/animals/30483.html; Stranahan, *Susquehanna, River of Dreams*, 118 (intruder), 119 (quoting Nathaniel Parker Willis, *Letters from under a Bridge* (1840)).

16. Joseph L. Arnold, *The Evolution of the 1936 Flood Control Act* (Fort Belvoir, Va.: U.S. Army Corps of Engineers, Office of History, 1988), 4–5.

17. Swamp Act, 9 Stat. 352, 352, § 1 (Mar. 2, 1849); 53 Cong. Rec. H7779 (daily ed. May 10, 1916) (statement of Rep. Tilson) (removes the mask); Karen M. O'Neill, *Rivers by Design: State Power and the Origins of U.S. Flood Control* (Durham, N.C.: Duke University Press, 2006), 129 (fully compatible), 146 (greatest); Sandra B. Zellmer, "A New Corps of Discovery for Missouri River Management," *Neb. L. Rev.* 83 (2004): 305.

18. 79 Cong. Rec. 14296 (1935) (statement of Sen. Tydings); Editorial, "After the Deluge," *N.Y. Times*, Mar. 22, 1936, E8; *see also* Arnold, *The Evolution of the 1936 Flood Control Act*, 65.

19. Flood Control Act of 1936, Pub. L. No. 74-738, 49 Stat. 1570, 1573–74, §§ 1, 2, & 5; Arnold, *The Evolution of the 1936 Flood Control Act*, viii, 91.

20. William C. Kashatus, "'One Flood against Another,'" *Citizens' Voice*, June 24, 2007 (quoting Rep. Flood). According to the accepted meteorological measurements, Agnes was a tropical storm, rather than a hurricane, by the time it reached central Pennsylvania. Everyone referred to it as a hurricane, though, so I will follow that nomenclature here.

21. Wolensky, *Better Than Ever!*, 11 (thousands), 17 (quoting de Toqueville's *Democracy in America*), 93 (interview with Judge Max Rosenn).

22. Wolensky, *Better Than Ever!*, 22 (slow, reluctant); Mary Russell, "Romney, Angry Flood Victims Tangle," *Wash. Post*, Aug. 10, 1972, A1; "Nixon Sending Romney to Check Flood-Aid Snag at Wilkes-Barre," *N.Y. Times*, Aug. 8, 1972, 36 (quoting a memorandum written by President Nixon).

23. 118 Cong. Rec. 26872 (1972) (statement of Sen. Scott); Wolensky, *Better Than Ever!*, 21 (entirely inadequate), 26 (quoting "Remarks of the President in a Radio Speech on Additional Disaster Relief," July 12, 1972).

24. 42 U.S.C. § 4002(a)(6) (public interest); *Small Business Disaster Loans—Hearings before the Subcomm. on Small Business of the Senate Banking, Housing and Urban Affairs Comm.*, 92d Cong., 2d Sess. (1972), 74 (testimony of Sen. Schweiker); Stranahan, *Susquehanna, River of Dreams*, 136, 138; Wolensky, *Better Than Ever!*, 84 (National Catastrophic Disaster Insurance Act), 95 (interview with Judge Rosenn).

25. Brubaker, *Down the Susquehanna*, 98 (green light), 99 (lower Mississippi and dams all over the place), 124 (empty swimming pool); Water Resources Development Act of 1986, Pub. L. No. 99-662, 100 Stat. 4082, 4124 § 401 (authorizing the Wyoming Valley Levee Raising Project).

26. *West Branch Valley Flood Protection Ass'n v. Stone*, 820 F. Supp. 1 (D.D.C. 1993).

27. Susquehanna River Basin Compact, § 6.6.

28. 42 U.S.C. § 4002(b)(1) (NFIA); "Comprehensive Wildlife Conservation Strategy (CWCS) Plan," 475 (blaming the lack of zoning); Stranahan, *Susquehanna, River of Dreams*, 126 (quoting the Corps of Engineers), 139; Wolensky, *Better Than Ever!*, 13–14, 54–55 (defining the floodplain); Brubaker, *Down the Susquehanna*, 76 (quoting Dan Bauman of Bloomsburg, Pennsylvania's complaint about realtors versus developers).

29. 155 Cong Rec H1841, H1988 (daily ed. Feb. 23, 2009) (itemizing 2009 appropriations); Press release, "SRBC Calls on Congress to Restore Funding for Susquehanna Flood Forecast and Warning System," Apr. 1, 2005, http://www.srbc.net/pubinfo/press/docs/FF&WSResolutionMarch05.pdf; Press release, "Mikulski Announces Commitment to Fighting for Federal Investment in Susquehanna River Basin Commission," June 17, 2005, http://mikulski.senate.gov/Newsroom/PressReleases/record.cfm?id=239055.

30. Pa. Stat. at Large, ch. DCXXVII, 1770–71, 36–37; *Mayor and City Council v. Harlow*, 98 A. 852, 853, 854 (Md. 1916) (quoting Act of the Legislature of 1797, Chapter 99).

31. H.R. 92, 39th Cong., 1st Sess. (1866); Stranahan, *Susquehanna, River of Dreams*, 51.

32. Memorandum of Secretary of War, Mar. 8, 1904.

33. Brubaker, *Down the Susquehanna*, 178.

34. *Pennsylvania Water & Power Co. v. Federal Power Comm'n*, 123 F.2d 155 (D.C. Cir. 1941); *Mayor & City Council v. Harlow*, 98 A. at 853.

35. FERC, "Final Environmental Impact Statement for License Amendment: Holtwood Hydroelectric Project" (Nov. 2008), http://www.ferc.gov/industries/hydropower/enviro/eis/2008/11-14-08.asp, xix; "PPL to Expand Holtwood Hydroelectric Plant in Lancaster County," *PA Environmental Digest*, Jan. 18, 2008, http://www.paenvironmentdigest.com/newsletter/default.asp?NewsletterArticleID=8484 (McGinty); Press release, "Proposed Expansion of PPL Hydroelectric Plant Takes Major Step Forward," Jan. 17, 2008, http://www.pplweb.com; In re PPL Holtwood, LLC, Consent Order and Agreement (PADEP Nov. 21, 2007).

36. Stranahan, *Susquehanna, River of Dreams*, 243 (greatest fish highway); *Susquehanna Canal Co. v. Wright*, 159 (quoting Smith's diary); George Brown Goode, *The Fisheries and Fishery Industries of the United States* (Washington, D.C.: Government Printing Office, 1887), vol. 1, 646 (settlers).

37. *Carson v. Blazer*, 2 Binn. 475 (Pa. 1810) (riparian owner); *id.* at 488 (Brackenridge, J., dissenting); Richard Gerstell, *American Shad: A Three-Hundred-Year History in the Susquehanna River Basin* (State College, Pa.: Pennsylvania State University Press, 1998), 100 (more than seventy-five laws); Bump, *Down the Historic Susquehanna*, 347 (lamentations).

38. 16 U.S.C. § 803(a) (Federal Power Act); Stranahan, *Susquehanna, River of Dreams*, 272 (quoting the administrative judge).

39. In re Philadelphia Elec. Power Co. & Susquehanna Power Co., 38 F.E.R.C. P61,003, P61,006, P61,008–09 (FERC 1987).

40. Atlantic States Marine Fisheries Commission, "Review of the Atlantic States Fisheries Commission Fishery Management Plan for Shad and River Herring (*Alosa spp.*) 2007 (2007)," 3, http://www.asmfc.org; Pennsylvania Fish and Boat Commission, Susquehanna River American Shad, http://www.fish .state.pa.us/shad_susq.htm; Pennsylvania Fish and Boat Commission, "Migratory Fish Restoration and Passage on the Susquehanna River," n.d., 3, http://www.fish.state.pa.us/pafish/shad/migratory_fish.pdf.

41. Brubaker, *Down the Susquehanna,* 125; Paul E. Kanjorski, "Deflating the Myths about the Inflatable Dam," *Times-Leader* (Wilkes-Barre, Pa.), Apr. 30, 2006; Gannett Fleming, p. ES-14.

42. In re Wilkes-Barre Inflatable Structure, No. 2003-01240-13 (U.S. Army Corps of Engineers, Baltimore District, Feb. 14, 2008), 96, http://www.nab.usace .army.mil/Regulatory/News/WBIS13Feb08.pdf; Bill O'Boyle & Jennifer Learn-Andes, "Get Out of Dam Project Now: County Now Would Have to Pay $6 Million in Local Cost Share Because Project's Cost Has Gone Up, Commissioner Says," *Times-Leader* (Wilkes-Barre, Pa.), Feb. 16, 2008 (quoting Rep. Kanjorski); Kanjorski's Statement about Army Corps of Engineers' Decision to Reject Inflatable Dam, Feb. 14, 2008, http://kanjorski.house.gov/index.php ?option=com_content&task=view&id=1042&Itemid=.

43. SRBC Information Sheet, "Pennsylvania Agricultural Consumptive Water Use," rev. Jan. 2007, 1, http://www.srbc.net/pubinfo/docs/Agricultural %20Water%20Use%20(1_07).pdf.

44. H.R. Res. 1444, 110th Cong., 2d Sess. (2008) (introduced by Rep. English); SRBC, Review and Approval of Projects, 73 Fed. Reg. 78618, 76819 (2008); Marcellus Shale Public Hearing: Pennsylvania House of Representatives Environmental Resources and Energy Comm. (Sept. 30, 2008), 2 (testimony of Thomas W. Beauduy), http://www.srbc.net/whatsnew/docs/SRBCTestimony 93008.pdf; SRBC, "Accommodating a New Straw in the Water: Extracting Natural Gas from the Marcellus Shale in the Susquehanna River Basin," Feb. 2009, 3 (previously unused rule), http://www.srbc.net/programs/docs/ Marcellus%20Legal%20Overview%20Paper%20(Beauduy).pdf.PDF; SRBC, "SRBC Information Sheet: Natural Gas Well Development in the Susquehanna River Basin," http://www.srbc.net/programs/docs/ProjectReview Marcellus%20Shale12-2008.pdf (Jan. 2009); Independent Oil & Gas Ass'n of N.Y., "Homegrown Energy: The Facts about Natural Gas Exploration of the Marcellus Shale," http://www.marcellusfacts.com/pdf/homegrownenergy .pdf, 1 (500 trillion cubic feet).

45. Water Resources Development Act of 1986, Pub. L. No. 99-662, § 1135, as amended by Water Resources Development Act of 1996, Pub. L. No. 104-404; SRBC Information Sheet, "Whitney Point Environmental Restoration Project," rev. Sept. 2005, 1, http://www.srbc.net/pubinfo/docs/Whitney %20Point%20_revised%20Sept%202005_.pdf.

46. Brubaker, *Down the Susquehanna,* 22 ("sweating bullets," quoting a local resident); 35 (Garbage Disposal and "no city").

47. American Rivers, "America's Most Endangered Rivers of 2005: Ten Rivers Reaching the Crossroads in the Next 12 Months" (2005), 7, http://www.americanrivers.org/site/DocServer/AR_MER_2005.pdf?docID=1261.

48. "Rep. Kanjorski Welcomes National Attention to Susquehanna River," *US Fed News*, Apr. 13, 2005.

49. Brubaker, *Down the Susquehanna*, 53–55 (Knox Mine disaster); Bump, *Down the Historic Susquehanna*, 90 (wondrous prosperity).

50. *Commonwealth v. Barnes & Tucker Co.*, 371 A.2d 461 (Pa. 1977); *Commonwealth v. Barnes & Tucker Co.*, 319 A.2d 871 (Pa. 1974); *Pennsylvania Coal Co. v. Sanderson*, 6 A. 453, 459 (Pa. 1886); Act of Aug. 23, 1965, P.L. 372, § 4(3) (finding of mine drainage damage); Clean Streams Law, 1937 Pa. Laws 1987 (codified as amended at 35 Pa. Cons. Stat. §§ 691.01-1001); *Water Pollution Control: Hearings before the House Comm. on Public Works*, 80th Cong., 1st Sess. 219 (1947) (statement of Andrew B. Crichton, president of Johnstown Coal and Coke Co.); Joseph L. Sax, "The Limits of Private Rights in Public Waters," *Envtl. L.* 19 (1989): 473, 476; Note, "Statutory Stream Control," *U. Pa. L. Rev.* 100 (1951): 225, 235; Note, "An Examination of Sanderson v. Pennsylvania Coal Company," *Dickinson L. Rev.* 18 (1913): 1, 11.

51. SRBC Information Sheet, "Abandoned Mine Drainage Remediation Strategy for the West Branch Susquehanna Watershed," Nov. 2006, 1, http://www.srbc.net/pubinfo/docs/West%20Branch%20Strategy%20(11_06).pdf.

52. *Commonwealth v. Scantena*, 498 A.2d 1314, 1317 (Pa. 1985); Stranahan, *River of Dreams*, 150.

53. *United States v. Alcan Alum. Co.*, 964 F.2d 252, 256, 259 (3d Cir. 1992).

54. *Id.* at 269–70; *Alcan Aluminum Corp. v. Butler Aviation-Boston, Inc.*, 57 ERC (BNA) 1232 (M.D. Pa. 2003) (rejecting Alcan's lawsuit against the settling parties); *United States v. Alcan Aluminum Corp.*, 892 F. Supp. 648 (M.D. Pa. 1995) (holding Alcan jointly and severally liable), *aff'd*, 96 F.3d 1434 (3d Cir. 1996) (unpublished table decision), *cert. denied*, 521 U.S. 1103 (1997); John Copeland Nagle, "CERCLA, Causation, and Responsibility," *Minn. L. Rev.* 78 (1995): 1493, 1516–21 (reviewing the implications of the Third Circuit's decision).

55. *Metropolitan Edison Co. v. People against Nuclear Energy*, 460 U.S. 766 (1983) (NEPA); *Sholly v. NRC*, 651 F.2d 780 (D.C. Cir. 1980), vacated, 459 U.S. 1194 (1983) (venting litigation); J. Samuel Walker, *Three Mile Island: A Nuclear Crisis in Historical Perspective* (Berkeley: University of California Press, 2004), 48 ("did not incite"), 225 (Lancaster suit); Bonnie A. Osif, Anthony J. Baratta, & Thomas W. Conkling, *TMI 25 Years Later: The Three Mile Island Nuclear Power Plant Accident and Its Impact* (University Park: Pennsylvania University Press, 2004), 35 (psychologists), 46 (water disposal).

56. In re TMI Litig., 193 F.3d 613 (3d Cir. 1999); Stranahan, *Susquehanna, River of Dreams*, 212.

57. "Comprehensive Wildlife Conservation Strategy (CWCS) Plan," at 473.

58. Chesapeake Bay Program, "Chesapeake 2000," June 28, 2000, 4, 12, http://www.chesapeakebay.net/pubs/chesapeake2000agreement.pdf.

59. New York State Department of Environmental Conservation, "New York State Tributary Strategy for Chesapeake Bay Restoration: An Interim Plan Based on the Chesapeake Bay Program Watershed Model," Sept. 2007, 10, http://www.dec.ny.gov/docs/water_pdf/cbaystratfinal.pdf; Brubaker, *Down the Susquehanna*, xiii.

60. 72 Penn. Stat. § 8703-E (2008) (Resource Enhancement and Protection Act tax credits); Chesapeake Bay Foundation, "Voices of Agriculture: A Summary of Fourteen Listening Sessions with Pennsylvania Producers," Apr. 2006, 3–4, http://www.cbf.org/site/DocServer/VoicesofAg.pdf?docID=5383.

61. Chesapeake Bay Foundation, "Forested Buffers: The Key to Clean Streams," *Forest Leaves* 16, No. 3 (Winter 2007), 1, http://rnrext.cas.psu.edu/PDFs/FLWinter2007.pdf; Broome County Soil & Water Conservation Dist., *Conservation Update* 9 (Spring 2007): 2.

62. *Commonwealth of Pa., Dep't of Envtl. Resources v. USPS*, 13 F.3d 62 (3d Cir. 1993); *Pennsylvania Agriculture and County Life 1640–1840* (quoted in "Pa. Stream ReLeaf," 1).

63. Mary R. Owens, ed., *Bay Smart, A Citizen's Guide to Maryland's Critical Area Program* (Annapolis: Critical Area Commission for the Chesapeake and Atlantic Coastal Bays, 2007), 11, http://www.dnr.state.md.us/criticalarea/download/baysmart.pdf; Chesapeake Bay Foundation, "The Critical Area Act: Intent, Reality, and the Need for Reform," Feb. 2008, 1 (variances).

64. Harford County, "Harford County 2004 Master Plan and Land Use Element Plan," May 2004, iv, http://www.harfordcountymd.gov/PlanningZoning/landuseplan/Plan/Part1_ExecSumTableContents.pdf; Harford County, "Citizen's Guide to Harford County's Agricultural Land Preservation Program," http://www.harfordcountymd.gov/PlanningZoning/LandPreservation.html.

65. Chesapeake Bay Foundation, "Addressing Sprawl and Land Use in Pennsylvania," n.d., 5, http://www.cbf.org/site/DocServer/sprawl_white_paper_for_pennsylvania.pdf?docID=8263.

66. "Comprehensive Wildlife Conservation Strategy (CWCS) Plan," 487.

67. Brubaker, *Down the Susquehanna*, 50 (learned a lesson).

68. Susquehanna Gateway National Heritage Area Act, S. 49, 111th Cong., 1st Sess. (2009).

69. SRBC, Comprehensive Plan for the Water Resources of the Susquehanna River Basin (Dec. 2008), 73, http://www.srbc.net/planning/ComprehensivePlanwithAppendicesFINALDec2008.pdf.

70. Congressman C. A. Dutch Ruppersberger, "Appropriations Requests," http://dutch.house.gov/approps.shtml.

71. Ronald D. Utt, "Closing Unneeded and Obsolete Independent Governmental Agencies," http://www.heritage.org/Research/GovernmentReform/bg1015.cfm, 14 (Jan. 25, 1995) (Heritage Foundation report); SRBC, press release, "Congressman Holden Secures $1 Million for SRBC to Enhance Flood Mitigation, Protect Water Supplies and Manage Low River Flows," Mar. 16, 2009, http://www.srbc.net/pubinfo/press/docs/HoldenPressConf31609.pdf.

CHAPTER 5. LIGHTS OUT

1. David H. Townsend, "A Brief History of Alamogordo," in David H. Townsend, Clif McDonald, & Mose C. Cauthen eds., *Our First Hundred Years* (Alamogordo, N.M.: Holloman Air Force Base, 1998), 2; Robert H. Sholly, "Alamogordo, New Mexico: A Case Study in the Dynamics of Western Town Growth," May 1971 (M.A. thesis, University of Texas at El Paso), 120 (speculation scheme).

2. Lesley S. King, *Frommers' New Mexico* (Hoboken, N.J.: Wiley, 8th ed. 2005), 344 ("Alamegeddin"); Mose C. Cauthen, "The Birth of a Military Base: One Man's Memories—How Holloman Air Force Base Got Its Start," in Townsend, McDonald, & Cauthen, *Our First Hundred Years,* 16 (telegram to Sen. Chavez).

3. City of Alamogordo, City of Alamogordo's Annual Report for 2007, 1; Alamogordo Chamber of Commerce, "Alamogordo, New Mexico, USA," n.d., 1.

4. 15 U.S.C. § 473 (purposes); Forest Service Organic Act of 1897, 30 Stat. 11, 34–35, codified as amended at 16 U.S.C. §§ 473 et seq.; Act of March 3, 1891, ch. 561, 26 Stat. 1095, 1103; GORP, Lincoln National Forest, New Mexico, http://gorp.away.com/gorp/resource/us_national_forest/nm_linco.htm (recreational mecca).

5. *Forest Guardians v. USFS,* No. CIV-00-490 JP/RHS & No. CIV-00-1240 JP/RHS (D.N.M. Apr. 14, 2003).

6. Healthy Forests Restoration Act of 2003, Pub. L. No. 108-148, 117 Stat. 1887, § 2(1) (codified at 16 U.S.C. § 6501(1)); *Sierra Club v. Bosworth,* 510 F.3d 1016 (9th Cir. 2007); Robert B. Keiter, "The Law of Fire: Reshaping Public Land Policy in an Era of Ecology and Litigation," *Envtl. L.* 36 (2006): 301, 344; Bryan Bird & Elicia Whittlesey, "Born of Fire: The National Fire Plan in the Southwest," Oct. 2007, 3, 16, http://www.fguardians.org/support_docs/report_born-of-fire_10–07.pdf (Forest Guardians report).

7. Beth Gilbert, *Alamogordo: The Territorial Years, 1898–1912* (Albuquerque: Starline Printing. 1988), 85–86.

8. U.S. Forest Service, Press Release, "Lincoln National Forest and BLM's Ft. Stanton Area to Re-Open July 2nd," June 26, 2008, http://www.publiclands.org/firenews/pressreleases/NM.php?id=EkEuVpkpypuSGACjUj (quoting Mayor Venable).

9. U.S. Department of Agriculture, "Environmental Assessment for Sacramento Mountains Defoliation Project, Sacramento Ranger District, Lincoln National Forest," 2008, http://www.fs.fed.us/r3/lincoln/projects/sac-defol/EA_sacramento_mtns_defoliation_04122008.pdf, 51–52, 59.

10. *Forest Guardians v. Kempthorne,* No. 1:08-cv-00011-RMU (D.D.C. Apr. 15, 2008) (stipulated settlement agreement); *Forest Guardians v. Kempthorne,* No. 1:08-cv-00011-RMU (D.D.C. filed Jan. 3, 2008); Endangered and Threatened Wildlife and Plants, 90-Day Finding on a Petition to List the Sacramento Mountains Checkerspot Butterfly (*Euphydryas anicia cloudcrofti*) as Endangered with Critical Habitat, 73 Fed. Reg. 74123 (2008); Endangered and

Threatened Wildlife and Plants, Withdrawal of the Proposed Rule to List the Sacramento Checkerspot Butterfly as Endangered with Critical Habitat, 69 Fed. Reg. 76428 (2004); Endangered and Threatened Wildlife and Plants, Proposed Endangered Status for the Sacramento Checkerspot Butterfly and Proposed Designation of Critical Habitat, 66 Fed. Reg. 46575 (2001); Otero County (N.M.) Ordinance No. 01-05 (2005); FWS, Otero County, The Village of Cloudcroft, and U.S. Forest Service, Conservation Plan for the Sacramento Mountains Checkerspot Butterfly (*Euphydryas anicia cloudcrofti*) (Albuquerque, N.M.: FWS, 2004), 38, http://www.fws.gov/southwest/es/NewMexico/documents/SMCB_Final_11_1_05.pdf; Bill English, "What Will 2009 Bring Us?" *Alamogordo Daily News*, Jan. 1, 2009 (annual migration); Bill English, "Butterflies Aren't Free, You Know?" *Alamogordo Daily News*, Dec. 11, 2008 (deep fried).

11. Environmental Assessment for Pinyon/Juniper Opening Maintenance, Sacramento Ranger District, Otero County, N.M., 2, 5.

12. William Belknap Jr., "New Mexico's Great White Sands: Feathery Dunes of Snow-white Gypsum in a 140,000-acre 'Sandbox' Make This Area Unique among National Monuments," *National Geographic*, July 1957, 113; Carl. P. Russell, "The White Sands of Alamogordo: A Dry Ocean of Granular Gypsum Billows under Desert Winds in a New National Playground," *National Geographic*, Aug. 1935, 250.

13. David H. Stratton, *Tempest over Teapot Dome: The Story of Albert B. Fall* (Norman: University of Oklahoma Press, 1998) (biography of Fall and his career); Dietmar Schneider-Hector, *White Sands: The History of a National Monument* (Albuquerque: University of New Mexico Press, 1993), 52–69 (describing the national park proposals).

14. *Fall v. United States*, 49 F.2d 506 (D.C. Cir. 1931) (affirming Fall's bribery conviction); 62 Cong. Rec. 10064 (1922) (statement of Rep. Bursum); *Mescalero National Park Project: Hearing before the House Comm. on Indian Affairs*, 76th Cong., 4th Sess. (1923), 49–50 (testimony of Robert Sterling Yard); Dietmar Schneider-Hector, "A.B. Fall's All-Year National Park," *New Mexico Historical Rev.* 68 (July 1993) (describing the national park proposals).

15. Antiquities Act of 1906, 16 U.S.C. § 431; 40 Cong. Rec. 7888 (1906) (statement of Rep. Lacey); Robert W. Righter, "National Monuments to National Parks: The Use of the Antiquities Act of 1906," *Western Historical Q.* (Aug. 1989): 284 (describing the debate over the Antiquities Act).

16. *Mountain States Legal Foundation v. Bush*, 306 F.3d 1132 (D.C. Cir. 2002), *cert. denied*, 540 U.S. 812 (2003) (upholding President Clinton's national monument designations); Hal Rothman, *Preserving Different Pasts: The American National Monuments* (Urbana & Chicago: University of Illinois Press, 1989), xi, xiii (describing the Antiquities Act).

17. Pres. Proc. 2025, 261 (Jan. 18, 1933) (President Hoover's national monument proclamation); Rothman, *Preserving Different Pasts*, 89–118 (chapter on "second-class sites").

18. Belknap, "New Mexico's Great White Sands," 137.

19. *White Sands Ranchers of New Mexico v. United States,* 18 Cl. Ct. 13, 17 (1988); White Sands Fair Compensation Act, H.R. 3408, 101st Cong., 1st Sess. § 2(4) (proposed finding of inadequate compensation); *White Sands Fair Compensation Act of 1989: Hearing before the Subcomm. on Administrative Law and Government Relations of the House Judiciary Comm.,* 101st Cong., 1st Sess. (1990), 91 (statement of Assistant Attorney General Myles Flint), 117 (statement of G. B. Oliver Jr. on behalf of the White Sands Ranchers of Alamogordo, N.M.).

20. Schneider-Hector, *White Sands,* 135 (quoting the executive order), 136 (quoting George Fitzpatrick, editor of *New Mexico*).

21. Susan M. Kain, "White Sands National Monument: White Animals at White Sands," http://www.nps.gov/whsa/naturescience/white-animals-at-white-sands.htm (last updated Sept. 16, 2007).

22. Schneider-Hector, *White Sands,* 24–27 (wolves and oryx).

23. UNESCO World Heritage Centre, World Heritage Information Kit (June 2008), 9, 17, http://whc.unesco.org/documents/publi_infokit_en.pdf.

24. Otero County, N.M., Ordinance No. 07-05, § 1(2) (2007); Rene Romo, "No, Thanks; Otero County Doesn't Want U.N. World Heritage Designation for White Sands," *Alamogordo Daily News,* Aug. 26, 2007, B1 (U.N. closure); Karl Anderson, "Steve Pearce on Pause," *Alamogordo Daily News,* Aug. 16, 2007 (Pearce); Steve West, "Designation Would Be a Good Thing, and an Honor," *Alamogordo Daily News,* Oct. 31, 2007 (misinformation); Harold A. Teeter, Letter, *Alamogordo Daily News,* Sept. 12, 2007 (environmentalists and albino bugs); J. P. Krzenski, "WHS Opponents Have Shot Us All in the Foot," *Alamogordo Daily News,* Sept. 8, 2007 (embarrassed); J. P. Krzenski, "Opposition Seems Based on Paranoia," *Alamogordo Daily News,* Aug. 25, 2007; William R. Moyers, "U.N. Can't Be Trusted at WSNM, or Anywhere," *Alamogordo Daily News,* Aug 11, 2007 (entrance fees); J. P. Krzenski, "Conspiracy People See Big Risk in Heritage Site," *Alamogordo Daily News,* July 29, 2007.

25. World Heritage Information Kit, 5; Press release, "Secretary Kempthorne Selects New U.S. World Heritage Tentative List," Jan. 25, 2008, http://www.doi.gov/news/08_News_Releases/080122a.html.

26. UNESCO Convention Concerning the Protection of the World Cultural and Natural Heritage, Nov. 16, 1972, 27 U.S.T. 37, T.I.A.S. No. 8226, arts. 4–6; Erica J. Thorson, "On Thin Ice: The Failure of the United States and the World Heritage Committee to Take Climate Change Mitigation Pursuant to the World Heritage Convention Seriously," *Envtl. L.* 38 (2008): 139, 164–65; UNESCO, World Heritage: About World Heritage, http://whc.unesco.org/en/about (belong to people).

27. *American Land Sovereignty Protection Act: Hearings before the House Comm. on Resources,* 105th Cong., 1st Sess. (1997), 7 (statement of Rep. Jerry Solomon); Otero County, N.M., Ordinance No. 07-05, 1(2) (2007); John Charles Kunich, "World Heritage in Danger in the Hotspots," *Ind. L.J.* 78 (2002): 619, 638;

Mathew Machado, "Mounting Opposition to Biosphere Reserves and World Heritage Sites in the United States Sparked by Claims of Interference with National Sovereignty," *Colo. J. Int'l Envtl. L. Y. B.* (1997): 120; Janet White, "Withdraw White Sands Application," *Alamogordo Daily News*, Nov. 24, 2007 (buffer zones).

28. *American Land Sovereignty Protection Act Hearings,* 191 (statement of Jeremy A. Rabkin, Dep't of Government, Cornell University).

29. Ekirch, *At Day's Close,* 3, 6, 12, 71, 207.

30. Catherine Rich & Travis Longcore, "Introduction," in Catherine Rich & Travis Longcore, eds., *Ecological Consequences of Artificial Night Lighting* (Washington, D.C.: Island Press, 2006), 1.

31. Elizabeth M. Alvarez del Castillo, David L. Crawford, & Donald R. Davis, "Preserving our Nighttime Environment: A Global Approach," in Hugo E. Schwarz, ed., *Light Pollution: The Global View* (Dordrecht: Kluwer Academic Publishers, 2003), 65; Kendrick Frazier, *People of Chaco: A Canyon and Its Culture* (New York: W. W. Norton, rev. ed. 1999), 189 (quoting Don Talayesva, Sun Chief).

32. Timothy Ferris, *Seeing in the Dark: How Amateur Astronomers Are Discovering the Wonders of the Universe* (New York: Simon & Schuster, 2002); Pablo Daud Miranda, "Discurso/Speech by Representante CONAMA," in Schwarz, *Light Pollution,* 4–5 (our skies); Alvarez del Castillo, Crawford, & Davis, "Preserving," 65 (vital part of environment).

33. Apache Point Observatory, http://www.apo.nmsu.edu/Images/07bwbrochure .pdf. The bylaws of the Alamogordo Astronomy Club are online at http://www .zianet.com/aacwp/PDF/AAClub%202006%20Bylaws.pdf.

34. Ekirch, *At Day's Close,* 72, 82; Sholly, *Alamogordo, New Mexico,* 49–50 (electric lighting in Alamogordo).

35. The International Dark-Sky Ass'n, "IDA Mission and Goals," http://www .darksky.org/mc/page.do?sitePageId=56411&orgId=idsa.

36. Pierantonio Cinzano, Fabio Falchi, & Christopher D. Elvidge, "Global Monitoring of the Night Sky Brightness by Satellites and the State of the Night Sky in Chile," in Schwarz, *Light Pollution,* 22 (99 percent of Americans); Bob Mizon, *Light Pollution: Responses and Remedies* (London: Springer, 2002), 43 (glare); *The American Heritage Dictionary of the English Language* (Boston: Houghton Mifflin, 1996), 1402.

37. Alvarez del Castillo, Crawford, & Davis, "Preserving," 62.

38. *Loggerhead Turtle v. County Council of Volusia,* 148 F.3d 1231 (11th Cir. 1998), *cert. denied,* 526 U.S. 1081 (1999); City of Alamogordo, "City Commission Work Session," May 6, 1985, 3 (plants); Travis Longcore & Catherine Rich, "Synthesis," in Longcore & Rich, *Ecological Consequences,* 425 (general ecological effects of night lighting); Letter from Robert L. Gent, President, IDA Board of Directors to USEPA Administrator Steven Johnson, Jan. 4, 2008, http://data.nextrionet.com/site/idsa/Gent%20Letter%204%20Jan%20 08%20Rev2.pdf (carbon dioxide).

39. Alan Hale, "Dark Skies a Blessing in Sac Mountains," *Alamogordo Daily News*, Feb. 26, 1999, 5B.

40. Night Sky Protection Act, N.M.S.A. §§ 74-12-1 to 74-12-10.

41. International Dark-Sky Ass'n, "Model Lighting Ordinance," http://www.darksky .org/mc/page.do?sitePageId=58880.

42. City of Alamogordo, "City Commission Regular Meeting Minutes," Oct. 23, 1990, 12–13 (summarizing testimony of Kurt Anderson and of Donna Nueva on behalf of the Alamogordo Amateur Astronomers); City of Alamogordo, "City Commission Work Session," 1.

43. Alamogordo, N.M., Ordinance No. 805, An Ordinance Adopting a New Chapter 18.5 to the Alamogordo City Code Regulating the Installation of Outdoor Lighting (Dec. 11, 1990).

44. Alamogordo, N.M., Ordinance No. 1057, Amending the Outdoor Lighting Ordinance (Apr. 13, 1999); Alamogordo, N.M., Ordinance No. 1030, Amending § 31-01-040 of the *Code of Ordinances* and Having to Do with Outdoor Lighting (Apr. 14, 1998); Alamogordo, N.M., Ordinance No. 397, Amending Chapter 31 of the *Code of Ordinances* concerning Outdoor Lighting (Apr. 22, 1997).

45. City of Alamogordo, "October 1990 City Commission Minutes," Oct. 1990, 15 (Commissioner Wynham); Sharon Anderson, "Dark Sky Ordinance Again Comes under the Spotlight," *Alamogordo Daily News*, July 8, 1996, 1 (quoting Paul Carnes and city attorney Becky Ehler).

46. Alamogordo, N.M. Code § 1-01-100(a) (general penalty provision).

47. *Whiteco Outdoor Advertising v. City of Tucson*, 972 P.2d 647 (Ariz. Ct. App. 1998).

48. Mizon, *Light Pollution*, 163; International Dark-Sky Ass'n, "How to Talk to Your Neighbor Who Has a Bad Light," 1997, http://data.nextrionet.com/site/ idsa/iso25.pdf.

49. Mizon, *Light Pollution*, 161 (blaming retailers).

50. 33 U.S.C. § 1251(a)(1) (goal of the Clean Water Act); Amitai Aviram, "The Placebo Effect of Law: Law's Role in Manipulating Perceptions," *Geo. Wash. L. Rev.* 75 (2006): 54; Michael S. Kirsch, "Alternative Sanctions and the Federal Tax Law: Symbols, Shaming, and Social Norm Management as a Substitute for Effective Tax Policy," *Iowa L. Rev.* 89 (2004): 863, 921–30. The critiques of symbolic environmental legislation include Joshua D. Sarnoff, "The Continuing Imperative (But Only from a National Perspective) for Federal Environmental Legislation," *Duke Envtl. L. & Pol'y F.* 7 (1997): 225, 288–91; John P. Dwyer, "The Pathology of Symbolic Legislation," *Ecology L.Q.* 17 (1990): 233; David Schoenbrod, "Goals Statutes or Rules Statutes: The Case of the Clean Air Act," *UCLA L. Rev.* 30 (1983): 740; and James A. Henderson Jr. & Richard N. Pearson, "Implementing Federal Environmental Policies: The Limits of Aspirational Commands," *Colum. L. Rev.* 78 (1978): 1429.

51. *Small Business Compliance with Federal Regulations: Hearing before the Investigations and Regulation and Paperwork Subcomms. of the House Economic and Educational Opportunities Comm.*, 104th Cong. 1st Sess. (1995); Elva K. Sterreich,

"Era Ends Thursday as Business Owner Retires," *Alamogordo Daily News*, Mar. 13, 2008; Anderson, "Dark Sky Ordinance Again Comes under the Spotlight," 1 (quoting Lattauzio's comments on customer safety).

52. Mark T. Adams & William Wren, "Preserving the Night Sky at McDonald Observatory," in Schwarz, *Light Pollution*, 179; San Pedro Creek Estates, "Covenants," http://www.sanpedrocreek.com/covenants.html.

53. *Whorton v. Mr. C's*, 687 P.2d 86, 89 (N.M. 1984); *id.* at 90 (Stowers, J., dissenting); *Mason v. Farmer*, 456 P.2d 187 (N.M. 1969); *Alamogordo Improvement Co. v. Prendergast*, 109 P.2d 254 (N.M. 1940); *Alamogordo Improvement Co. v. Hennessee*, 56 P.2d 1127 (N.M. 1936); David H. Townsend, "Alamogordo and the Block 50 Covenant," *Pioneer* 10 (2006): 62–68 (describing the *Safeway* case).

54. Paula A. Franzese, "Does It Take a Village? Privatization, Patterns of Restrictiveness and the Demise of Community," *Vill. L. Rev.* 47 (2002): 553, 560.

55. *2006 NPS Management Policies*, 44; *Mich. Comp. L.* § 322.821–26 (dark sky preserve); Black Canyon of the Gunnison, "Visitor Guide, Darkness in Danger," Summer 2005, 5; National Park Service, "The Endangered Night Sky Darkness Project in Chaco Culture National Historical Park," http://www.nps.gov/archive/chcu/nightskyprogram.htm.

56. *United States v. Alamogordo Lumber Co.*, 202 F. 700 (8th Cir. 1912) (describing the land title litigation).

57. Alamogordo, N.M., Code § 28-03-033 (water conservation); *City of Alamogordo v. Christopher*, No. CV-05-019 (N.M. 12th Jud. Dist. Ct. Apr. 7, 2008) (upholding city's water rights); Sloan Digital Sky Survey Project Book, http://www.astro.princeton.edu/PBOOK/site/site.htm (Apache Point Observatory proposal).

58. *Lee v. United States Air Force*, 354 F.3d 1229 (10th Cir. 2004); U.S. Air Force, "Proposed Expansion of German Air Force Operations at Holloman AFB, New Mexico, Final Environmental Impact Statement," Apr. 1998, vol. 3, 6:78 (outsiders); 6:112 (liberal judge); 6:115 (abomination).

59. Tiner J. Limancusa, "The Federalization of a Western Frontier Town: Alamogordo, New Mexico, 1942–1946," *Pioneer* 8 (Spring/Summer 2004): 40 (quoting Ethel Ortega Olson's "ghost town" comment), 60 (federalization).

60. Ferris, *Seeing in the Dark*, 294; Bob Unger, "President's Message," *Alamogordo Astronomy Club: June 2006 Newsletter*, 1, http://www.zianet.com/aacwp/Newsletters/Current.pdf.

CONCLUSION

1. Michael P. Vandenbergh, "Order without Social Norms: How Personal Norm Activation Can Protect the Environment," *Nw. U. L. Rev.* 99 (2005): 1001, 1004.

2. Vision 100—Century of Aviation Reauthorization Act, Pub. L. No. 108-176; 117 Stat. 2490, 2543, § 404 (2003).

3. Matthew Klingle, *Emerald City: An Environmental History of Seattle* (New Haven, Ct.: Yale University Press, 2007), 3; William Cronon, *Changes in the Land: Indians, Colonists, and the Ecology of New England* (New York: Hill & Wang, rev. ed. 2003), 7.

4. J. B. Ruhl, "Climate Change and the Endangered Species Act: Building Bridges to the No-Analog Future," *B.U. L. Rev.* 88 (2007): 1, 50 n.200 (explaining adaptive management); J. B. Ruhl, "Regulation by Adaptive Management—Is It Possible?," *Minn. J. L. Sci. & Tech.* 7 (2005): 21; Alejandro Esteban Camacho, "Can Regulation Evolve? Lessons from a Study in Mal-adaptive Management," *UCLA L. Rev.* 55 (2007): 293, 344–57.

5. Timothy Ferris, *Seeing in the Dark: How Amateur Astronomers Are Discovering the Wonders of the Universe* (New York: Simon & Schuster, 2002), xvi; Zygmunt J. B. Plater, "Law and the Fourth Estate: Endangered Nature, the Press, and the Dicey Game of Democratic Governance," *Envtl. L.* 32 (2002): 1, 3.

ADAK ISLAND

Adak Alaska Photography: http://www.orneveien.org/adak/index.htm

Adak Update: http://www.adakupdate.com

Alaska Maritime National Wildlife Refuge: http://alaskamaritime.fws.gov

Aleut Corporation: http://www.aleutcorp.com

Aleut Real Estate, L.L.C., "Adak Island Resources": http://www
.aleutrealestate.com/index.php?option=com_content&view=article
&id=18&Itemid=19

NAVSTA ADAK, Web log by Bob Rich: http://navstaadak.blogspot.com

North Pacific Fishery Management Council: http://www.fakr.noaa.gov/
npfmc/default.htm

COLTON

Center for Community Action and Environmental Justice: http://www
.ccaej.org

City of Colton: http://www.ci.colton.ca.us

Colton Super Block: http://www.ci.colton.ca.us/Documents/Econ/CSB
_files/frame.htm#slide0352.htm

Living on the Dime Inland Mexican Heritage: http://www.mexican
heritage.org

U.S. Fish and Wildlife Service: http://www.fws.gov

NORTH DAKOTA'S BADLANDS

Dakota Prairie National Grasslands: http://www.fs.fed.us/r1/dakotaprairie/.
Dakota Resource Council: http://www.drcinfo.com
North Dakota Game and Fish Department: http://gf.nd.gov
Theodore Roosevelt National Park: http://www.nps.gov/thro

SUSQUEHANNA RIVER

Atlantic States Marine Fisheries Commission: http://www.asmfc.org
Chesapeake Bay Foundation: http://www.cbf.org
Federal Energy Regulatory Commission: http://www.ferc.gov
Pennsylvania Department of Environmental Protection: http://www
    .depweb.state.pa.us
Pennsylvania Fish and Boat Commission: http://www.fish.state.pa.us
Susquehanna River Basin Commission: http://www.srbc.net
Upper Susquehanna Coalition: http://www.u-s-c.org
Wilkes-Barre Riverfront Project: http://www.luzernecounty.org/county/
    major_projects/riverfront-project

ALAMOGORDO

Alamogordo Astronomy Club: http://www.zianet.com/aacwp
Apache Point Observatory: http://www.apo.nmsu.edu
City of Alamogordo: http://www.ci.alamogordo.nm.us/site4.aspx
Holloman Air Force Base: http://www.holloman.af.mil
International Dark-Sky Association: http://www.darksky.org/mc/page.do
Lincoln National Forest: http://www.fs.fed.us/r3/lincoln/index.shtml
Mescalero Apache Tribe: http://www.innofthemountaingods.com/
    mescalerohistory1.asp
National Solar Observatory Sacramento Peak Facilities: http://nsosp.nso
    .edu
New Mexico Heritage Preservation Alliance Night Sky Program: http://
    www.nmheritage.org/sky/index.php
New Mexico Skies: http://www.nmskies.com
Otero County Administrator: http://www.co.otero.nm.us/MiscDept/
    admin.htm
UNESCO World Heritage Information Kit: http://whc.unesco.org/
    documents/publi_infokit_en.pdf
White Sands National Monument: http://www.nps.gov/whsa
WildEarth Guardians: http://www.wildearthguardians.org

CPSIA information can be obtained
at www.ICGtesting.com
Printed in the USA
JSHW050545210722
28307JS00002B/218